William C. Nichols
Editor

Family Therapy Around the World: A Festschrift for Florence W. Kaslow

Family Therapy Around the World: A Festschrift for Florence W. Kaslow has been co-published simultaneously as *Journal of Family Psychotherapy*, Volume 15, Numbers 1/2 2004.

Pre-publication REVIEWS, COMMENTARIES, EVALUATIONS . . .

"CLINICIANS, FAMILY SCIENCE RE-SEARCHERS, POLICY MAKERS, EDUCATORS, AND STUDENTS IN MANY DISCIPLINES WILL ALL BENEFIT from this rich book. This unique book brings together scholars from over 15 countries and they clearly demonstrate how family therapy and systemic thinking has made a positive difference in the world."

Jerry Gale, PhD
Director
Marriage and Family Therapy
Doctoral Program
Department of Child and Family
Development
The University of Georgia
Athens, GA

"A FITTING AND FASCIN-ATING TRIBUTE to Florence Kaslow. . . focused on the professional but infused with the personal. Readers will find A WEALTH OF INFORMATION regarding the challenges and practices of work with and research on families in a variety of cultural contexts, offered by therapists residing in widely differing parts of the planet. A particularly significant aspect of each chapter is the provision of a window into the world in which the authors live and work, enabling both a better understanding of the specific perspective described and a greater comprehension of global diversity in general. Editor Bill Nichols' effort to demonstrate his regard for a very respected colleague succeeds in many meaningful ways."

Dorothy S. Becvar, PhD, MSW
Associate Professor
School of Social Service
St. Louis University

"Should be REQUIRED READ-ING IN ANY COURSE ON MULTICULTURAL ISSUES IN COUNSELING AND FAMILY THERAPY and will expand the thinking of seasoned therapists as well. What a fitting tribute to the extraordinary contributions and pioneering international outreach of Florence Kaslow's life and work! The festschrift offers AN EXCITING PALETTE OF INTERNATIONAL PERSPECTIVES on the development of family therapy in 15 different countries. While every chapter is distinct and will be savored on its own, together these 16 chapters paint an exciting picture of the richness of theories and techniques evolving from each writer's particular cultural and historical context."

Ingeborg Haug, DMin
Clinical Director
Associate Professor of Marriage
and Family Therapy
Fairfield University

The Haworth Press, Inc.

Family Therapy
Around the World:
A Festschrift
for Florence W. Kaslow

Family Therapy Around the World: A Festschrift for Florence W. Kaslow has been co-published simultaneously as *Journal of Family Psychotherapy*, Volume 15, Numbers 1/2 2004.

The *Journal of Family Psychotherapy* Monographic "Separates"
(formerly the *Journal of Psychotherapy & the Family* series)*

For information on previous issues of the *Journal of Psychotherapy & the Family* series, edited by Charles R. Figley, please contact: The Haworth Press, Inc., 10 Alice Street, Binghamton, NY 13904-1580 USA.

Below is a list of "separates," which in serials librarianship means a special issue simultaneously published as a special journal issue or double-issue *and* as a "separate" hardbound monograph. (This is a format which we also call a "DocuSerial.")

"Separates" are published because specialized libraries or professionals may wish to purchase a specific thematic issue by itself in a format which can be separately cataloged and shelved, as opposed to purchasing the journal on an on-going basis. Faculty members may also more easily consider a "separate" for classroom adoption.

"Separates" are carefully classified separately with the major book jobbers so that the journal tie-in can be noted on new book order slips to avoid duplicate purchasing.

You may wish to visit Haworth's website at . . .

http://www.HaworthPress.com

. . . to search our online catalog for complete tables of contents of these separates and related publications.

You may also call 1-800-HAWORTH (outside US/Canada: 607-722-5857), or Fax 1-800-895-0582 (outside US/Canada: 607-771-0012), or e-mail at:

docdelivery@haworthpress.com

Spirituality and Family Therapy, edited by Thomas D. Carlson, PhD, and Martin J. Erickson, MS (Vol. 13, No. 1/2 and 3/4, 2002). *"One of the best books I have read on this topic. . . . Provides an excellent mix of theoretical, clinical, and research chapters. I strongly recommend this text for clinicians and students alike. . . . A first-rate piece of scholarship." (Joseph Wetchler, PhD, Professor and Director, Marriage and Family Therapy Program, Purdue University Calumet; Editor,* Journal of Couple & Relationship Therapy*)*

Multi-Systemic Structural-Strategic Interventions for Child and Adolescent Behavior Problems, edited by Patrick H. Tolan, PhD (Vol. 6, No. 3/4, 1990).* *"A well-written, informative, practical guide for clinicians interested in utilizing multi-systemic, structural-strategic interventions for child and adolescent behavior problems and for dysfunctional family patterns." (Journal of Marital and Family Therapy)*

Minorities and Family Therapy, edited by George W. Saba, PhD, Betty M. Karrer, MA, and Kenneth V. Hardy, PhD (Vol. 6, No. 1/2, 1990).* *"A must for those who are interested in family therapy and concerned with handling the problems of minority families. A particularly thought-provoking book for the novice who knows little about the area." (Criminal Justice)*

Children in Family Therapy: Treatment and Training, edited by Joan J. Zilbach, MD (Vol. 5, No. 3/4, 1989). *"The range of clinical material presented in this volume provides a powerful and vivid addition to an important and often neglected area of family therapy. . . . Lively, illustrative, and convincing." (Carol C. Nadelson, MD, Professor and Vice Chairman of Academic Affairs, Department of Psychiatry, Tufts University School of Medicine)*

Aging and Family Therapy: Practitioner Perspectives on Golden Pond, edited by George A. Hughston, PhD, Victor A. Christopherson, EdD, and Marilyn J. Bonjean, EdD (Vol. 5, No. 1/2, 1989).* *Experts provide information, insight, reference sources, and other valuable tools that will contribute to more effective intervention with the elderly and their families.*

Family Myths: Psychotherapy Implications, edited by Stephen A. Anderson, PhD, and Dennis A. Bagarozzi, PhD, MSW (Vol. 4, No. 3/4, 1989).* *"A marvelous international collection of papers on family myths–their development, process, and clinical implications." (American Journal of Family Therapy)*

Circumplex Model: Systemic Assessment and Treatment of Families, edited by David H. Olson, PhD, Candyce S. Russell, PhD, and Douglas H. Sprenkle, PhD (Vol. 4, No. 1/2, 1989).* *"An excellent resource for the Circumplex Model." (The Family Psychologist)*

Women, Feminism, and Family Therapy, edited by Lois Braverman, ACSW (Vol. 3, No. 4, 1988).* *"Get the book, have it at your fingertips, and you will find it hard to put down." (Australian Journal of Marriage & Family Therapy)*

Chronic Disorders and the Family, edited by Froma Walsh, PhD, and Carol M. Anderson, PhD (Vol. 3, No. 3, 1988).* *"An excellent text, for it thoughtfully explores several of the critical issues confronting the field of family systems medicine. . . . It should have a long shelf life for both clinical and scholarly work." (Family Systems Medicine)*

The Family Life of Psychotherapists: Clinical Implications, edited by Florence W. Kaslow, PhD (Vol. 3, No. 2, 1987).* *"A first in the field, these innovative contributions by outstanding therapists/trainers will enable family therapists to understand and explore the reciprocal influences between the therapist's personal family system and professional life." (Jeannette R. Kramer, Assistant Professor of Clinical Psychiatry and Behavioral Science, Northwestern University Medical School)*

The Use of Self in Therapy, edited by Michele Baldwin, PhD, MSW, and Virginia Satir (Vol. 3, No.1, 1987).* *"Recognized masters share insights gathered over decades on how the person the therapist is the fulcrum around which therapy succeeds. Thirty-six masters, from Kierkegaard to Buber to Satir and Rogers . . . this collection of scholarly work imparts lasting information." (American Journal of Family Therapy)*

Depression in the Family, edited by Arthur Freeman, PhD, Norman Epstein, PhD, and Karen M. Simon, PhD (Vol. 2, No. 3/4, 1987).* *Here is the first book focused on treating depression through the family system.*

Treating Incest: A Multiple Systems Perspective, edited by Terry S. Trepper, PhD, and Mary Jo Barrett, MSW (Vol. 2, No. 2, 1987).* *"Both theoretical and clinical aspects of intrafamily sexual abuse are covered in this important book which stresses the need for a systemic approach in working with incestuous families." (Journal of Pediatric Psychology)*

Marriage and Family Enrichment, edited by Wallace Denton, EdD (Vol. 2, No.1, 1986).* *"A practical book. A good introduction to the history, philosophy, and practice of this group-based approach." (The British Journal of Psychiatry)*

Family Therapy Education and Supervision, edited by Fred P. Piercy, PhD (Vol. 1, No. 4, 1986).* *"Written by authors who are well-known and well-represented in the family therapy literature (Beavers, Duhl, Hovestadt, Kaslow, Keller, Liddle, Piercy, and Sprenkle) . . . individual chapters are well-presented and offer valuable, concrete guidelines." (Journal of Family Psychology)*

Divorce Therapy, edited by Douglas H. Sprenkle, PhD (Vol. 1, No. 3, 1985).* *"While focusing on the specific area of divorce, the book in fact adds richly to a more general knowledge of family dynamics." (The British Journal of Psychiatry)*

Computers and Family Therapy, edited by Charles R. Figley, PhD (Vol. 1, No. 1/2, 1985).* *"An ideal resource for clinicians who have a systemic orientation in their practice and who are intrigued with how recent developments in home computers might be applied as an adjunct to their clinical work." (Canada's Mental Health)*

Family Therapy Around the World: A Festschrift for Florence W. Kaslow

William C. Nichols
Editor

Family Therapy Around the World: A Festschrift for Florence W. Kaslow has been co-published simultaneously as *Journal of Family Psychotherapy*, Volume 15, Numbers 1/2 2004.

The Haworth Press, Inc.

New York • London • Victoria (AU)
www.HaworthPress.com

Family Therapy Around the World: A Festschrift for Florence W. Kaslow has been co-published simultaneously as *Journal of Family Psychotherapy*™, Volume 15, Numbers 1/2 2004.

The development, preparation, and publication of this work has been undertaken with great care. However, the publisher, employees, editors, and agents of The Haworth Press and all imprints of The Haworth Press, Inc., including The Haworth Medical Press® and Pharmaceutical Products Press®, are not responsible for any errors contained herein or for consequences that may ensue from use of materials or information contained in this work. Opinions expressed by the author(s) are not necessarily those of The Haworth Press, Inc. With regard to case studies, identities and circumstances of individuals discussed herein have been changed to protect confidentiality. Any resemblance to actual persons, living or dead, is entirely coincidental.

Cover design by Marylouise E. Doyle.

Library of Congress Cataloging-in-Publication Data

Family therapy around the world : a festschrift for Florence W. Kaslow / William C. Nichols, editor.
    p. cm.
    "Family therapy around the world : a festschrift for Florence W. Kaslow has been co-published simultaneously as Journal of family psychotherapy, Volume 15, Numbers 1/2 2004."
    Includes bibliographical references and index.
    ISBN 0-7890-2514-0 (hard cover : alk. paper) – ISBN 0-7890-2515-9 (soft cover : alk. paper)
    1. Family psychotherapy. 2. Kaslow, Florence Whiteman. I. Kaslow, Florence Whiteman. II. Nichols, William C. III. Journal of family psychotherapy.
RC488.5.F336 2004
616.89'156–dc22
                                                   2004010866

Indexing, Abstracting & Website/Internet Coverage

Journal of Family Psychotherapy

This section provides you with a list of major indexing & abstracting services. That is to say, each service began covering this periodical during the year noted in the right column. Most Websites which are listed below have indicated that they will either post, disseminate, compile, archive, cite or alert their own Website users with research-based content from this work. (This list is as current as the copyright date of this publication.)

Abstracting, Website/Indexing Coverage . . . . Year When Coverage Began

- *Biology Digest (in print and online)* **1992**
- *Biosciences Information Service of Biological Abstracts (BIOSIS)*
  a centralized source of life science information
  <http://www.biosis.org> . . . . *****
- *CNPIEC Reference Guide: Chinese National Directory*
  of Foreign Periodicals **1995**
- *Educational Research Abstracts (ERA) (online database)*
  <http://www.tandf.co.uk> **2002**
- *EMBASE/Excerpta Medica Secondary Publishing Division*
  <http://www.elsevier.nl> **1992**
- *Environmental Sciences and Pollution Management (Cambridge*
  Scientific Abstracts Internet Database Service)
  <http://www.csa.com> . . . . *****
- *e-psyche, LLC <http://www.e-psyche.net>* **2001**
- *Family Index Database <http://www.familyscholar.com>* **2001**
- *Family & Society Studies Worldwide*
  <http://www.nisc.com> **1996**
- *Family Violence & Sexual Assault Bulletin* **1992**

(continued)

Special Bibliographic Notes related to special journal issues
(separates) and indexing/abstracting:

- indexing/abstracting services in this list will also cover material in any "separate" that is co-published simultaneously with Haworth's special thematic journal issue or DocuSerial. Indexing/abstracting usually covers material at the article/chapter level.
- monographic co-editions are intended for either non-subscribers or libraries which intend to purchase a second copy for their circulating collections.
- monographic co-editions are reported to all jobbers/wholesalers/approval plans. The source journal is listed as the "series" to assist the prevention of duplicate purchasing in the same manner utilized for books-in-series.
- to facilitate user/access services all indexing/abstracting services are encouraged to utilize the co-indexing entry note indicated at the bottom of the first page of each article/chapter/contribution.
- this is intended to assist a library user of any reference tool (whether print, electronic, online, or CD-ROM) to locate the monographic version if the library has purchased this version but not a subscription to the source journal.
- individual articles/chapters in any Haworth publication are also available through the Haworth Document Delivery Service (HDDS).

Family Therapy Around the World: A Festschrift for Florence W. Kaslow

CONTENTS

ABOUT THE EDITOR

William C. Nichols, EdD, a marital and family therapist and Diplomate in Clinical Psychology, is a Clinical Member, Approved Supervisor, Fellow, and Past President of the American Association for Marriage and Family Therapy (AAMFT). He is a charter member of the American Family Therapy Academy (AFTA), a charter member and Past President of the International Family Therapy Association (IFTA), Past President of the National Council on Family Relations (NCFR), and a Fellow in both the American Psychological Association (APA) and the American Psychological Society (APS). He was in full-time private practice for nearly 25 years and taught and supervised post-doctoral, doctoral, and master's students in MFT programs, and also post-degree professionals for 35 years at Florida State University, the Merrill-Palmer Institute, and elsewhere.

Dr. Nichols was the Founder and first editor of the *Journal of Marital and Family Therapy* and former editor of *Family Relations,* and is current editor of *Contemporary Family Therapy.* He authored or edited eight MFT and therapy books, wrote the first model licensing laws, co-wrote the national licensing examination, and chaired a state licensing board for seven years.

Preface:
Florence W. Kaslow, PhD:
An Appreciation

For decades Florence W. Kaslow has been a tremendous force for the initiation and development of family therapy across the globe. Besides remaining an active practitioner, editor, author, teacher, researcher, and an energetic participant in professional organizations in her own country, the United States, she has traveled around the world, teaching, lecturing, promoting international family therapy cooperation and collegiality and increased quality of service delivery and training among practitioners, mentoring younger professionals at home and abroad, and co-founding and nurturing the International Family Therapy Association.

Although Florrie Kaslow has been awarded a variety of honors, including the American Psychological Association's Distinguished Contribution to Applied Psychology Award in 1990, the decision of Bill Cohen, publisher, and Terry Trepper, editor of the *Journal of Family Psychotherapy*, to offer this volume dedicated to her and her work in international family therapy, a Festschrift honoring her and her work, is an entirely appropriate recognition of her magnificent contributions to family therapy around the world.

Kaslow has gone far beyond simply traveling to distant lands and demonstrating her own particular treatment orientation, beyond essentially advocating and demonstrating her own approach. Instead, she has focused on the needs of people and families in dealing with their problems and the needs and understanding of professionals, including encouraging colleagues from other lands to share what they know and practice with others. One of her many books, for example, was the *International Book of Family Therapy* (1982), an edited work in which professionals from a variety of nations contributed examples of their work and knowledge. Another was *Together Through Thick and Thin: A Multinational Picture of Long-term Marriages* (Sharlin, Kaslow, &

[Haworth co-indexing entry note]: "Preface: Florence W. Kaslow, PhD: An Appreciation." Nichols, William C. Co-published simultaneously in *Journal of Family Psychotherapy* (The Haworth Press, Inc.) Vol. 15, No. 1/2, 2004, pp. xxiii-xxv; and: *Family Therapy Around the World: A Festschrift for Florence W. Kaslow* (ed: William C. Nichols) The Haworth Press, Inc., 2004, pp. xv-xvii. Single or multiple copies of this article are available for a fee from The Haworth Document Delivery Service [1-800-HAWORTH, 9:00 a.m. - 5:00 p.m. (EST). E-mail address: docdelivery@haworthpress.com].

Hammerschmidt, 2001), an international research report on studies in eight countries in the Middle East, Western Europe, North America, South America, and Africa, co-authored with colleagues from Israel and Germany.

Urged by Virginia Satir at a meeting of East-West therapists in Eastern Europe in 1987 to undertake the challenging but important task of organizing a world organization for family therapists, Florrie Kaslow tackled the undertaking with customary energy and efficiency–and large amounts of hard work and use of personal contacts to gain cooperation and participation among colleagues from many lands. The result was the International Family Therapy Association, which she served as first president and continued to nurture and support to this writing in 2003. During IFTA's world family therapy congresses she has brought together survivors of the Holocaust of World War II, creating a dialogue between descendants of perpetrators and children of victims (Kaslow, 1995, 1997) as they have met in small intensive, powerful, and healing discussion groups.

This tribute to Florence Kaslow contains papers from 13 different countries. It is representative, and not an all-inclusive presentation of materials from her colleagues. Except for space limitations, there would have been contributions from a significant number of other nations. We have in this Festschrift a varied collection of articles, ranging from descriptions of the current status of family therapy or the development of theory in a given land to presentations of case examples to reports of research. This variety and granting of freedom to contributors to present their own ideas and contributions is entirely consistent with Florrie Kaslow's encouragement of colleagues to develop their own approaches to their work and to their dedication to families and to dealing with human and family problems and needs. Similarly, I am not going to offer descriptions or evaluations of their work, but am going to let them speak for themselves through their writing.

On a personal note, I first became acquainted with Florrie more than a quarter century ago when she succeeded me as editor of what is now the *Journal of Marital and Family Therapy*. I worked closely with her on the IFTA board of directors for seven years, 1996-2003, as well as being involved in various writing projects, both as editor of a journal in which she has published articles and as a contributor to books she has edited. Besides being bright–which is obvious, she combines great ideas with an amazing amount of hard work and unswerving dedication to the tasks and goals she accepts. Perhaps what I appreciate most about Florrie from our work together is that she has been at all times a consummate professional who can be trusted to deliver on what she promises–and deliver on time! I can trust her to do what she says she will do. Editing this collection is an expression of the regard in which I view her.

Florrie, we appreciate you. We're glad you came our way, in our time. Many careers are different and improved because of your energetic and dedicated activities.

William C. Nichols
Editor

REFERENCES

Kaslow, F. W. (Ed.) (1982). *International book of family therapy.* New York: Brunner/Mazel.

Kaslow, F. W. (1995). Descendants of Holocaust victims and perpetrators: Legacies and dialogue. *Contemporary Family Therapy, 17,* 275-290.

Kaslow, F. W. (1997). A dialogue between descendants of perpetrators and victims. *Israel Journal of Psychiatry, 34(1),* 44-54.

Sharlin, S. A., Kaslow, F. W., & Hammerschmidt, H. (2001). *Together through thick and thin: A multinational picture of long-term marriages.* New York: Brunner/Mazel.

Introduction to Family Therapy
Around the World:
A Festschrift for Florence W. Kaslow

I am most pleased to present a special, double issue of the *Journal of Family Psychotherapy*, "Family Therapy Around the World: A Festschrift for Florence W. Kaslow," edited by William C. Nichols, EdD. Dr. Nichols, himself a luminary in the field of marriage and family therapy, took on the task of collecting papers from around the world which celebrate the life and work of Florence Kaslow, with affection and energy. What he has assembled is an amazing body of work demonstrating the profound influence Dr. Kaslow has had on the field of marriage and family therapy all over the world.

It is most fitting that this honoring of Dr. Kaslow's work occur in the *Journal of Family Psychotherapy*. Back in 1988, Dr. Kaslow was one of the original founding Advisory Board members of the *Journal*, along with Douglas Sprenkle, Charles Figley, and myself. Dr. Figley, who was the founding editor in a previous incarnation called the *Journal of Psychotherapy and the Family*, was about to retire from the editorship. I had been appointed Editor by The Haworth Press, and had asked these three giants in marriage and family therapy journal editing to help design a format for the *Journal* which would be different from all others currently being published. Our goal was to create a journal which would be read and *used* by practitioners in clinical practice, while keeping the high academic and scientific standards required of all mainstream journals. The result of this meeting was the format of the *Journal*, which is for all intents and purposes the same as designed back in 1988; that is, a journal which focuses on case studies, treatment reports, and strategies for clinical practice. Not only has this shown to be a useful format for the *Journal*,

[Haworth co-indexing entry note]: "Introduction to Family Therapy Around the World: A Festschrift for Florence W. Kaslow." Trepper, Terry S. Co-published simultaneously in *Journal of Family Psychotherapy* (The Haworth Press, Inc.) Vol. 15, No. 1/2, 2004, pp. 1-2; and: *Family Therapy Around the World: A Festschrift for Florence W. Kaslow* (ed: William C. Nichols) The Haworth Press, Inc., 2004, pp. 1-2. Single or multiple copies of this article are available for a fee from The Haworth Document Delivery Service [1-800-HAWORTH, 9:00 a.m. - 5:00 p.m. (EST). E-mail address: docdelivery@haworthpress.com].

http://www.haworthpress.com/web/JFP
Digital Object Identifier: 10.1300/J085v15n01_01

but it has spawned a number of books and book series with a similar focus. Dr. Kaslow was a driving force in the early vision and development of the *Journal*.

Dr. Kaslow was also instrumental in the *Journal*'s next major step. During the mid-1990s, Dr. Kaslow began working with members of the Board of Directors of the International Family Therapy Association (IFTA) on a plan to adopt the *Journal* as the official journal of that association. IFTA had grown significantly, and the Board felt it was time to have its own journal, to serve as a vehicle for dissemination of clinical family therapy ideas and practices to its worldwide membership. Dr. Kaslow felt strongly that the *Journal of Family Psychotherapy* was the ideal journal for this purpose, especially with its strong clinical and practitioner focus. Beginning with Volume 8, in 1997, the *Journal of Family Psychotherapy* became the official journal of the International Family Therapy Association. Since that time, the *Journal* has focused increasingly on research and practice of family therapy from around the world. Again, Dr. Kaslow was the force that made this relationship between IFTA and the *Journal* possible.

Finally, I would add a personal note. Florence Kaslow has had a profound impact on my career and the career of scores of other psychologists, family therapists, and others in all of the mental health disciplines. She seems to know everyone in the entire field! More important, she has used her friendships and "connections" for the good of all. Her ability to bring divergent groups of professionals together has led to the founding, growth and development of leading academic journals, some of the most important books in our field, and national and international associations and divisions of associations. She is tireless, focused, and caring. I am *so* pleased to present this wonderful compendium of tributes, both to the work and the person, of Dr. Florence Kaslow.

Terry S. Trepper, PhD
Editor
Journal of Family Psychotherapy

Family Life in the Context of Chronic Stress and Dramatic Social Transformation in Yugoslavia

Branko Gačić
Vera Trbić
Milan Marković
Lazar Nikolić

SUMMARY. This paper describes the situation in Belgrade, Yugoslavia, during the 1990s. An ecosystemic paradigm was used in its concep-

---

Branko Gačić, Vera Trbić, Milan Marković, and Lazar Nikolić are affiliated with the University Clinical Center, Belgrade, Yugoslavia.
Address correspondence to: Branko Gačić, Jurija Gagarina 261/IV, 11070 N. Beograd, Serbia (E-mail: gacic@eunet.yu).

The authors appreciate very much Dr. Florence Kaslow's activities as a leading expert in the family therapy field. She gave valuable theoretical and practical contributions in developing family therapy theoretical framework and its application in this region of the world. Special appreciation is expressed to Dr. Kaslow for her sincere understanding and fruitful collaboration during the past difficult times in Yugoslavia. From the very beginning, Dr. Kaslow constantly supported the YAFTA's (Yugoslav Association for Family Therapy) active participation in all activities of the International Family Therapy Association. The authors are grateful to Dr. David Olson, formerly of the University of Minnesota, Family Social Science, for his constant support during the past decade and on this project.
The first version of this paper was presented at the 7th World Family Therapy Congress, Guadalajara, Mexico, October 1995.

[Haworth co-indexing entry note]: "Family Life in the Context of Chronic Stress and Dramatic Social Transformation in Yugoslavia." Gačić, Branko et al. Co-published simultaneously in *Journal of Family Psychotherapy* (The Haworth Press, Inc.) Vol. 15, No. 1/2, 2004, pp. 3-18; and: *Family Therapy Around the World: A Festschrift for Florence W. Kaslow* (ed: William C. Nichols) The Haworth Press, Inc., 2004, pp. 3-18. Single or multiple copies of this article are available for a fee from The Haworth Document Delivery Service [1-800-HAWORTH, 9:00 a.m. - 5:00 p.m. (EST). E-mail address: docdelivery@haworthpress.com].

http://www.haworthpress.com/web/JFP
Digital Object Identifier: 10.1300/J085v15n01_02

tualization and operationalization at multisystem levels of context. Description is based on research performed on 50 "normal" families under chronic stress and persistent crises, as well as on the authors' personal and professional experience, both as participants and observers faced with everyday, new stressful life events. The families have modified their system functioning on cohesion dimension (enmeshment) and on flexibility dimension (chaos), activating and mobilizing families' strengths, resources, and resilience to survive and to adapt to persistent/chronic stressful life in the context of global crisis of the society. A dramatic social transformation–greatly modified social structure, different dominant social actors, a new "logic" of functioning, and new social problems and contradictions–leave its stamp on everyday life. At the same time, families have confirmed their strengths and resilience in the past difficult times as a basis for our hope and optimism for the progress in the future. *[Article copies available for a fee from The Haworth Document Delivery Service: 1-800-HAWORTH. E-mail address: <docdelivery@haworthpress.com> Website: <http://www.HaworthPress.com>*

KEYWORDS. Family crisis, Circumplex Model, Belgrade ecosystemic, biopsychosocial model, FACES, Yugoslavia (Serbia, Montenegro)

The Yugoslav society in the 1990s was to a great extent a destroyed society, where the basic institutions (of state, economy, culture) were fundamentally destroyed; this is supported by many empirically confirmed facts. The people in Yugoslavia were inundated in waves under the impact of numerous persistent stresses and consequences of chronic crisis, including United Nations sanctions and isolation between 1992 and 2000. A huge social devastation resulted in existential pauperization of individuals and their families, affecting all parts of the society, the center and the periphery, cities and the country, and all social strata–of course, not all of them with the same effects or consequences. In the circle of pauperization we find families different from each other to the point of incomparability in terms of size of losses, quality of potential resources for recovery, and capabilities to put these potential resources to use for their own benefit: from those who lost their lifelong hard currency savings in the collapse of the banking system, but retained their status positions and connections, to those who have lost their usual monthly income (salaries, pensions, disability allowances, welfare allowances) and thus chances for a normal subsistence, to those who have lost everything–home, job, position, even their basic needs provisions (Bolčić & Milić, 2002). They all suddenly found themselves out in the open, struggling to ensure their daily existence. A host of new, innovative, and ingenious family and individual coping strategies have surfaced.

This paper describes an actual situation during the 1990s[1] in Belgrade, the capital of both former SFRY and FRY, now Serbia and Montenegro,[2] that has more than two million citizens (including a few hundred thousand refugees). During the last decade of the 20th century, Belgrade was not formally at war, but was surrounded by it, being a "crossroad" between war (100 miles west) and peace (100 miles northeast).

Our research is based on the survey performed on 50 "normal" families under chronic stress, and official data about the larger social context, as well as on our personal and professional experience, both as participants and observers, faced everyday with the new stressful life events.

Using ecosystemic paradigm, research, and clinical work on the relationship between various mental health problems and family life/functioning in the context of society has a long tradition in Belgrade, Yugoslavia (Gačić, 1986, 1995). We conceptualized our ecosystemic model on the fact that "any living system is always interlinked with others, in mutual interaction." It is operationalized at five interconnected levels: individual, marital/family, local community, national/state level, and international/world level.

Our theoretical orientation is the Ecosystemic Integrative Biopsychosocial Approach, which includes family with its individuals (and dyads), "horizontal," microsystemic network (i.e., nuclear and extended family, relatives, friends, neighbors, colleagues, health/social professionals, and so on), and "vertical," macrosystemic–widest and highest societal context (state-national) in which they are all incorporated. We believe that "vertical" dimension of social context is especially important, powerful, and decisive for family life in this situation. Thus, we take into consideration five multisystem levels of context in interrelation: individual, family, local community, societal/state level, and international/world level (see Figure 1; Gačić, 1986, 1992; Landau & Stanton, 1995). Now, first we shall describe shortly the societal context and then move to the family/individual level, aiming for better understanding of this constant interplay.

SOCIETAL CONTEXT IN YUGOSLAV CRISIS

A phrase we have repeated a hundred times, "Our difficult situation" (in all spheres of life), that denoted chaotic situation in Yugoslavia during the 1990s should be decoded. The social context of crisis was very complex and under an influence of destructive events/processes and a combination of multiple internal (Yugoslav) and external (international) factors in interaction:

FIGURE 1

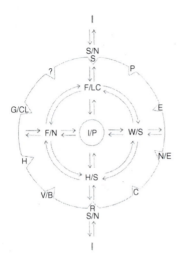

Multiple levels of context:

I/P = Individual/Person Level

F = Family Level

LC = Local Community Level:
Friends, Neighbourhood (F/N),
Work (W), School (S)
Health/Social Services (H/S)
Systems in Local Community (LC)

S/N = Societal/National/State Level:
Social (S), Political (P),
Economical (E), Nation/Ethnic (N/E),
Cultural (C), Religious (R),
Value/Belief System (V/B),
Historical (H), Geographical (G), Climate (CL),
and Other ("Invisible") Factors (?)

I = International/World Level

Ecosystem
Multisystem levels of context (Eco-map)
(Garčić B.; Belgrade Ecosystemic Approach to Alcoholism [ESTA] Belgrade-YU, 1992.)

Internal, Yugoslav Crisis Variables

These include a dozen factors inside the country as follows:

- *Social Factors:* Increased crime, violence, and corruption at all levels, including bureaucracy, collapse of legal system in new reality, "civilization periphery," everyday stressful situations.
- *Political/Ideological Turmoil:* An authoritarian system, "totalitarian collectivistic mentality" and ideology, patterns of mass/collective behavior with group phenomena, in spite of formal pluralism and multiparty system with "left" and "right" extremism ("patriots" and "traitors"). The previous system has still persisted with Yugo-nostalgia for old times. State monopoly over media, control and lack of information, information blockade, disinformation, and mass-media propaganda and manipulation have also had a determining role in an epidemic of ethno-nationalism, as a "mental infection" in Yugoslavia.

- *Economic Factors:* Hyperinflation, pauperization, and polarization to "new rich-new poor" citizens with the disappearance of the middle class; average salary about $50 per month, lack of satisfaction of basic human, existential needs: food, electricity, heating, elevator use, consumer goods, medications, telephone problems, city transportation, and problems with gasoline, and so on. Unemployment with a "black market" and "gray/underground" economy has been dominant, paradoxically helping ordinary people in supplying goods essential for everyday living. The word survival completely replaced the word life!
- *Ethnic/National Factors:* National romanticism became super-patriotism or nationalistic chauvinism with severe multiethnic conflicts, as well as collective intoxication by ethno-nationalistic ideology assuming dimensions of dependence on ideas.
- *Cultural Factors:* Positive tradition has been transformed into conservatism and "mythomanic kitsch"; fatalistic attitude and low tolerance for differences in opinion have been omnipresent. A dominating saying is: "Our truth/justice wins!"
- *Religious Factors:* Old conflict between Orthodox, Catholic, and Muslim populations was activated. The Orthodox Church maintained its national Serbian identity, but it is still oriented to the past too much, bringing confusion in believers.
- *Value/Belief System, Moral Norms and Standards:* These are in big change and confusion, so some extremes and aggressive/asocial behavior have become acceptable, even normal. In our opinion, these enormous value systems conflicts and moral crises create the most serious factor and problem, especially for young people.
- *Historical Characteristics and Specifics:* Generally known as a nation of warriors fighting for centuries against someone who has been threatening our freedom and independence; all conflicts being resolved by sacrifice and heroism, these are considered as traditional patriotic qualities. Frequent wars, destruction, compulsory migrations have been a part of the search for national identity, with inevitable intermingling with other cultures. All that leads to backwardness in modernization and civilization.
- *Geographical, Climate, and Other "Invisible" Factors:* For example, Yugoslavia is on the crossroads of the Balkans and Europe, which represents a specific and sensitive position.

All that was happening during the 1990s. The fact that the former Yugoslavia was a leading country in East Europe and had a solid income of $3,500 per capita (in 1989) has made it even harder (Jankulov, 1993). Recent investigation of public opinion has shown that today 4/5 of the citizens have been dissatisfied with the economic situation and standard of living in this country (Pantić, 1995). Our results correlate with statement of Boss (1988) about the catastrophic influence of chronic stress on family state and individual health. Thus, there have been practically no basic conditions for personal and social functioning. The standard of living is at existential/human minimum, seriously limiting the individual and social life of all people. Such a catastrophe has certainly borne mass frustration, dissatisfaction, insecurity, fears, conflicts and anomie.

External, International Factors

These are Balkan contexts and mentality specifics, and central and east European post-socialism countries had an important part in the crisis, together with the efforts of the European community, superpowers, and the United Nations. In general, they all had "good intentions," but their ways of action were inadequate, one-sided, ineffective, and even counterproductive. Thus, a solution became a problem.

These are some of the main factors and circumstances which, interwoven and combined, make the very complex and complicated dynamics of chronic Yugoslav crisis. We believe that some of these factors are unrecognized and underestimated. Their importance and hierarchy are interchangeable, both generally and specifically for each concrete case, in space and time, because "every day something new and problematic happens." That means that one factor is constantly present and dominant, producing/contributing to chronic stress. Also, there is a risk of generalizations and stereotypes. Thus, the process of destruction has continued in waves, in characteristic oscillations and phases, in complexities of various variables. The final result culminated in a fact that all people were under chronic stress. It has become a typical part of the everyday lifestyle.

THE LEVEL OF FAMILY AND INDIVIDUAL LIFE: "NORMAL" FAMILIES UNDER CHRONIC STRESS

Here, we shall present our research of "normal" families under chronic stress that we performed during 1994 and 1995 in Belgrade.

- The main goal of this pilot explorative study was to examine and define eventual changes in family life/functioning under chronic stress during the 1990s in the surrounding of civil war, global crisis, and destruction in

Belgrade. Indirectly, gathered data would show the sensitivity and usefulness of Olson's FACES-III Scales on our samples, because it was used during the last decade in Yugoslavia, but has not been standardized in our country (Marković, 1995).

- The sample consisted of N = 50 "normal," nonclinical, intact families with at least one child older than 12 years (adolescent). Family members' ages ranged from 12 to 66 years. All the families were permanent residents of Belgrade. Their property and income were in the medium range, with generally good housing conditions. About two-thirds of the families owned a car. About 4/5 of the women were employed, and nearly all the men, except three who were retired. Sociodemographic characteristics of the sample are statistically typical for the population in Belgrade. Average age and education years of family members are given in Table 1.
- Methods and Instruments were drawn from the Circumplex Model of Marital and Family Systems (Olson, Sprenkle, & Russell, 1989, 1993) and has been used as the framework in this study. The main instrument was the self-report measure, the Family Adaptability and Cohesion Evaluation Scale (FACES-III). At that time, we did not apply the Clinical Rating Scale (CRS). In addition, sociodemographical data were obtained.

The sample was tested with above-mentioned instruments at the end of 1991 and the beginning of 1992, before the global social, economic, and war crisis in Yugoslavia (Trbić & Gačić, 1992).

After more than three years (at the end of 1994 and the beginning of 1995), the same group of families was retested with FACES-III. The sample consisted of a total of 50 families, N = 50 (four families were lost, i.e., moved, a member was absent, and so on). The families were also questioned about real and ideal (desirable) states on FACES-III in order to derive a discrepancy between real and ideal, thereby creating an assessment of family satisfaction. In addition, a questionnaire related to the stressful life events in the previous crisis period was constructed for this research. Basic results of these two tests are given in Table 2.

TABLE 1. Age and Education of the Testees

	Age	Education years
Wife	37.6	10.8
Husband	41.6	11.4
Adolescent	13.2	6.2

The results of Table 2 are illustrative of Olson's Circumplex Model and are presented in Figure 2 and Figure 3.

As can be seen from the presented results, during slightly more than three years, the families moved significantly, both on the cohesion and adaptability dimension. Using the norms for such families with adolescents–32-43 for cohesion (center–37, 1) and 20-29 for adaptability (center–24, 3), it is easy to calculate the distances from the center or balanced area of the Circumplex Model. The data are presented in Table 3.

The basic finding was that the families changed their family type significantly on both dimensions of the model, with more changes on the cohesion dimension than on the flexibility dimension. While the families in 1991/1992 were located in balanced type (flexible-connected), in 1994/1995 they were located in the unbalanced family type since they were enmeshed on the cohesion dimension and chaotic on the adaptability dimension. Distance from the center has been moved to the right and upward (toward the mentioned extreme family types) for more than 8 points (12.9 − 4.7 = 8.2). That means that they changed in a negative direction, from a balanced (flexible-connected) type to the extreme or unbalanced (chaotic-enmeshed) type.

It should be noted that, although such significant shifting occurred, the family discrepancy score did not change, indicating that the whole family moved together. Family members did not become distant according to their perceptions. What attracts attention is the drastic change of adolescents' estimation (see Figure 2), who changed their position by 10 points on cohesion and 8 points on the flexibility dimension. That means that the shift is greater on cohesion dimension than on flexibility dimension, which will be discussed later in this paper.

TABLE 2. Basic Results of the Test (1991/92) and Retest (1994/95) of N = 50 Families

COHESION	1991/92	1994/95 REAL	IDEAL
Wife	39.4	41.4	38.1
Husband	40.5	45.5	38.8
Adolescent	36.3	46.5	39.8
FLEXIBILITY			
Wife	28.5	34	24
Husband	30.2	35.2	26.3
Adolescent	27.4	35.6	28.1

FIGURE 2

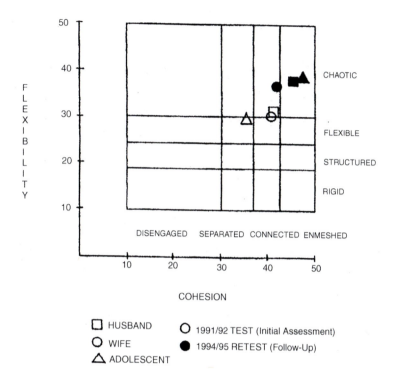

DISCUSSION

We believe that described global social, economic, and political crises with the chronic stress in Yugoslav context had the most massive and decisive influence on the change of family system, relations, and functioning. In summary, we found the following:

Cohesion

Under crises, families increased their cohesion dramatically. The emotional bonding between the family members increased and that seemed to be most dramatic for the adolescent. Perhaps it is also a developmental phenomenon for adolescence, with a real lack of differentiation and separation. The parents increased their care and control because the situation was unsafe and life-threatening. Thus the stress is doubled, both developmentally and situationally.

FIGURE 3. Family System: Current and Ideal State

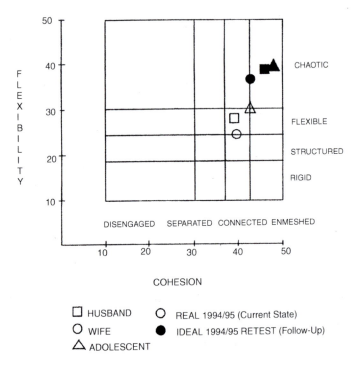

We see the increased family cohesion as "pseudo-cohesion" or "pseudo-mutuality" which is not the result of healthy and mature togetherness, but a symbiotic relationship (from fear, difficulties and reduced social contacts, and so forth). As we used to say, "a snail retreats into his house when faced with danger." This solidarity is based on the idea that "we are stronger together." So, here increased cohesion is a form of family adaptation to stress.

Significant changes on both dimensions of the model showed that the families reacted to the stress by increasing mutual bonding and closeness, at the price of individualization and separation. The fact that the adolescent most drastically feels those changes implies that under the influence of the crisis, the family has changed the pattern of upbringing to increase family cohesion.

In addition to the interpretation of the results of our research, our experience confirms an impressive tradition of mutual help and support in trouble, between family and extra family systems/network in local community (friends, neighbors) who share everyday problems. For example, homemade "blockade

TABLE 3. Basic Results: Test and Retest (Follow-Up)

	1991/92	1994/95 REAL	IDEAL
Family mean on cohesion	38.7	44.5	38.9
Family mean on flexibility	28.7	34.9	26.1
Family distance from center	4.7	12.9	2.7
Family discrepancy score	3.4	3.6	3
Family type	Balanced: Flexible-connected	Extreme: Chaotic-enmeshed	Balanced: flexible-connected

pie and cake" with few ingredients, as a treat for the whole network, was a strategy for survival.

Flexibility

On the flexibility dimension, the family did not manage to remain efficient in the formation and flexibility of family rules in such a chaotic societal context. This change for the worse was shown most in adolescents' estimations, though not so drastically as on cohesion dimension. These changes on flexibility dimension are, because of that, harder to explain. We could say that this is the point of "negative adaptability" because "the family must be ready for anything," i.e., sudden unpredictable events/stresses, and react instantly.

In the last decade in this country, different researchers have found the same tendency towards increasing cohesion (smaller in adaptability dimension) in many family systems with chronic disorders (alcoholic, addictive, adolescents, psychosomatic, and, recently, refugee families) (Gačić, 1993; Marković, 1995; Vlajković, 1992).

Communications

Communications, as a third facilitating dimension of Olson's Circumplex Model, are low quality, superficial, avoid real-life topics, and are focused on secondary, peripheral, naive, harmless themes, with contradictory messages and confusion, but avoiding open conflicts. We believe that they apply short-term strategies in order to survive "from today to tomorrow" (in analogy with Alcoholics Anonymous, AA). Communications are a mixture of positive (empathy, support) and predominantly negative communication (double bind, criticism).

The Ideal Picture

The families' position on the ideal picture indicates that they were generally on the expected level and family members were very realistic in their wishes and expectations. They inclined to a balanced system of flexibly connected family type (Figure 3), which was natural. Paradoxically, family satisfaction was good, despite the low quality of life, since families were probably thinking "it could be worse."

* * *

It is still an open basic question whether these families are normal and adjusting to the major stress or whether the family has become pathological and dysfunctional. According to Olson's Circumplex Model, families that are located in extreme positions are dysfunctional. However, we believe that temporary extreme positions of our families is functional–as a condition, a strategy to survive stressful life events, temporarily in a situation of instability, insecurity, uncertainty and unpredictability. So, we could say that this family is functional in a dysfunctional context, "normal in abnormal conditions." Under the huge impact of chronic stress, with no other choice, the family must activate all resources and family resilience in problem solving. That means "to find one's way to survive." Here, we add our important national saying that spite could be a motive to survive despite everything.

The Circumplex Model of Marital and Family Systems by Olson (1993) and colleagues is used as the theoretical foundation for analyzing the change in family systems. One hypothesis of the Circumplex Model is: "When a family system is under major situational or developmental stress, the family will modify its system in cohesion and flexibility to adapt to the stressor." In other words, a family system is expected to change its system under stress (second order change) in order to adapt and sometimes this means that the family will move to a more extreme family type. Generally, it is rather common for a family under major stress to become more cohesive (even enmeshed) and/or more flexible (even chaotic), which supports our conclusions. This also confirms our belief that the crisis is a challenge and a chance for activating potentials/resources/resilience for positive changes.

The family system is attacked both inside and outside, and affected/affecting both internal and external larger systems. Thus, the whole family becomes a unit of stress and the greatest natural resource for management and coping with stress-related problems. Considerable stress results in a large spectrum of complex health and psychosocial problems, common symptoms in these families both individual and collective, including distress, depression, anxiety, fear (rational/irrational), apathy, low self-esteem, cognitive difficulties, interpretative ideas, vulnerability, frustration, interpersonal intolerance, aggressiveness, exhaustion, PTSD (Post Traumatic Stress Disorder). In contrast to overreaction, denial is also frequent, typical in the process of adaptation and transition. Thus, we agree with Froma Walsh (1998) that various stressors/triggers imply different coping strategies based on families' strengths, resources, and resilience.

In our current domestic realities of fast and dramatic social changes where "everything is a problem," people live at an existential minimum with drastically reduced human needs, drastically limited personal and social life. Again, in these circumstances, everyday routine life is complicated and takes too much time and energy. Conformism is linked with dominant helplessness–inability to control situations and change things. So, in actual context, all these factors lead to anomie.

CONCLUSIONS

As we have emphasized, this work was conceptualized and operationalized within the framework of Belgrade Ecosystemic Model, on five multisystem interrelated levels of a Yugoslav crisis context: individual, family, local community, widest societal/national/state and international/world level. Now, we are more focused on the relationship between family and larger societal, state levels. Here, we have to note a clear gap between the family microsystem and extra family (society/state) macrosystem. However, they are interconnected and interdependent, stuck in a perfect balance, paradoxically, contributing to the chronicity of the crisis and quality of life's spiral decline. We believe that the interrelation: family-state systems include an implicit rule: "Quid pro quo" ("Mutual tolerance of ignorance"–each one minding its own business) as a basic long-term arrangement. The state regime does not care about the family and the family is allowed to do anything, and, in turn, the state does the same. Thus, our average "functional family" has a chance to survive. In other words, in such an ecological context, it seems more realistic to achieve first order change, with possibility of the second one having important implications for future life.

During the 1990s the family atmosphere was under strong influence of various problems, particularly material deprivation, conflicting needs, and feeling of existential insecurity, even endangerment. We made an open and honest effort to inform, to present some main characteristics of our transformation processes in the former FRY, now Serbia and Montenegro, where the old system is destroyed–the new is not built yet. It is clear that this story indicates that a high price is being paid by everybody. Thus, many open questions still remain, and further ecosystemic research of relationship within and between individual, family and society is needed.

In the preceding period the population of Serbia and Montenegro as a whole has suffered huge material, human and psychological devastation, so that rehabilitation and revitalization will take a very long time and deep structural reforms. Future research should deal with at least two issues: both about chronic, persistent stress effects (including prolonged reactions, such as "sleeper effect") and family life functioning in the future, after lifting-up of the U.N. sanctions–in conditions of social recovery. The question is whether getting out of this ghetto situation is going to be a stressogenic factor or if it will have some other, different effect.

The "return to the family" in this 10-year story going on in Serbia seems neither so permanent and stable nor so attractive and promising, either for individuals, families, or society. On both sides of the divide, the return is not a freely chosen commitment, but instead a result of constraint, hardship and distress. Genuine reconstruction can start when families are provided with prerequisites for a normal and relatively secure existence. Then the changed face of some post-modern family will emerge in its full force, a family whose transformation, with many standstills, turns and reversals, has been going on continuously under the shadow of dramatic historical events, hoping for a better life.

Many clinical and general (direct-indirect) implications emerge from these experiences and from our work, reflecting new trends; some of the more important are:

- The Belgrade Ecosystemic, Biopsychosocial Model is an appropriate and useful framework in conceptualization and operationalization of stress/crisis-related problems at multiple interconnected levels. We believe that the broadest family context (i.e., societal processes) is still neglected in understanding and treating people's problems, although their importance is still neglected in our field. The model also makes possible an awareness of more balanced interdependence of intrapsychic and interpersonal factors/levels within the (eco)system, implying the need of closer images between family therapy, psychiatry, psychology, sociology, and other relevant disciplines/professions.

- Today, in a new time of constant and dramatic social reality, changes, and uncertainties, new and complex human problems emerge, demanding new ways of thinking and practice. This is a time for new integrative models, as a combination or synthesis of old, classic models, and new postmodern ideas and actions. Thus we define our theoretical framework now as an integration of Ecosystemic/Multisystemic/Postmodern/Constructionist approaches practicing coherent, specific interventions under one umbrella–flexible and adapted to each concrete case. We emphasize here a new humanistic orientation of our ESTA Model focused on strengths, potentials, and resilience, rather than on deficits and pathology. Natural family and social networks and informal natural local community resources enabling comprehensive, collaborative, and joint actions are the powerful components of the therapeutic processes. In addition, the importance of therapist/team and client/family collaborative relationships, psychoeducation, and self-help materials are also obligatory parts of the treatment plan and program. We strongly believe that stress/disaster guidelines and interventions are needed more today than classical clinical programs.

- Besides these clinical implications, new possibilities for (multi)systemic prevention interventions are open, at all multisystemic levels of context. We believe that each therapeutic intervention has a preventive dimension/effect. Again, coordinated action and education of family and larger social systems, as well as network resources are important in promoting healthy lifestyle and human well-being, increasing new information, knowledge, and awareness in both persons in trouble and the general population. New ways of thinking and new ideas require a new language, new terminology such as meaning, belief system, empathy, tolerance, interconnectedness, contextualization, normalization, conversation/dialogue, stories, collaboration, negotiation, forgiveness, reconciliation, and so forth. These are the terms that are dominant in our vocabulary of today.

This paper is meant as a contribution to a more profound, scientific understanding of dramatic transformation of individual/family lives and social reality during the 1990s. For future analysts it will be a valid document on the social reality of Yugoslavia during the last decade of the 20th century.

NOTES

1. This paper was completed by the end of 1995. However, persistent stresses and crisis in Yugoslavia continued to the end of 2000 at all levels: individual, family and social. Three-month NATO bombing during 1999 was a culmination, a new "wave" in the series of stressful events with extremely negative consequences. A decade of accumulated stressful events brought the country into a catastrophic situation, destruction and impoverishment of the society, certainly rarely seen in the world. Without disputing the oft-cited claim that in Serbia, the 1990s were the years of blocked transition, blocked both in social-systemic terms and by those who ruled it, we have to note numerous social changes and say that in Serbia and Montenegro, too, the process of post-socialist transformation has been going on. This process was peculiar, different than in most other countries of the former "Soviet bloc" and marked by tragic events. But by its basic thrust this process has produced a new, post-socialist society at the be-

ginning of the 21st century. It was only on the basis of such actually changed society that the change of government and of the previous ruling political regime at the end of the year 2000 was possible, along with new reforms of the system and policies after 2000.

2. The Kingdom of Serbs, Croats and Slovenians was founded in 1918. In 1929 the country changed the name to Kingdom of Yugoslavia. The post World War II socialistic Yugoslavia was consisted of six republics: Serbia, Croatia, Bosnia and Herzegovina, Macedonia, Slovenia and Montenegro. The people have lived together for more than seventy years despite multiple social, economic, political, cultural, ethnic, and religious diversities. In 1991, after the breakup of the former state of SFRY, the process of disintegration was culminated in destructive processes of crisis, civil war and chaos. The third Federal Republic of Yugoslavia (FRY), founded in 1992, was constituted of two republics, Serbia and Montenegro. In March 2003, the FRY changed the name to Serbia and Montenegro.

REFERENCES

Bolčić, S., & Milić, A. (2002). *Serbia at the end of millennium: Destruction of society, change, and everyday life*. Belgrade: Institut za sociološka istraživanja Filozofskog Fakulteta.

Boss, P. (1988). Family stress. In M.B. Sussman & S.K. Steinmetz (Eds.), *Handbook of marriage and the family*. New York: Plenum Press.

Gačić, B. (1986). An ecosystemic approach to alcoholism: Theory and practice. *Contemporary Family Therapy, 8,* 264-278.

Gačić, B. (1992). Belgrade systemic approach to the treatment of alcoholism: Principles and interventions. *Journal of Family Therapy, 14 (2),* 103-122.

Gačić, B. (1993). Development of ecosystemic approach to alcoholism: 30 years of clinical experience and research in Belgrade. *Psihijatrija danas, III-IV,* Beograd.

Gačić, B. (1995). Belgrade ecosystemic model in alcoholism. *Alkoholizam, XXIX, 3-4.*

Jankulov, S. (1995). Personal Communication, Belgrade.

Landau-Stanton, J., & Stanton, M.D. (1995). Personal Communication, Rochester, NY.

Marković, M. (1995). Experience with Olson's Circumplex Model of marital and family systems. In press, Belgrade.

Mihailović, K. (1994). *Sanctions: Their causes, legitimacy, legality and effects.* Belgrade: SANU.

Olson, D.H. (1993). Circumplex Model of marital and family systems: Assessing family functioning. In F. Walsh (Ed.), *Normal family processes* (2nd ed.) (pp. 134-137). New York: Guilford Press.

Olson, D.H., Russell, C.S., & Sprenkle, D.H. (Eds.) (1989). *Circumplex Model: Systemic assessment and treatment of families.* New York: The Haworth Press, Inc.

Pantić, D. (1995). Personal Communication, Belgrade.

Trbić, V., & Gačić, B. (1992). *Alcoholic family system: Evaluation and treatment.* European Conference on the Family at Risk, London.

Vlajković, J. (1992). *Life crisis and its overcoming.* Belgrade: Nolit.

Walsh, F. (1998). *Strengthening family resilience.* New York: Guilford Press.

The Theme of the Family
in Contemporary Society
and Positive Family Psychology

Alexander Shapiro

SUMMARY. Social observers agree that a family is a focus for contemporary concerns. The author suggests that relying on the value dimension of the field of family therapy, which means working with such positive concepts as family resilience, reconciliation can help to defend families against their vulnerability to manipulation. New, positive forms of psychological practice are needed to work at the level of the family. The author also stresses the importance of reflecting on the family theme in psychology and blending ideas from positive psychology and family psychology. As both disciplines are rather new, they can benefit from constructive interaction. Some illustrations concerning the author's work with Russian families and Russian family culture are included. *[Article copies available for a fee from The Haworth Document Delivery Service: 1-800-HAWORTH. E-mail address: <docdelivery@haworthpress.com> Website: <http://www.HaworthPress.com> © 2004 by The Haworth Press, Inc. All rights reserved.]*

Alexander Shapiro is Senior Research Fellow, Institute of Preschool and Family Education, Russian Academy of Education, Moscow, Russia. He was a member of the board of directors of the International Family Therapy Association from 1997-2003. He is former chair of the family psychology and family therapy division of the Russian Psychological Association, and country representative of the International Family Psychology Academy.

Address correspondence to: Alexander Shapiro, Lenin Hills, Moscow University, cor. "K," apt. 122. Moscow, 119234, Russia (E-mail: shapalex@rbcmail.ru).

[Haworth co-indexing entry note]: "The Theme of the Family in Contemporary Society and Positive Family Psychology." Shapiro, Alexander. Co-published simultaneously in *Journal of Family Psychotherapy* (The Haworth Press, Inc.) Vol. 15, No. 1/2, 2004, pp. 19-38; and: *Family Therapy Around the World: A Festschrift for Florence W. Kaslow* (ed: William C. Nichols) The Haworth Press, Inc., 2004, pp. 19-38. Single or multiple copies of this article are available for a fee from The Haworth Document Delivery Service [1-800-HAWORTH, 9:00 a.m. - 5:00 p.m. (EST). E-mail address: docdelivery@haworthpress.com].

http://www.haworthpress.com/web/JFP
© 2004 by The Haworth Press, Inc. All rights reserved.
Digital Object Identifier: 10.1300/J085v15n01_03

KEYWORDS. Value dimension of family therapy, Russia, positive psychology, family psychology, positive family psychology

I was lucky to get acquainted with Dr. Florence Kaslow in 1994 at an International Family Therapy Association (IFTA) congress in Budapest, and since that time I have felt the importance of positive family-oriented value dimension in her professional work and in her social activities. I saw her lecturing, leading workshops and seminars, and taking part in meetings of the board of directors of IFTA. She spreads positive energy and positive values which give something to everyone around her. In particular, she gives colleagues an example of positive leadership and professionalism. She was at the beginning of the global movement of family therapy and family psychology, a globalist in a real positive sense. That is why the subject of this article fits well into the "Kaslow Festschrift."

FAMILIES IN CONTEMPORARY RUSSIA: ON THE EDGE OF NEGATIVITY AND POSITIVITY

The family theme is very important for humanity at large and for Russia in particular. The role of the family in contemporary Russia, fitting at the cross-section of individual life and social life, is very important, emphasizing the significance of education, children, old relatives, interpersonal communications, longing for intimate relationships with close people, patience, endurance, altruism, emotionality (Gaylin, 2001; Shapiro, 2000c; Tuson, 1985). Speaking geographically, we can say that the West is centered around individual life and the East around community life, and Russia, which is in the cross-section between East and West, is centered around the family theme.

Positive Family Values and Totalitarian Attitudes

Mama, a new Russian movie, portrays graphically the importance of positive family values as the opposite to totalitarian attitudes in society and in family relationships. The film is about a Russian family in which the mother has a very strong sense of individual resilience. She and her husband met at a little village train station at the end of World War II. Girls were strolling along the platform, making themselves as attractive as possible in order to catch the attention of soldiers passing by. She succeeded and they got married.

One child followed after another. The family did not have enough money to buy food or heat their home. The mother suggested stealing coal from the nearby train station. The father and the sons began to steal regularly and the local police did not disturb them, as they knew that the family was poor and they felt some compassion for them. But at one point the Moscow militia came after them, shooting the father and wounding him. After he recovered he was sent away to a prison camp for eight years. At this point, the mother, pregnant, decides to free the father and, in order to raise money for this purpose, sells their house and goes to Siberia where the camp is situated, with all their sons in tow. They decide that the eldest boy should be the one to negotiate with the guards. The guards take money and release the father, but only for a few seconds. In actual fact, the guards had simply planned to kill the father as a runaway after taking the money. But the boy notices their tricks and tries to protect his father. In the ensuing struggle, the father is killed and the son wounded in the spine and paralyzed.

And so the whole family returns without the father, or a home or money. But it so happens that they are all talented musicians, so the mother decides that they should form a band, become famous, and in this way earn enough money to live on. They succeed in becoming famous but not in earning enough money even to live on. At this point, the mother realizes that it is not going to be possible to live in Russia any longer, so she decides to go to the United States by hijacking an airplane. Her attempt fails. (This was a real case in the 1970s.) One son is killed and the remaining sons are sent to different orphanages, except for the paralyzed eldest, whom the mother advises to pretend to be insane. She reasons that there is no other way for him to survive in prison. The mother is so desperate at this point that she demands to be killed. However, the judge gives her a stiff 15-year jail sentence.

She survives those terrible years and wishes to liberate her son from the mental institution. The doctors are convinced that he really is insane and do not wish to release him. She sends a cable to all five of her other sons, calling them to a family reunion. They somehow succeed in liberating their brother and in the final scenes, the family is on the train to their old village. The mother asks her oldest son why he is still pretending to be insane. The son responds, with wisdom, that he is doing it only to avoid her domineering advice which he declares has always had a very negative effect on all the members of the family. The mother is shocked by what he says and begins to cry. At the station, she starts making confessions to her sons. Although at first all have gloomy expressions, they all begin laughing. There is some soot on the bench, the very same bench that she had been sitting on when she first met her husband. She flashes back to the moment when she had used this soot to make herself attractive for him. But now the soot makes her face dirty in a comical way. As the mother sees how amusing she looks, she also starts laughing, in recognition of her own weakness and the need for building new (equal, non-manipulative, tolerant) relationships with this family, stressing the importance of family (not just individual) resilience and its positive potential and positive resource for its members.

This movie illustrates that a whole family can be happy even in a situation of extreme adversity (Walsh, 1998), such as the many generations of Soviet cultural negativity. It is not easy to avoid the effects of what one has lived through, which are fixed in the consciousness of whole generations, in the specifically negative Soviet culture, the main components of which were psychological closedness, economic helplessness, and lack of creativity in all spheres. On the other hand, for our people family relations were (or could be) a real island of positivity, goodness, and humanity in a cruel and manipulative world. That is why to overcome the legacy of totalitarianism in our families, we must undertake a positive reframing of the experience of every post-Soviet family, reveal its hidden positive resources (Kroupin, 2000; Long & Shapiro, 2001; Shapiro, 1998a, 1998b, 2000a). My conviction is that family resilience has the potential to facilitate a return to individual and social strengths here in Russia.

The Influence of History on the Generations

A family case (Shapiro, 1999b, 2000b, 2000c) illustrates how history has influenced the private lives of the people, in different generations of one Russian family. Positive change factors and negative obstacles to changes which exist in attitudes, cultural values, and patterns will be identified through analyzing the clinical work with this family.

> The mother of a 13-year-old boy came to us three years ago, complaining that her son was doing poorly in school and had many conflicts with her and her mother. Neither she nor her son knows their father. Work began with this "no-father-cross-generational family pattern," one of the "lessons" totalitarian experience had taught many Soviet families. It was evident that the relationship between the two women was very bad, and they competed with one another to control the boy. Grandmother felt herself to be an unhappy victim and the mother saw herself in the role of "Cerberus" in the family.

As a result of the therapy, the mother and grandmother understood how important their reconciliation was for the boy, for themselves, for future generations. They also understood that in order to reconcile with each other, they needed to reconcile with their own past. What caused this understanding? As they talked about the history of their family, it gradually emerged that this family, like so many in Russia, had suffered from "Stalin purges."

This family typifies the transgenerational experience of many other Russian families who developed the attitude that "too strong and overcontrolling women" had to take over the role of the 50 million men who were killed in the USSR in the period between the middle of the 1930s and the beginning of the 1950s, either in the war where Stalin used Russian soldiers as "cannon-fodder" or in the "Stalin purges," as a result of which we now had approximately five million fatherless children in Russia. Stalin and the Soviet totalitarian regime devalued men, women, and families in the USSR. The people of our country very much need reconciliation with their cultural gender roles. In particular, being "strong" and being "in control" ("empowering" and "overpowering") are two different things; perhaps people should be strong, but it is not a good idea to control everything or victimize others, to be violent.

In this particular family, the grandmother hated her late mother, and this led to bad relations with her daughter. When the grandmother's father was taken away and persecuted, his wife began an affair with her neighbor. At the time, she did not know the truth about her husband. In fact, many Russian wives of persecuted and "disappeared" husbands did not know at first what had actually happened to them. During the sessions (we used the psychodramatic technic "empty chair"), the boy's mother learned of the shame felt by the grandmother following this tragic event. This realization helped her to reconcile her feelings about her grandmother and her mother as well.

To illustrate how those three women saw the situation in 1938, three pictures drawn by my daughter Elena are presented in Figures 1-3. These pictures represent materials gained from performing several family therapy technics such as family sculpture and family choreography. They show how one member of the family sees his or her family as a whole.

Later both women "threw away" the fathers of their children in divorces that are unexplainable from analyzing the actual conflicts between the partners. The "no-father pattern" persists in spite of evidence to suggest that the conflicts between partners were manageable.

Our clinical case also effectively illustrates how families have to reflect on their history in order to be healthy psychologically. This process of reconciliation which is based on family resilience phenomena is one of the most important aspects of transitional process in Russia on the family level. Each family has a heritage of different experiences and values from the country's past. We may assume, stressing the value dimension of the transitional process in Russia, that there is obvious mutual dependence between the dominant content of moral-psychological regulators (MPRs) in the family and the broader social context in which this family is embedded.

Negative MPRs in the society engender negative MPRs in the family. Russia's totalitarian experience reduced the value of the person and deformed the essence of the family in the USSR. The tyranny of "education by fear" set family members against each other (in this case–between a mother and her daughter),

FIGURE 1. The mother of the boy blames her grandmother for committing adultery.

FIGURE 2. The grandmother is understanding, feeling that "Mother just helped the family survive."

FIGURE 3. The great grandmother's shame.

but failed to destroy the family as an "island of positivity," "shared experience," and "kindness." Now, although Russia has come through a positive transformation, everything is in crisis here (according to Scharwiess [2002], a disorientation so typical of transition!), including the family. The economic and political situation produces a real survival challenge for many Russian families who must restore old identities, and create new ones. The social history carried by multigenerational families provides a base for new beginnings.

Russian Families in Transition

A healthy family is necessary for a healthy society and vice versa: in order to make the family more healthy we have to make society more positive and vice versa. Moreover, the role of the family for society (at societal level) can be positive and/or it can be negative depending on the family sub-themes we are taking into account; we can concentrate on violence, manipulation, conflicts, or gender inequality, or we can concentrate on identity development, tolerance, reconciliation, and family resilience.

There are some specifics of our cultural inheritance which we must take into account: for instance, the absence in Russia of a developed democratic tradition. Democracy has not been a positive value here, neither in families, which were most often closed, authoritarian, and undemocratic, nor in community life which as a whole did not support a diversity of voices. The Russian people, faced with poverty prior to the revolt but possessing a unique Russian resilience, struggled with the "new" Russian way. Should we continue with this idea or should we adopt other values? And at the same time could we overcome this contemporary clash of values and avoid the bloody totalitarian method of conflict resolution–another October revolution?

Many Russians, in this transitional period, are overwhelmingly preoccupied with business and making money. Commerce has become a prime value, reflecting the materialistic attitude which was predominant in Soviet times, the difference being that it now is being expressed far more aggressively and openly as people experience increasing difficulty finding positive alternatives to those "purely materialistic" attitudes. A glaring example is the advertising industry, which is urging families to chase after external goods which purportedly will improve their daily lives. Since the majority of people do not have much money, it is natural that every problem becomes one of economics. One might get the impression that there are no social interactions other than those having money at their root.

The contextual side of communication between people is seriously neglected and the meaning of any voluntary activity has been lost (Shapiro, 1998b, 1999a, 2001). Another danger is manipulation of the family's spiritual needs

(Shapiro, 1997b, 1999a; Stander, Piercy, Mackinnon, & Helmeke, 1994). So the negative and the positive approaches are fighting each other in Russian mentality, Russian society, and Russian families. Because of negativity, which is very widespread here, a positive approach is important for all social areas in Russia, including family life.

FAMILY THERAPY AS A POSITIVE APPROACH TO PSYCHOTHERAPY AND ITS POTENTIAL FOR HELPING RUSSIAN FAMILIES

Russia is a very special place now; it is a microcosm, in even more evident form, of all the problems of the contemporary world. Examples include economic collapse, the yawning gap between the poor and the rich, and the painful tragedy in Chechnya. Russia's main hope today is in our society, which after having been numbed by totalitarianism, is finally turning not just in words, but also in real acts toward responsible individuals and toward a positive understanding of the family. Still, our people and our families need special (transitional) psychological help to remove the incrustation of totalitarianism from our souls.

Benefits of Family Therapy

Family therapy, because of its positive potential and focus on family relationships, may be the most effective method of psychological help in Russia. Family therapy came into existence with the understanding (e.g., Minuchin, Whitaker, Satir, Ackerman, Haley, and others) that if a family is provided with the necessary professional support, it is capable of helping its members with its own resources, not the contrary, i.e., aggravating the distress of the individual. In its historical development family therapy has intensified psychotherapy's opposition to traditional psychiatry. For instance, group psychotherapy developed under the value attitude that the real personal growth is possible only in an environment of strangers, certainly not in one's own family, and that escaping from the family was important in becoming a "real person." Family therapy pursues the power of "positivity" that makes the therapeutic potential of intrafamilial interrelations capable not only of shielding a person from the negative sides of life but also of helping him or her to deal with psychological problems (Shapiro, 1996, 1997b, 1999b, 2000c).

Family therapy attempts to work with broad segments of the population, not just with the traditional clients of psychotherapists (the middle class in Western countries). The founders of family therapy attempted to deal with this task by relying less on the invention of sophisticated technical means and more on personal experience, the spiritual-existential vision displayed in intrafamilial relations, and the principle of equality between the family and the therapist (the therapist does not regard himself or herself as being free of problems), encouraging clients to rely on their own resources and cultivating the positively human in the individual, a self-awareness of the individual as a person, not as a tool, a means, or a thing (Walsh, 1998; Nichols, Pace-Nichols, Becvar, & Napier, 2000). As for the techniques, such cultural devices as legends, histories, tales, and psychotechnical instruments such as the "circular interview" and "positive redefinition of symptoms" have been used in work with families, and have helped to create in the clients of family therapists a positive vision of present, past, and future (Gaylin, 2001; Sharlin, Kaslow, & Hammerschmidt, 2000; Szapocznik & Kurtines, 1995). These approaches would provide Russian families with acceptable ways to address their history and adjust/adapt to the new Russia.

The cornerstone of family therapy is congruent, mutually accepting, and empathetic interpersonal interaction, which it regards as an asset of relations within the family. We should also mention the flexibility of the relational system: psychotherapist-individual-family-society (Tuson, 1985). Despite the fact that the family is the focal point of the psychotherapist's efforts, he or she does not limit himself or herself to helping the individual through the family but also helps the family through the individual and fosters a productive relationship of both with the surrounding community, while at the same time drawing on the resources of the individual and on the resources of the broader socioeconomic and cultural context in which the family and the individual are embedded. On the other hand, family therapy is an intercultural approach to straightening out intrafamilial relations as the field itself represents the diversity of theories technics, methods, and values.

The positive essence of family therapy at the core of its value dimension is very evident, and it is very meaningful for psychotherapeutic help on the level of family level and on the societal level. This includes "win-win" (not "win-lose") approaches to resolving conflicts and the positive potential every family has as well as such concepts as reconciliation, resilience, and tolerance. Our conviction is that no single author has a monopoly on a positive approach because it is the essence of family therapy itself (Peseschkian, 1980; Shapiro, 1997b).

Barriers to Establishing Family Therapy in Russia

Family therapy in Russia has two challenges: being a part of contemporary family therapy and being "in Russia." A healthy professional community is as important for survival here in Russia as are healthy families. In the extraordinary situation in Russia today, there is an urgent need to emphasize family therapy not primarily as a body of therapeutic techniques or scientific methods but rather as a value-oriented profession having very strong sociocultural dimensions; professionals in this field have to direct themselves to the positive resources of the family as well as to the positive resources of professional community. The value dimension can help us to look at our profession not only in the framework of solving its immediate problems but in a more global perspective. Our conviction is that only if it can function this way will it have the possibility to become a beacon of hope in this country and become applicable to the reality being experienced in everyday life here.

Individual mindset toward therapy. In the process of providing psychological help to contemporary Russian families, it is necessary in the first instance (before using sophisticated techniques of whatever kind) to endeavor to cultivate what is "positively human" in human beings. We also need an image of a positive family, protecting the individual at all stages of his or her life path from the manipulative actions of the particular social group of which he or she is a part, in which the struggle for resources often is more important than human life itself. A positive family opens a man/woman to the world by bringing the individual into contact with the polyphony of human values and traditions. This is a point of special relevance for contemporary Russian society, which is under the dangerous influence of centrifugal forces of an unending struggle for territory, for humanitarian help, and for various cultural prerogatives. One Russian poet wrote: "I am tired of the 20th century, of its bloody rivers, I don't need human rights, because I am not human being any more."

In addition to the need to develop a family therapy profession in Russia valued by the professional and the people, there is a need to expand the current medical model for treating sick people and to include working with "healthy" people who want to improve the quality of their lives and solve emotional problems. In Soviet times the communist party claimed to resolve all problems, including those that were psychological or purely personal. If a couple or person were having marital difficulties or trouble raising their children, the party organs called that person in for an "exploratory discussion." This led Russian clients to have a tendency to be passive and to transfer responsibility for treatment to the power holder (in therapy, the therapist) the expectation of fast and wonderful healing and recovery. Only a small part of the Russian population can even think about using therapists. The poor majority are using "homemade devices" which can be positive (such as "friendly talks") or negative (such as "alcohol").

Therapists' needs for a positive approach. Our clinical case cited above gave good evidence for the fact that families have to reflect on their history in order to be healthy psychologically. What about the "professional family" of family therapists? You can say that the family therapy community in Moscow needs the same kind reconciliation as well, and at least some of the conflicts inside it exist because of the country's totalitarian past. Such reconciliation is one of the most important aspects of any transitional post-totalitarian process, no matter what level is considered (individuals, families, or society at large). Yes, here in Russia we have the same problems as professionals in other parts of the world, but we have some special problems as well. One of them is connected with Stalinist stereotypes not only inside the families we are working with but also in parallel inside the family therapy community itself. The post-totalitarian syndrome affected everything and everyone here–society, families, individuals, and not only our clients need special transitional psychological help to remove the incrustation of totalitarianism from their souls, but professionals as well, including myself, of course (Shapiro, 1998b, 1999a, 2001a).

We may suggest that psychological aid to the Russian family should require the professional to have some positive traits in terms of existential values, and that the corresponding professional community should have features of a commune that functions on the basis of positive values. The concept of "positivity," in addition to the above aspects, is also essential for other facets of psychological work with the family in today's Russia, as a possible philosophical basis for interaction among family psychologists, the educational system, religious communities, and social services endeavoring to overcome the information barrier between Western professionals and our own.

Analyzing certain tendencies in Russian society and Russian mentality, we may conclude that the positive approach in family therapy is very meaningful here, mainly because of the need to overcome the negative legacy of totalitarianism in our country.

SOME PERSONAL PERSPECTIVES: ON THE WAY TO POSITIVE FAMILY PSYCHOLOGY

The Family Theme and Positive Psychology

All the stages of a person's life, all the most important existential problems of humankind, are represented, in one form or another, in the family theme which is important for contemporary psychology especially in the context of its search for humanistic values (Gaylin, 2001; Nichols et al., 2000; Szapocznik & Kurtines, 1995; Kaslow, 1990). If we speak about the 21st century as a humanistic one, it is important to have in mind that the family will be important to psychology, because psychology will be obliged to be closer to life instead of trying to manipulate and boundlessly interfere with it. The modern family is mainly a psychological, not sociological or economic, reality. We believe that contemporary family is primarily a "personal device," that every person needs the family dimension in his or her life and it is his or her individual decision what form the family should take. Also every human being needs the positive family environment on each step of his or her life-span development (Doherty & Baptiste, 1993; Gaylin, 2001; Tuson, 1985).

"Positivity" as the essence of family therapy provides a humanistic challenge for contemporary psychology. There is evident commonality between the fundamental values of family therapy and positive psychology, a "new science of strength and resilience" as Martin Seligman, founder of positive psychology, called it (Seligman & Csikszentmihalyi, 2000). Positive psychology considers its aim building human strength. There is a reservoir of human strengths and virtues (courage, optimism, hope, honesty, perseverance, resilience, rationality, insight, realism, capacity for pleasure, putting troubles into perspective, finding purpose) that make it possible to resist psychological problems. These are the same aspects of human strength that family therapy uses to support the family with difficulties and this is in accordance with the value-oriented approach of family therapy (Gaylin, 2001; Walsh, 1998).

The "positivity" concept provides continuity with the humanistic psychological tradition of viewing the individual as a complex whole, with many facets shaped by life itself, endowed with a capability for continuous development, self-fulfillment, and responsibility for the choices he or she makes. The values of family therapy also stress the people's capacity to overcome defects, problems, and symptoms, as in the unique and irreplaceable positive qualities constituting Russian psychologist Lev Vygotsky's "zone of proximate development" and "social situation of development." The role of Russian philosophical and psychological theoretical tradition in this connection also is very important; my conviction is that Vygotsky's, Bakhtin's, and V. Soloviev's theories may be helpful in this direction as well as the experience of contemporary family therapy with such positive concepts as "tolerance," "reconciliation," and "family resilience" (Shapiro, 1997a, 1997c, 1999a, 1999c).

The Concept of Positivity in Evolutionary Psychology

The concept of positivity is very important also for the development of family psychology, to discover an adequate methodological language which can deal with the epistemological, social, ethnic, and moral perspectives of psychological research on families; to overcome the one-sided and negative views of family process, in particular to combat its biologicalization and sociologicalization. The essence of positivity is human specificity–that is, what makes human beings different from other species–connected to the question of the unique nature of the human being in all cultural, historical, and evolutionary complexity (DeKay, 2000; Shapiro, 1997a, 1997b, 1997c, 1999c). Vygotsky's general cultural/historical approach to solving the nature/nurture dilemma is helpful in providing a critical analysis of contemporary sociobiology (e.g., E. Wilson, R. Dawkins), even though it is seen as being in contradiction to the evolutionary/genetic model.

The evolutionary/genetic process is acknowledged to be a positive essential of pre-human life, while creativity is considered to be a positive essential of individual human and family life. The uniqueness of any individual in pre-human living matter has significance for reproduction, in that a single organism is a passive tool in the life of its kin in the evolutionary-genetic process. But in order to be included in the "unity in diversity" of sociocultural processes, an individual human acquires such "productive" positive qualities as exclusiveness, self-worth, and self-sufficiency, which bridge the boundary between the individual human being and his or her kin which is typical of all other living matter. The value of the "individual" organism in nature is defined by sociobiologists in terms of its contribution to the reproduction of the genetic material in the population to which it belongs. The less similarity the genotype of one organism has to that of another organism, the more it is likely to regard another as a lifeless part of its environment, to be used as part of the struggle for life. However, the life of nature has its own intrinsic positive harmony.

Human life, on the other hand, becomes unharmonious and negative, and it needs adequate positive cultural support, which for centuries was provided mainly by conventional religion. Relying solely on his instincts, the human being can become the most cruel "individual organism," to which the terrible history of the 20th century provides incontestable proof.

Creativity in family relationships, the capacity for which is inherent in the potential of every human being, is the basis of a healthy family. A human is a productive being doomed to creativity in his or her existence, including in intrafamilial relations, which define the psychological specificity of a "positive model of the family." Creativity based on personal experience constitutes the essence of the psychotherapist's professional work with the family. Unlike all other living creatures, what is positive in man is not inscribed in a genetic program, as sociobiologists believe: It is governed by such positive concepts as good, truth, beauty, love, unity in diversity, universalism, creativity, dialogue, and non-manipulativeness, in short, positively oriented moral-psychological regulators of intrafamilial relationships. These serve as the foundation for a "positive model of the family" and as a solid starting point for giving a positive direction to family psychology.

Spirituality, Positivity, and Psychological Theory

Throughout human history existed religion, a social institution which represents the cumulative wisdom of humankind which supported positive tendencies, and was oriented toward unity and harmony in intrafamilial relations, and opposed cruel, manipulative tendencies in interpersonal relations among family members. Behind many family conflicts is the question of the meaning of life, for which secular humanism has no universal answer (it is a very up-to-date issue for contemporary Russia). Traditional religions, however, coped quite effectively with such issues by providing man and woman with purely spiritual support plus psychological support in the strict sense to free people from fear, especially the fear of death, and to define positive regulators for intrapersonal, interpersonal, and broader social contexts. Such support is very essential for interrelations not only within large social groups but also in direct interpersonal interactions, especially among relatives within the family.

In the 19th century, human life became so complex that the effectiveness of the psychological guidance offered by religion to the individual and the family became very doubtful. Very often, in the past two centuries, religion itself became a moral psychological problem because of fanaticism, intolerance, and cruelty toward dissidents and doubters. If religion is deaf to everyday human needs, joys, and sorrows of the soul, then people will flee from traditional religiosity into the negativism of atheism and vulgar materialism (which can assume both communist and strictly capitalist market forms, although it remains essentially manipulative in either case) or turn to new radical anti-psychological negative religiosity, which takes advantage of people's psychological crises (including their interpersonal relations within the family) to indoctrinate them with dogma and to control their minds (Shapiro, 1997b; Stander et al., 1994).

Being positive does not necessarily mean being happy and not paying attention to the negative sides of human existence. Being positive means to be real, to deal with all aspects of a given situation, not just taking into account only a part of it, to reconcile several different subcultures in one cultural unit. The modern world teems with the most varied, sometimes conflicting, cultural-normative orientations, some that have never before existed. People work, rest, get ill, communicate, have fantasies, not only in different parts of the world but also each in his or her own way (one model of individual behavior is no better and no worse than others!); diversity is evident in each and every social body, from the state and the work collective down to, most especially, the family. Every individual tends to look at the world through the prism of his or her own experience, that concrete system of culture in which he grew up and in which his or her personality was formed. In particular, in our interpersonal relations, we often are wary of unfamiliar customs, values, and behavioral patterns of those close to us, and that obstructs a positive, accepting, and supporting attitude toward the other (Shapiro, 1997c; Taggart, 1982).

The experience of family therapy teaches us how to understand and tolerate differences. Even within one family, people often live in different worlds and do not understand each other. Family therapy stresses the importance of hearing the voices of everyone in the family, including children and old people. In the framework of such a model of relationships, tension and conflicts are possible (in families and in family therapy sessions), but there also exist other types of interactions: acceptance, care and support–the latter helps to tolerate conflicts and tension as existential reality, and not be afraid of them. In this connection it is not surprising that family therapists are very sensitive to current political events. That is why postmodern, narrative and spiritual approaches are so widespread now in our field. These promote an underlying attitude toward other people which manifests itself in giving them the right to be different, to have and speak out their own points of view, even if such points of view differ from those generally accepted in a given group.

Therefore, the experience of family therapy brings us to the necessity to give a deeper definition of the "positivity" concept in comtemporary psychology. It is important to be "positive even" in this sense of embracing all aspects and developing an integral picture of a given problem. But why is the issue so difficult, why is it a real challenge for contemporary psychological theory? The answer, I suggest, is because of its interdisplinary nature, because the fact that the issue has its own history and its strong connection to human experience. We have to take into account that nowadays there are many "negative" psychologists who even use "positive" wording in manipulative ways. For instance, advertising widely uses the psychologically shallow concept of "positive imagery." This was very brightly depicted in the movie *American Beauty.* One important task of contemporary psychological theory is to create an adequate language which can be understood not only by professionals, but also by the people (clients, customers, readers) who need our knowledge. Neither a "bird language" only for psychologists nor, on the other hand, one operating exclusively at the level of lay-persons would be suitable for this purpose.

The contemporary world is very complex. It is more complex than in earlier centuries when religion played the same role played now by psychology. That is why contemporary psychology has the theoretical mission of rethinking the psychological role of religion (and spirituality at large) in contemporary society. Spirituality had and still has psychological potential, and is universal in essence; it has been an important unifying factor for all people, operating often as a condition for harmony. In particular, human beings have to understand that they are not slaves to those who are close to them and who often have a tendency to manipulate them. Nor should they act as slaveowners and manipulators.

There is a fundamental contradiction in the idea of positivity: Is it possible to integrate all aspects of reality in the context of a particular value system, and if not, how can a common understanding between value systems be reached? From its very beginning, the science of psychology developed as a secular pursuit far removed from the traditional (in particular, religious) values of society. Today it is necessary to search for bridges betweeen secular scientific psychology and traditional spiritual systems. In this sense we may consider humanistic psychology as a challenge to scientific psychology and positive psychology as a challenge to humanistic psychology. It is important in this connection to do some theoretical work on the issue. A good start is to analyze the positive philosophy of Augustus Compte, not only those of his works which became a source for 19th century positivism and contemporary neo-positivistic movements, but also those which deal with his idea of a "religion of humanity." In this connection it is very interesting to analyse the criticism of Compte undertaken by the Russian "silver age" philosopher Vladimir Soloviev (Shapiro, 2001b).

CONCLUSION

This article is devoted to analyzing the role of the family theme in contemporary society and in contemporary psychology. Florence Kaslow helped the theme to spread worldwide in a non-manipulative way, in particular into Russia. The significant role of a professional family–professional organizations, local and international–is quite evident. Florence often spoke about "the international family of family therapists" (Kaslow, 2002), and that we need positive family therapy and family psychology community on both national and international levels as we need an image of positive family.

The family theme is very important for contemporary human existence and therefore for contemporary psychology, in particular for positive psychology (Aspinwall, 1998; Aspinwall, Richter, & Hoffman, 2001; Csikszentmihalyi, 1993; Seligman & Csikszentmihalyi, 2000). Family psychology is still an empirical discipline and needs a theoretical basis very urgently; my assumption is that the concept of positivity gives such a basis. Positive family psychology can be considered a part of both positive psychology and family psychology. It is on their cross-section; both disciplines are rather new, so they can benefit from their current intersections on a large scale.

REFERENCES

Aspinwall, L. G. (1998). Rethinking the role of positive affect in self-regulation. *Motivation and Emotion, 22*, 1-32.

Aspinwall, L. G., Richter, L., & Hoffman, R. R. (2001). Understanding how optimism "works": An examination of optimists' adaptive moderation of belief and behavior. In E. C. Chang (Ed.), *Optimism and pessimism: Theory, research, and practice* (pp. 217-238). Washington: American Psychological Association.

Csikszentmihalyi, M. (1993). *The evolving self.* New York: HarperCollins.

DeKay, W. T. (2000). Evolutionary psychology. In W. C. Nichols, M. A. Pace-Nichols, D. S. Becvar, & A. Y. Napier (Eds.), *Handbook of family development and intervention* (pp. 23-40). New York: John Wiley and Sons.

Doherty, W. J., & Baptiste D. (1993). Theories emerging from family therapy. In P. Boss, W. J. Doherty, R. LaRossa, W. R. Schumm, & S. K. Steinmetz (Eds.), *Sourcebook of family theories and methods: A contextual approach* (pp. 505-529). New York: Plenum Press.

Gaylin N. (2001). *Family, self and psychotherapy: A person-centered perspective.* Ross-on-Wye, NY: PCCS Books.

Kaslow, F. (Ed.) (1990). *Voices in family psychology. Vol. 1, 2.* Newbury Park, CA: Sage Publications.

Kaslow F. W. (2002). History of family therapy: Evolution outside of the U.S. IFTA Home Page. (www.ifta-familytherapy.org).

Kroupin, G. (2000). New Americans from Russia. In W. C. Nichols, M. A. Pace-Nichols, D. S. Becvar, & A. Y. Napier (Eds.), *Handbook of family development and intervention* (pp. 305-309). New York: John Wiley and Sons.

Long, J., & Shapiro, A. (2001). My spouse the alien: Working with cultural complaints in cross-cultural couples. In *Travelling through time and space.* Abstracts of 4th European Conference on Family Therapy. Budapest, p. 70.

Nichols, W. C., Pace-Nichols, M. A., Becvar, D. S., & Napier, A. Y. (Eds.) (2000). *Handbook of family development and intervention.* New York: John Wiley and Sons.

Peseschkian, N. (1980). *Positive family therapy.* Berlin: Springer-Verlag.

Scharwiess, S. (2002). The 'Five-Mountain' Diagram: Summarizing psychological challenges of transitional societies. In *A decade of dialogue: Psychological dimensions of transition in central Europe since 1989* (pp. 210-218). Berlin: Systems in Transition.

Seligman, M. E. P., & Csikszentmihalyi, M. (2000). Positive psychology: An introduction. *American Psychologist, 55,* 5-14.

Shapiro, A. (July 4-10, 1996). *A positive experiential approach to the psychology of intrafamily relationships and family therapy: Some theoretical considerations.* Presented at the Eighth World Congress of the International Family Therapy Association.

Shapiro, A. (1997a). Family therapy and psychological theory interconnections: Indifference or collaboration? Is there a need for theoretical family psychology? *The International Connection, 10(2),* 7-11.

Shapiro, A. (1997b). The concept of positivity in family therapy and the task of psychological assistance to the contemporary Russian family. *Journal of Russian and East European Psychology, 35,* 73-92.

Shapiro, A. (1997c). *Family psychology and L. S. Vygotsky's concept of "the social situation of development" "Vygotsky in theory–Vygotsky in practice."* Proceedings from the Vygotsky Seminar in Trondheim 1996. Trondheim, Norway, pp. 29-32.

Shapiro, A. (1998a). *A challenging situation for contemporary Russian family: Unity in diversity? Psychotherapy of the 21st century.* The First World Conference of Positive Psychotherapy. Moscow-St. Petersburg 1997. Conference proceedings. Wiesbaden, Germany, pp. 230-233.

Shapiro, A. (1998b). From Russia with despair, hope and love, the new "family therapy chosen land." *The International Connection, 11(1)*, 5-6.

Shapiro, A. (May 13-15, 1998c). *Family violence as cultural-historical phenomenon.* Reader of the 7th "Systems in Transition" Conference. Overcoming violence–Persons, families and societies. Dusseldorf, pp. 109-110.

Shapiro, A. (1999a). The value dimension in Russian family therapy. *The International Connection, 12(1)*, 11-14.

Shapiro, A. (April 13-17, 1999b). *Family resilience as a value of contemporary Russian family therapy.* Abstract of paper presentation at 1999 IFTA World Family Therapy Congress. Akron, Ohio, USA.

Shapiro, A. (September 1-5, 1999c). *L. S. Vygotsky's concept of "the social situation of development" and family psychology.* Proceedings of paper presentation at 9th European Conference on Developmental Psychology Human Development. Speze, Greece, p. 121.

Shapiro, A. (May 23-25, 2000a). *Family life education and post-Soviet youth.* International Conference on Post-Soviet Youth: A Comparative Study. Conference abstracts. Jerusalem, pp. 86-89.

Shapiro, A. (June 14-17, 2000b). Reconciliation as a key concept for contemporary Russian society and for Russian family therapy. In *Reconciliation: New voices for a new era.* International Family Therapy Association World Family Therapy Congress. Final programme and abstracts. Oslo, Norway, p. 25, ab. 178.

Shapiro, A. (August 4-8, 2000c). *Russian family in transition.* A paper for 2000 American Psychological Association Annual Convention (Washington, DC), Division 43 "Psychology of peace." A handout.

Shapiro, A. (May-June 2001a). *Case example on reconciliation process. Family therapy professional community in Moscow: Is reconciliation possible?* Abstract of paper presentation at 2001 Systems in Transition Conference. Praha, pp. 53-54.

Shapiro, A. (2001b). Theoretical problems of contemporary family psychology and V. Soloviev's philosophy. In *Philosophy of psychology: Back to the roots* (pp. 56-65). Moscow: Smisl (in Russian).

Sharlin, S., Kaslow, F. W. & Hammerschmidt, H. (2000). *Together through thick and thin: A multinational picture of long term marriages.* New York: The Haworth Press, Inc.

Stander, V., Piercy, F., Mackinnon, D., & Helmeke, K. (1994). Spirituality, religion and family therapy: Competing or complementary worlds? *American Journal of Family Therapy, 22(1)*, 27-41.

Szapocznik, J., & Kurtines, W. (1995). Family psychology and cultural diversity: Opportunities for theory, research, and application. In N. Goldenberg & J. Veroff (Eds.), *The culture and psychology reader* (pp. 808-824). New York: New York University Press.

Taggart, M. (1982). Values, ethics, legalities and the family therapist: II. Linear versus systemic values: Implications for family therapy. *Family Therapy Collections*, Vol. 1, 23-39.

Tuson, G. (1985). Philosophy and family therapy: A study in interconnectedness. *Journal of Family Therapy, 7*, 277-294.

Walsh, F. (1998). *Strengthening family resilience.* New York: Guilford Press.

Sense of Coherence as a Meta-Theory for Salutogenic Family Therapy

Kjell Hansson
Marianne Cederblad

SUMMARY. Resilience has during the last ten years been more and more put into focus. One concept in this domain is "salutogenesis," coined by Aaron Antonovsky. He claimed that sense of coherence is a vital ingredient in resilience. The sub-concepts of sense of coherence (SOC) are comprehensibility, manageability and meaningfulness that can all be used in a meta model of family therapy. In a lot of research, SOC has shown to be closely correlated to both psychiatric and physical health. We think these concepts are of great interest and importance in forming a meta-theory for family therapy. *[Article copies available for a fee from The Haworth Document Delivery Service: 1-800-HAWORTH. E-mail address: <docdelivery@haworthpress.com> Website: <http://www.HaworthPress.com> © 2004 by The Haworth Press, Inc. All rights reserved.]*

Kjell Hansson is Professor, Department of Social Work, Lund University, Ragnar Lodbroks Gränd, 16, 22475, Lund, Sweden (E-mail: Kjell.Hansson@soch.lu.se).

Marianne Cederblad is Professor Emeritus, Department of Child and Youth Psychiatry, Lund University, Sweden.

The authors present this article to honor Dr. Florence Kaslow. She has several times conducted highly appreciated teaching in Sweden and has put attention on resilience and multiperspectives in family psychology. The authors want to support these perspectives by presenting this article. Dr. Kaslow has also done an important review of the family therapy education program at Lund University. The authors also want to thank Dr. William Nichols for his great help in editing and commenting on this article.

[Haworth co-indexing entry note]: "Sense of Coherence as a Meta-Theory for Salutogenic Family Therapy." Hansson, Kjell, and Marianne Cederblad. Co-published simultaneously in *Journal of Family Psychotherapy* (The Haworth Press, Inc.) Vol. 15, No. 1/2, 2004, pp. 39-54; and: *Family Therapy Around the World: A Festschrift for Florence W. Kaslow* (ed: William C. Nichols) The Haworth Press, Inc., 2004, pp. 39-54. Single or multiple copies of this article are available for a fee from The Haworth Document Delivery Service [1-800-HAWORTH, 9:00 a.m. - 5:00 p.m. (EST). E-mail address: docdelivery@haworthpress.com].

http://www.haworthpress.com/web/JFP
Digital Object Identifier: 10.1300/J085v15n01_04

KEYWORDS. Resilience, salutogenic, sense of coherence, positive psychology, family therapy

When Freud laid the foundations of modern psychotherapies, he based his theories on the scientific thinking of his times. His theories about psychic energy were based on the theories of physics and mechanics of the 19th century. Salvador Minuchin (1993) says in *Family Healing* that the conception that there in some way was a store of psychic energy seemed to be more connected to hydraulics than to children. This ambition to base psychiatric theory in the current scientific theories of other disciplines has continued. When family theory started, its practical work was based on clinical, empirical practice but the theoretical explanations have been borrowed from cybernetics and linguistic theory. Von Bertalanffy's and Prigogine's writings in the field of biology and chemistry were applied to the family. So was the biological research of Maturana. The anthropologist Bateson became a founding father, and philosophers such as Bertrand Russell and Wittgenstein were used to explain phenomena of the therapeutic process. Structural family therapy was deeply inspired by another anthropologist, Levi-Strauss, who belonged to the philosophical school of constructivism. Later experts have developed the use of narratives, a concept borrowed from the French philosopher Rinceur. Recent family therapy writers talk about de-constructivism in therapy, falling back on writings from another French philosopher, Derrida.

The aim in this article is to present an alternative perspective in family therapy and to present some of the empirical support for this perspective.

AN ALTERNATIVE PERSPECTIVE BASED ON RESILIENCE RESEARCH

Strangely enough, little interest in family therapy has been focused on the current development in the health sciences, which focuses on "salutogenesis," the origins of health, stress resilience, and coping. One exception, however, is the research done by Froma Walsh (1998, 2003). If we wish to help families to become healthy and growth producing, scientific studies of individuals and families who themselves have managed to develop well under adverse conditions ought to be an adequate base for development of new therapeutic interventions.

Since the 1970s many researchers studying children of psychotic parents, mainly schizophrenics, have shifted their focus from looking at risk factors to looking at factors explaining stress resilience (Bleuler, 1978; Kaufmann et al., 1979; Anthony, 1974; Garmezy, 1974, 1981; Graham et al., 1973; Fischer et al.,

1987; Musick et al., 1987; Worland et al., 1987; Seifer et al., 1992). Interest in stress resilience was expanded to studies of children growing up in other high-risk environments such as inner city slums (Garmezy & Nuechterlein, 1972; Garmezy, 1987; Wyman et al., 1992; Gribble et al., 1993), children from low socioeconomic groups (White, 1985), children at risk for abuse and neglect (Farber & Egeland, 1987), and children from multiproblem families (Lösel et al., 1992).

Two early studies starting in the 1950s on normal children also described stress resilience and coping (Murphy & Moriarty, 1976; Werner et al., 1977, 1982, 1989, 1992, 2001). In the famous Kauai study, Emmy Werner focused on the 30% of her cohorts who were considered at risk because they had experienced four or more child psychiatric factors before the age of two years. She followed her cohort longitudinally until they reached the age of 40.

Individual factors found by different investigators in increasing resilience in children and adolescents are:

- A good social capacity (i.e., sociability). This is described as being socially open, cooperative, and having open, kind, and calm behavior (Rutter, 1979; Rutter et al., 1979; Garmezy, 1981; Garmezy & Rutter, 1983; White, 1985; Werner, 1989).
- Positive self-esteem and autonomy. Many researchers consider self-esteem (Bleuler, 1978; Rutter, 1979; Garmezy, 1981; Garmezy & Rutter, 1983; Werner, 1985) and autonomy to be phenomena furthering stress resilience (Garmezy, 1981; Anthony, 1974; Werner, 1985).
- Successful coping (i.e., the capacity to solve problems and handle developmental and traumatic crises) (Garmezy, 1981; Murphy & Moriarty, 1976; Rutter, 1979; Anthony, 1974; Werner, 1985; Lösel, Kolip, & Bender, 1992).
- Intelligence and creativity (Garmezy, 1981, 1987; Rutter, 1979; White, 1985; Anthony, 1974; Lösel, Kolip, & Bender, 1992; Offord, 1974).
- Development of special interests and hobbies during childhood (Werner, 1985).
- Inner locus of control and good impulse control and high activity and energy (Murphy & Moriarty, 1976; Werner, 1985).

Resilient environmental factors proposed were aspects of family composition such as being the only child in the family during the first four years of life (Hirschi, 1969) or the family having four or fewer children spaced more than two years apart. Werner (1985) listed steady employment by the mother as a protective factor. "Required helpfulness" was a protective factor, since it allowed the child to develop a feeling of self-worth, self-reliance, and autonomy

(Bleuler, 1978; Rachman, 1979). A significant other (i.e., an adult outside the family that the child could connect with and identify with, who could be a role model, a source of support, and a compensation for insufficient parenting) has been shown to be important (Mead, 1962; Rutter, 1979; Garmezy, 1981; Garmezy & Rutter, 1983; Kauffman, 1979). Werner (1985) also pointed out that having additional caretakers besides the mother is a protective factor. Care by siblings, grandparents, and the availability of kin and neighbors for emotional support were important in her study.

Certain qualities of the inner life of the family were found to be protective. Clearly defined delineation of subsystems within the family (Garmezy, 1981; Garmezy & Rutter, 1983) and structured rules in the household (Coopersmith, 1967; West, 1973; Werner, 1985; Gramezy, 1987; Gribble et al., 1963; Wyman et al., 1992) increased resilience, while a high degree of involvement in family entanglement was destructive (Hoover & Franz, 1972). Having a "trusting and intimate relationship" with at least one parent was a protective factor (Anthony, 1974; Beardslee, 1989; Rutter, 1979; Seifer et al., 1992; White, 1985). The importance of a positive parent/child relationship in early childhood characterized among other things by open and trustful communication as well as shared values between the generations have also been stressed by Werner (1985).

From the family perspective, Walsh (1998, 2003) in her study of normal families has arrived to very much the same resilient variables and results. The fact that different research perspectives show the same results strengthens the validity of these studies.

These studies were mainly done within the fields of developmental psychology and child psychiatry. The medical sociologist Aaron Antonovsky focused on adults who remained somatically and mentally healthy under conditions of severe stress. He developed the concept of "sense of coherence" in the framework of what he called "the salutogenic model" (Antonovsky, 1979, 1987). He proposed that it be used for the orientation, which seeks to understand the emergence of health. The sense of coherence is the answer to the salutogenic question, and is defined as:

A global orientation that expresses the extent to which one has a pervasive, enduring though dynamic feeling of confidence that:

1. The stimuli deriving from one's internal and external environments in the course of living that are structured, predictable, and explicable (comprehensibility),
2. the resources are available to one to meet the demands posed by these stimuli (manageability), and
3. these demands are challenges, worthy of investment and engagement (meaningfulness) (Antonovsky, 1987, p. 19).

The person with a strong sense of coherence confronting stressors, Antonovsky hypothesized, is capable of clarifying and structuring the nature of the stressor, believes that the appropriate resources are available and can be mobilized to deal successfully with the challenge, and is motivated to deal with it. Such an orientation to life, he proposed, allows the selection of appropriate coping strategies and provides a solid base for maintenance and strengthening of health and well-being.

EMPIRICAL SUPPORT FOR THE SALUTOGENIC PERSPECTIVE

Our own studies (Cederblad et al., 1994, 1995a+b, 1996; Dahlin et al., 1990), based on the concepts previously mentioned, comprised 590 participants first studied at the age of 0 to 15 years in 1949 as part of a longitudinal population study in an area of southern Sweden. Out of the 590 children, 221 had experienced at least three risk factors for negative psychosocial development. These individuals were re-interviewed when they were between 40 and 55 years of age. We used multiple ways of assessing their mental health. All filled in the Hopkin's Symptom Checklist, which covers 90 items describing different kinds of mental health problems, and a Quality of Life Scale measuring satisfaction with material conditions, interpersonal relations, and inner feelings. An in-depth interview was performed with each individual. Based on that, two independent raters assessed their psychosocial health using Luborsky's Health Sickness Rating Scale. Correlations were found between the sense of coherence questionnaire and a variety of potential health-promoting factors. The same health-promoting factors also correlated directly with the different measures of positive mental health. A stepwise regression analysis showed that 60 percent of the variance in health was explained by the concept sense of coherence measured by Antonovsky's questionnaire. This concept was totally dominating among the potential health factors, regardless of measurement method.

Another study in southern Sweden (Andersson et al., 1993) assessed 657 teenagers, 13-16 years of age, randomly selected from the population. There, we tried to analyze the connection between the sense of coherence concept and different family factors, using self-rating questionnaires, which were filled in by the teenagers about their own families. The questionnaires were Moos and Moos' Family Environment Scale, Olson's FACES (Family Environment and Cohesion Adaptability Scale), a Swedish scale measuring family climate, and a Swedish questionnaire measuring EE (Expressed Emotion). There were medium high correlations between a high sense of coherence and closeness in the family, expressiveness, interest in recreation, and organization. There were also moderately high negative correlations between a high sense of coherence and the measurement of distance, chaos, isolation, conflict, attribution (using scapegoating), emotional over-involvement, and critical remarks. A multiple regression analysis showed that 38% of the variances of the sense of coherence was explained by the family factors. High closeness, low chaos, and low attribution contributed most to a high sense of coherence.

Other studies have shown the same association between a high sense of coherence and positive mental health. Margalit and co-workers (1989) found that parents of children with a physical handicap have a lower sense of coherence and a lower satisfaction with family life than parents of normal children. Petrie and Brook (1992) studied 150 patients who were hospitalized for depression and suicidal behavior. The group was followed up after six months. The sense of coherence was a better prediction instrument than degree of depression, self-esteem, or feelings of hopelessness when assessing the prognosis. Kalimo and Vuori (1990) showed in a longitudinal epidemiological study of 706 individuals, who were between 31 and 44 years of age at the time of the investigation, that high sense of coherence was associated with competence and satisfaction with life.

We suggest that such a powerful health concept as the sense of coherence is a valuable base for health promoting family therapy. Our studies have also shown that various family factors are connected to the individual sense of coherence disposition in a family member. We have started to use a salutogenic model of family therapy based on the sense of coherence at our own clinic.

AN ALTERNATIVE MODEL FOR FAMILY THERAPY

Perhaps the most interesting question is the difference between this salutogenic family therapy approach and other family therapy approaches that have been influencing the field in recent years. We think that it is very important that a family approach or model have some kind of scientific empirical background, where we know that the variability or dimensions we are trying to influence have something to do with the individual's and family's physical health and psychiatric health. As Antonovsky puts it, "First of all we have to question ourselves about what we actually ask in a family therapy session." From a salutogenic perspective we ask questions about what has influenced your well-being. What has influenced your health? What influences your health today? From a pathogenic perspective we ask families, "What is the problem? What has caused the problem?" (1987, p. 3). These are two very different approaches that create different pictures in the heads of the family members.

Research from the Lundby study (Cederblad et al., 1994, 1995a+b, 1996; Dahlin et al., 1990) have shown that a high-risk history explains about one-third of the outcome 40 years later. This means that the history explains only 33% of the actual situation, which leaves us with several other possibilities to explain the health in a given situation. We need a couple of other possibilities than risk factors to make a fuller description of the actual situation. From this research we also learn that the more salutogenic recourses the individual has in his high-risk childhood the better life they get 40 years later. That indicates that treatment in this area should take several salutogenic factors into consideration.

Whatever salutogenic factors we work with in a salutogenic family therapy, we think it is important that we use several agents to change and improve facilitate the actual salutogenic factors. When working with salutogenic meta-theory with families, we have to take into consideration all the resilience factors that previous research has found concerning the family.

Different family therapy schools have focused on some of these, but in order to work in a salutogenic framework, we have to pick techniques from different schools and integrate them into our therapy.

Structure, subsystems, and roles are important. Structural and strategic family therapy can contribute with effective techniques. Clear and supportive communication is important. To build hope is important since having hopeful and positive expectations about the future is an important resilience factor. Both Satir and others have stressed the importance of "positive reframing" and have pointed out positive intent by reformulation. Effective appropriate and flexible coping methods are essential to resilience building. Many useful coping techniques are basic in the methods of de Shazer, White, and Tomm.

As shown in Figures 1, 2, and 3, the concept of sense of coherence is built up by three sub-concepts: comprehensibility, manageability, and meaningfulness. In a therapeutic situation, we think it is very important to work with these three concepts through different kinds of therapeutic intervention with one or more of the salutogenic factors. The reason for that is, as shown earlier, if we could change the salutogenic factors, it is probably possible to gain better health for the patient. The salutogenic theory with the concept of sense of coherence could be a meta-model in therapeutic work.

Comprehensibility. In looking at comprehensibility, it is possible to use several of the existing therapeutic models, each of which has salutogenic parts that we can use when we work with the different factors. Virginia Satir, for example, with her way of working with communication could raise the amount of comprehensibility in a family. Salvador Minuchin's way to intervene also can influence the comprehensibility.

FIGURE 1. Salutogenic Possibilities in Different Family Therapeutic Models Regarding Comprehensibility

Family therapeutic models	Salutogenic parts in the model	Therapeutic interventions from this model
Virginia Satir	Works with the communication. Works to a certain extent with insight.	Clarifies if the different family members understand one another using the therapist as an interpreter of the communication.
Salvador Minuchin	Has a row of different educational statements in the treatment.	Often explains "circularities," how one can see different connections or patterns in the family, etc.
Steve de Shazer	Relates to the patient's description of the problem. Concrete situations.	Asks about concrete situations. Asks about specific occasions or behaviors.
Karl Tomm	A humane attitude in general. The patients shall produce the knowledge.	Reflective questions which give the patient a new knowledge.
Michael White	Careful. Everybody must understand what is going on. Tries to find methods and metaphors that can be understood by relatively small children.	Externalization. Takes concrete measures in order to help a child. Everyone can take part and understand what they can do.

FIGURE 2. Salutogenic Possibilities in Different Family Therapeutic Models Regarding Manageability

Family therapeutic models	Salutogenic parts in the model	Therapeutic interventions from this model
Virginia Satir	Points out positive possibilities in relations and communication that could be possible to change.	Works with small parts of a communication or parts of a pattern in the present situation.
Salvador Minuchin	Discusses concrete parts of a behavioral sequence. Homework for training new ways.	Keeps limited interventions possible for the families to accomplish by solving tasks.
Steve de Shazer	Works with parts of solutions, not with a whole problem at the same time.	Works with relatively limited changes in behavior that the patient him/herself can manage.
Karl Tomm	Often works with the limit of one problem at a time.	Asks reflective questions about a defined area that directly could be a matter of coping to a situation differently.
Michael White	Reattributes by putting the problems outside the patient. Helps the family to see positive sides of, for example, the child.	Externalization. By this method one helps the family in a new way to deal with a difficult situation in order not to become personally attributed.

FIGURE 3. Salutogenic Possibilities in Different Family Therapeutic Models Regarding Meaningfulness

Family therapeutic models	Salutogenic parts in the model	Therapeutic interventions from this model
Virginia Satir	Tries to activate all family members in order to make the therapeutic work meaningful.	Creates sculptures and investigates thoroughly if the sculptures correspond with the experiences of the individuals.
Salvador Minuchin	Joins the family in order to be able to understand the family and increase their experiences of a meaningful change.	Joining. Often works with the symptom as a basis. Places the solution of the problem within the family.
Steve de Shazer	Acts on the needs from the clients/families and what they experience as problems.	Acts on the things that work, investigates how this is done. Points out differences that could give meaningful information.
Karl Tomm	Works with the problems that the family wants to work with.	Reflective questions. It is up to the patient and the family to look for the meaningful questions.
Michael White	Keeps to the presented problem. Tries to find openings that are meaningful for the patient and the family to go on with.	Externalizes. Makes a point of questioning the patient and the family about what measures that could be included in the treatment and checks that they are meaningful.

Manageability. The same pattern prevails with regard to manageability. For example, Steve de Shazer, in his solution-focused model, works with specific parts of the problem. That means that you could increase the individual's or the family's manageability in the situation.

Meaningfulness. Karl Tomm can use his way of looking at the problem with his reflective questioning to increase the meaningfulness in the treatment situation for the family, for instance.

Salutogenic theory with the concept of sense of coherence can be a meta-model in therapeutic work. In a therapeutic situation we think it is very important to work with the three sub-concepts of sense of coherence–comprehensibility, manageability, and meaningfulness–through different kinds of therapeutic interventions with one of more of the salutogenic factors. As noted, if we can change the salutogenic factors it is probably possible to reach better health for the patient. We can use several of the existing therapeutic models, each of which has salutogenic parts that can be used with the different factors.

For example, Satir's way of working with communication can raise the amount of comprehensibility in the family, as can Minuchin's different kinds of intervention. With regard to manageability, de Shazer's solution-focused work with specific parts of the problem can increase the individual's or the family's manageability in the situation. Karl Tomm's use of reflective questioning can increase meaningfulness in the treatment situation for the family. Michael White's way of working increases the meaningfulness for the family by keeping track of the problems family members themselves have presented. (The different suggestions collected from different models are only suggestions and not a total description of the respective models.)

In these ways we can use the theory of sense of coherence and the theory of salutogenesis as a meta-model when we treat individuals or families. One of the most important differences between other theoretical models and a salutogenic approach, including an approach where we use the different models, is that we always take under consideration salutogenic parts. What causes health instead of what causes problems? We also use the results from research where we now know that we have a lot of different factors that probably are more health-promoting than other factors. For example, if we manage to increase the person's inner locus of control, the person probably will get better health.

We are using this salutogenic model in a couple of treatment projects at the department of child and youth psychiatry at the University of Lund (Sweden). One project is with adolescents between 13 and 18 years of age. We call this project Absolute Salutogenesis; both the investigation and the treatment of the adolescents and their families lean heavily on salutogenic principles. The investigation focuses on competences more than weaknesses. For example, if the staff plays hockey with the adolescents, they do not stop the game when the youngsters make trouble. Instead, they stop the game when the adolescents do not make trouble, taking a time out and asking the youth: What happens now when you don't lose control over your aggressiveness and don't make trouble? Can you explain why you don't do that? What kind of resources did you use in this situation? In salutogenic family therapy we are trying to work with the salutogenic episodes where the individual and the family are acting in a health-promoting way like the example above, where the young person manages to retain self-control, rather than focusing on the problem situations, which were much more frequent. We systematically analyze individual competences, intelligence, temperaments, locus of control, etc., family characteristics found in studies on resilience to promote health such as clearly delineated subsystems, structured rules and roles, open supportive communications, etc. The treatment focuses on enhancing such health-promoting factors that are missing on different levels of life. We focus also on the family as a stress-buffering supportive system increasing its sense of coherence.

DISCUSSION

Theories of psychotherapies have usually developed from patient contacts within the care system. In these contexts we don't encounter the stress-resilient individuals. The salutogenic theory formation is based on epidemiological studies on high-risk families outside the care system which give new answers on how treatment could be carried out. Rutter (2000) wrote based on his epidemiological studies, "Even with most severe stressors and adversities, it is unusual for more than half of the children to develop significant psychopathology" (Rutter, 2000, p. 651). That points out that it is important to look for other possible explanations for different individual developmental results. It is not only risk factors that are interesting!

In postmodern society, life is becoming more and more complex, and the speed of change increases, and preserved sense of coherence is of utmost importance for the individual in order to keep reasonable health. Many researchers have shown that the stress in today's society has increased. A well known Swedish stress researcher pointed out that our biological stress reactions are still the same as when they developed during the stone age, but they are not as well adapted to the stressors of a modern information age (Levi, 2002). "Biologically a cave man is sitting in front of the computer" (Levi, 2002, p. 19). That gives us as human beings a lot of problems, but it also points out our fantastic adaptation ability!

To sum up, we emphasize that the salutogenic perspective contributes to our understanding in the following ways:

Treatment Based on Suitable Research

A consistent ambition in this article has been to try to present a treatment approach where health research is the basis for a planned treatment. Salutogenic family therapy differs from other family therapeutic models dealing with positive reformulation by giving outlines of the fields effective to work with. We believe that it is important for the survival of family therapy that the treatment we provide also is based on scientific premises that can be examined and revised. That borrowing family therapy theories from other fields like biology or philosophy might be hazardous is exemplified by the widely spread assumption among family therapists that instructive interaction is impossible in systemic family therapy. Several research findings on parent-child interaction in parent education have shown instructive methods are very effective in improving the relations between parents and children and changing the behavior of the children (Webster-Stratton 1998). What we know today is that in a longitudinal perspective, a row of salutogenic factors from a statistical point of view leads to good mental health.

A New Use of Language

The salutogenic perspective can contribute to an alternative use of language. We get from it words and concepts related to health and soundness. Typically, in care and treatment, pathogenic diagnoses and discussions dominate, and, partly depending on that, we do not use a language for alternative thinking. In line with contemporary social constructivism, the language in salutogenic treatment is an important aspect, not to say a determining factor, in treatment (Hoffman, 1992). This means that if we can acquire new concepts from the salutogenic theory, we will also acquire a new knowledge.

Emphasizing Resources and Possibilities

In salutogenic family therapy it is important to emphasize the salutogenic efficacies in a family. This can be short-term as we are asking for explanations and causes for well-being or the capacity for coping with a difficult situation, and not merely inquiring about the problems.

REFERENCES

Andersson, L., Balldin, T., & Rudnert, U. (1993). *Högstadieungdomars känsla av sammanhang och temperament. En jämförande studie av KASAM och EAS.* Socialhögskolan, Lunds universitet. (In Swedish).

Anthony, E.J. (1974). The syndrome of the psychological invulnerable child. In: Anthony, E.J. & Koupernik, C. (Eds.), *The child in his family.* Vol. III. New York: Wiley, 529-544.

Antonovsky, A. (1979). *Health, stress and coping.* San Francisco: Jossey-Bass.

Antonovsky, A. (1987). *Unraveling the mystery of health.* San Francisco: Jossey-Bass.

Beardslee, W.R. (1989). The role of self-understanding in resilient individuals: The development of a perspective. *American Journal of Orthopsychiatry*, 59(2), 266-278.

Bleuler, M. (1978). *The schizophrenic disorders: Long-term patient and family studies.* New Haven: Yale University Press.

Cederblad, M., Dahlin, L., Hagnell, O., & Hansson, K. (1994). Intelligence and temperament as protective factors for mental health. A cross-sectional and prospective epidemiological study. *European Archives of Psychiatry and Clinical Neuroscience*, 245, 11-19.

Cederblad, M., Dahlin, L., Hagnell, O., & Hansson, K. (1995a). Salutogenic childhood factors reported by middle-aged individuals. Follow up of the children from the Lundby study grown up in families experiencing three or more childhood psychiatric risk factors. *European Archives of Psychiatry and Clinical Neuroscience*, 244, 1-11.

Cederblad, M., Dahlin, L., Hagnell, O., & Hansson, K. (1995b). Coping with developmental and traumatic crisis. Follow-up of children from the Lundby study grown up in families experiencing three or more childhood psychiatric risk factors. *Acta Psychiatrica Scandinavia*, 91, 322-330.

Cederblad, M. & Hansson, K. (1996). Sense of coherence–a concept influencing health and quality of life in a Swedish psychiatric at-risk group. *Israel Journal of Medical Science*, Vol. 32, Nos. 3-4, 194-199.

Coopersmith, S. (1967). *The antecedents of self-esteem.* San Francisco: W H Freeman.

Dahlin, L., Cederblad, M., Antonovsky, A., & Hagnell, O. (1990). Childhood vulnerability and adult invincibility. *Acta Psychiatrica Scandanavia*, 82, 228-232.

Fanshel, D. (1972). *Far from the reservation: The transracial adoption of American Indian children.* New York: Scarecrow Press.

Farber, E.A. & Egeland, B. (1987). Invulnerability among abused and neglected children. In: Anthony, E.J. & Cohler, B.J. (Eds.), *The invulnerable child.* New York: Guilford Press.

Fischer, L., Kokes, R.F., Cole, R.E., Perkins, P.M., & Wynne, L.C. (1987). Competent children at risk : A study of well-functioning offspring of disturbed parents. In: Anthony, E.J. & Cohler, B.J. (Eds.), *The invulnerable child.* New York: Guilford Press.

Garmezy, N. (1974). The study of competence in children at risk for severe psychopathology. In: Anthony, E.J. & Coupernik, C. (Eds.), *The child in his family*, Vol. III , 77-98, New York: Wiley.

Garmezy, N. (1981). Children under stress: Perspective on antecendents and correlates of vulnerability and resistance to psychopathology. In: Rabin, A.I., Aronoff, J., Barclay, A.M., & Zucker, R.A. (Eds.), *Further explorations in personality.* Wiley, New York, pp. 196-269.

Garmezy, N. (1987). Stress, competence, and development: Continuities in the study of schizophrenic adults, children vulnerable to psychopathology, and the search for stress-resistant children. *American Journal of Orthopsychiatry*, 57(2), 159-174.

Garmezy, N. & Nuechterlein, K. (1972). Invulnerable children: The fact and fiction of competence and disadvantage. *American Journal of Orthopsychiatry*, 42 , 328-329.

Garmezy, N. & Rutter, M. (1983). *Stress, coping and development in children.* New York: McGraw-Hill.

Graham, P. (1978). Child psychiatry recent epidemiological findings. *Arch franc Pédiat*, 35, 810-814.

Gribble, P.A., Cowen, E.L., Wyman, P.A., Work, W.C., Wannon, M., & Raoof, A. (1993). Parent and child views of parent-child relationship qualities and resilient outcomes among urban children. *Journal of Child Psychology and Psychiatry*, 34, 507-519.

Hirschi, T. (1969). *Causes of delinquency*. Los Angeles: University of California Press.

Hoover, C.F. & Franz, J.D. (1972). Siblings in the families of schizophrenics. *Archives of General Psychiatry*, 26, 334-342.

Kalimo, R. & Vuori, J. (1990). Work and sense of coherence–resources for competence and life satisfaction. *Behavior Medicine*, 76-88.

Kauffman, C., Grunebaum, H., Cohler B., & Gamer, E. (1979). Superkids: Competent children of psychotic mothers. *American Journal of Psychiatry*, 136(11), 1398-1402.

Levi, L. (2002). *Stressen i mitt liv*. Stockholm: Natur och Kultur (in Swedish).

Lösel, F., Kolip, P., & Bender, D. (1992) Stress-Resistenz im Multiproblem-Milieu. Sind seelisch widerstandfähige Jugendliche "Superkids"? *Z Klin Psychol*, XXI (1), 48-63.

Margalit, M., Leyser, Y., & Avraham, Y. (1989). Classification and validation of family climate subtypes in kibbutz fathers of disabled and nondisabled children. *Journal of Abnormal Child Psychology*, 17(1) 91-107.

Mead, G.H. (1962). *Mind, self and society. From the standpoint of a social behaviorist*. Chicago: University of Chicago Press.

Minuchin, S. & Nichols, M.P. (1993). *Family healing. Tales of hope and renewal from family therapy*. New York: Free Press.

Murphy, L.B. & Moriarty, A.E. (1976). *Vulnerability, coping and growth*. New Haven, CT: Yale University Press.

Musick, J.S., Stott, F.M., Spencer, K.K., Goldman, J., & Cohler, B.J. (1987). Maternal factors related to vulnerability and resiliency in young children at risk. In: Anthony, E.J. & Cohler, B.J. (Eds.), *The invulnerable child*. Guilford Press, New York, pp. 229-252.

Offord, D.R. (1974). School performance of adult schizophrenics, their siblings and agemates. *British Journal of Psychiatry*, 125, 12-19.

Petrie, K. & Brook, R. (1992). Sense of coherence, self-esteem, depression and hopelessness as correlates of reattempting suicide. *British Journal of Clinical Psychology*, 31, 293-300.

Rachman, S. (1979). The concept of required helpfulness. *Behavior Research and Therapy*, 17, 1-6.

Rutter, M. (1979). Maternal deprivation 1972-1978: New findings, new concepts, new approaches. *Child Development*, 50, 283-305.

Rutter, M. (2000). Resilience reconsidered: Conceptual considerations, empirical findings, and policy implications. In: Shonkoff & Meisels (Eds.), *Handbook of early childhood intervention*. New York: Cambridge, pp. 651-682.

Rutter, M., Manghan, N., Mortimore, P., & Ouston, J. (1979). *Fifteen thousand hours: Secondary schools and their effects on children*. Cambridge, MA: Harvard University Press.

Seifer, R., Sameroff, A. J., Baldwin, C., & Baldwin, A. (1992). Child and family factors that ameliorate risk between 4 and 13 years of age. *Journal of American Academy of Child and Adolescent Psychiatry*, 31, 893-903.

Walsh, F. (1998). *Strengthening family resilience*. New York: Guilford.

Walsh, F. (2003). Family resilience: A framework for clinical practice. *Family Process*, 42, 1-18.

Webster-Stratton, C. (1998). Preventing conduct problems in Head Start children: Strengthening parenting competencies. *Journal of Consulting and Clinical Psychology*, 66(5), 715-730.

Werner, E.E. (1985). Stress and protective factors in childrens' lives. In: Nicol, A.R. (Ed.), *Longitudinal studies in child psychology and psychiatry*. New York: Wiley & Sons.

Werner, E.E. (1989). High-risk children in young adulthood: A longitudinal study from birth to 32 years. *American Journal of Orthopsychiatry*, 59, 72-81.

Werner, E.E. & Smith, R.S. (1977). *Kauai's children come of age*. Honolulu: University of Hawaii Press.

Werner, E.E. & Smith, R.S. (1982). *Vulnerable but invincible: A longitudinal study of resilient children and youth*. New York: McGraw-Hill.

Werner, E.E. & Smith, R.S. (1992). *Overcoming the odds*. Ithaca: Cornell University Press.

Werner, E.E. & Smith, R.S. (2001). *Journeys from childhood to midlife. Risk resilience and recovery*. Ithaca: Cornell University Press.

West, D.J. & Farrington, D.P. (1973). *Who becomes delinquent?* London: Heinemann.

White, B.C. (1985). *The first three years of life*. Prentice Hall, Englewood Cliffs, NJ.

Worland, J., Weeks, D.G., & Janes, C.L. (1987). Predicting mental health in children at risk. In: Anthony, E.J. & Cohler, B.J. (Eds.), *The invulnerable child*. New York: Guilford Press.

Wyman, P.A., Cowen, E.L., Work, W.C., Raoof, A., Gribble, P.A., Parker, G.R., & Wannon, M. (1992). Interviews with children who experienced major life stress. Family and child attributes that predict resilient outcomes. *Journal of American Academy of Child and Adolescent Psychiatry*, 31(5), 904-910.

Development and Influences
on Family Therapy in Iceland:
Festschrift to Florence Kaslow

Toby Sigrun Herman

SUMMARY. This article is about the groundwork and the development of family therapy in Iceland. The primary pioneers in Iceland are recounted. The environmental, cultural, and social influences and the influences of the Sagas on Icelanders and therapy issues are discussed. The article culminates with an account of the VI Nordic Congress in Family Therapy in Reykjavik in August 2002. The Congress placed the members of the Icelandic Association of Professionals Working in Family Therapy (FFF) firmly within the Nordic alliance alongside colleagues in other Northern countries. The profile of the profession has changed dramatically in Iceland since 1988 when Florence Kaslow, founder of the International Family Therapy Association and acclaimed author, came to Iceland, helping the profession gain recognition and become more accessible. *[Article copies available for a fee from The Haworth Document Delivery Service: 1-800-HAWORTH. E-mail address: <docdelivery@haworthpress.com> Website: <http://www.HaworthPress.com> © 2004 by The Haworth Press, Inc. All rights reserved.]*

Toby Sigrun Herman is President-Elect of the International Family Therapy Association (2003-2005), Aegeisgata 10, 101 Reykjavik, Iceland (E-mail: toby@mr.is).

The author wishes to extend her sincere gratitude to Dr. Sigrun Juliusdottir and Dr. William C. Nichols for their help and encouragement, and to the persons who graciously provided interviews that contributed to understanding of the development of family therapy in Iceland.

[Haworth co-indexing entry note]: "Development and Influences on Family Therapy in Iceland: Festschrift to Florence Kaslow." Herman, Toby Sigrun. Co-published simultaneously in *Journal of Family Psychotherapy* (The Haworth Press, Inc.) Vol. 15, No. 1/2, 2004, pp. 55-70; and: *Family Therapy Around the World: A Festschrift for Florence W. Kaslow* (ed: William C. Nichols) The Haworth Press, Inc., 2004, pp. 55-70. Single or multiple copies of this article are available for a fee from The Haworth Document Delivery Service [1-800-HAWORTH, 9:00 a.m. - 5:00 p.m. (EST). E-mail address: docdelivery@haworthpress. com].

Digital Object Identifier: 10.1300/J085v15n01_05

KEYWORDS. Iceland, family therapy, FFF, VI Nordic Congress, Florence Kaslow

Family therapy is relative to all areas of working with individuals, families, and their wider networks. As the profession develops, the fundamental theory and its wide application promise a better way for families to relate to and respect each other. Theories of family therapy are also applicable to companies, institutions, and relations between and within nations. In working with families in different cultures as well as between nations, family therapists need to be sensitive to cultural differences. It is the author's hope that this article will give the reader some feeling for and understanding of the influences on the profession and its development in Iceland.

ICELAND: THE ENVIRONMENT AND THE PEOPLE

Iceland is the second largest island in the North Atlantic and the westernmost country of Europe. Four-fifths of the country is uninhabited. The population in December 2002 was a mere 288,201 (National Statistical Institute of Iceland, 2003). Iceland is warmed by the Gulf Stream and has a temperate climate. It is rich in hydrothermal and geothermal energy as well as fish within a 200 nautical mile zone.

The country is relatively safe in turbulent times and is becoming a favourite among travellers. Tourism has been one of the fastest growing industries in recent years. Iceland has no military. In 1949 it was one of the 12 founding nations of NATO. A NATO Defence Force along with the police and coast guard has provided the only means of defence since then. Iceland has a parliamentary form of government. The Althingi, the legislative assembly, established in 930, is the oldest functioning assembly in the world (CIA, 2002; Iceland Org., 2001).

The Icelandic people enjoy a rich cultural scene, a relatively stable economy, and a high standard of living. Life expectancy among males is the highest in the world, 78.2 years. For females, life expectancy is now 82.2 years, the ninth highest in the world. Ninety-nine percent of children are vaccinated, and infant mortality is the lowest in the world with fewer than three deaths per 1,000 live births (Directorate of Health, 2002).

Cultural activities such as theatre, music, and art are abundant. There is a city theatre, state theatre, opera company, symphony and many excellent art museums in Reykjavik, as well as theatres, orchestras, and other cultural activities in other parts of the country. These are only a few of the cultural attractions in this nation with a population equal to a small town in Europe or the Americas.

Literacy is among the highest in the world (Iceland Org., 2001). There are three daily national newspapers, and over 500 book titles are published every year. There is a research university, a teacher's university, and four colleges. Graduate training has, until now, been limited and obtained abroad or in the University of Iceland Continuing Education Centre. This has greatly improved and the emphasis is now on improving diversity in graduate work.

The People in the Land of Fire and Ice

The Icelandic people are no strangers to natural disasters. Many loved ones have been lost at sea. The last major avalanche that fell in Flateyri in the west of Iceland in 1995 claimed the lives of 20 people out of the population of 379. Rosa Thorsteinsdottir, family therapist and teacher, was at the time principal of a school near Flateyri. She and her husband Kjell Hymer, family therapist and pedagogue, took part in the rescue. They housed 20 people in their home in the aftermath of the tragedy, which affected every family in the area and grieved the nation. Thirty-four avalanches have fallen in or around Flateyri in the past 60 years (Thorsteinsdottir, 2003).

Earthquakes are frequent and Iceland is one of the most active volcanic countries in the world. A volcanic eruption off the coast of the Vestman Islands caused an island, Surtsey, to eventually rise to a height of 169 meters above sea level. The eruption ceased on June 5, 1967, after lasting three and a half years. One of the most destructive eruptions was in 1973 on Heimaey, the only inhabited island in the Vestman Islands (Kokelaar & Durant, 1983) (see Figure 1). Approximately one-third of the town of Vestmannaeyjar was destroyed. Restoration work went on nonstop, and gradually most of the inhabitants returned. The more elusive pain and disaster also affect the work of the family therapist in Iceland. The mother, for instance, who embraces her child, yet is tormented with guilt and depression; the loving husband that slowly becomes cold and distant; the emotionally and/or physically abused child; and the suicidal youth that have learned to mask their pain.

Total expenditure on health is high per capita, but there is much room for improvement. For example, only 0.1 to 0.2 percent of children receive the care they require at the Children Psychiatric Hospital, as opposed to 2.0% in other Northern countries (Department of Child and Adolescent Psychiatry, 2002; Directorate of Health, 2002). Only in 2003 have funds been approved to alleviate the situation. Death from self-inflicted injury is 9.9 per 100,000 and highest among young men (National Statistical Institute, 2002). External injury and poisoning are the most common causes of death in both men and women ages 15-29-years, as well as men ages 30-44. Men in Iceland are more

FIGURE 1

likely then women to die of accidental death and suicide. This difference is most pronounced in the 15-29-year-old range (Directorate of Health, 2002). Each suicide deeply affects families, schoolmates or colleagues. Every suicide can be expected to affect as many as 100 people.

Icelanders have been an extremely homogeneous population. A nationwide genealogical database of all living Icelanders stretching back to the settlement of the country 1,100 years ago is now available online. The database can be a valuable resource for the family therapist using family genograms. It permits a search for family relations generations back, and almost everyone is related in some way. It is no doubt due to the meager number of the population and the relationship between them that each loss of life is so deeply shared.

The paradox of fire and ice in a country that can seem magnificent as well as uninhabitable is mirrored in the people, who can seem difficult to approach, yet equally warm when they are approached. The people are extremely proud; they value their heritage, independence and their self-sufficiency and do not seek help easily (Gislason, 1990). Icelanders have a saying that translates literally, "I do not take my sorrow to the square." The meaning is that Icelanders bear pain and sorrow in silence and with stoic dignity. It can take time and knowledge of the culture and values to reach the people that need help the most.

The Sagas

There are an infinite number of past worlds; societies have highly differentiated pasts. Only the most elemental experiences are shared by all peoples, although in this century, shaping experiences are shared to a greater degree than ever before. Different cultures differ greatly on the way people should be treated, the relation to authority and social behaviour (Roberts, 2000). Family therapists will thus fare better if they know the societal and cultural influences of the culture they work in. In Iceland, insight into the mindset of the Icelander can be further found through the influence of the Sagas. Propensities toward the supernatural, stoicism, and pride, for instance, have roots in the Sagas.

Icelanders consider their language a link to their heritage but, more importantly, a source of identity and independence. They are proud of their language, which is spoken by a minute fraction of the world's population. Modern Icelandic still resembles the Old Norse, which many Icelanders can still read. Many can thus still read the original scripts of the Sagas even today. The Sagas instilled a tradition of reading and writing into the culture. They mix fact with fiction, myths, and legends and were an important precursor to the modern novel (Kristjansson, 1993).

Saga means story, and initially it was told verbally. The Sagas mirror the society and way of living of the early settlers who were Norsemen from Scandinavia and some Celts from the British Isles. During early times, there were no diversions except the Sagas and games of strength. The Sagas recounted tales of fighting, litigation, and family ties. When committed to writing, the Sagas documented detailed histories of individuals, illnesses, romances, offspring, and even behaviours (Kristjansson, 1988, 1993). The fascination with genealogy is still evident in the interest in the "Book of Icelanders," the genealogical database.

The Supernatural

Until 1000 AD when Christianity became mandatory, Icelanders believed in many deities, and belief in the supernatural was a significant part of the culture. The magical arts were primarily a female art and the practitioners were respected professionals (Ellis-Davidson, 1973). One form of magic was the art of determining destiny or the law of how things will be; these predictions and interpretations of dreams were used to prepare for the future. In Jomvikings Saga, for instance, Thyra interprets King Gorm's dreams and from it predicts that Denmark will endure nine devastating winters. King Gorm prepares Denmark, the prediction comes true, and Thyra becomes the "Savior of Denmark" (Hollander, 1989; Kristjansson, 1988, 1993).

Seidr, witchcraft, describes prophecy and a range of magic including malefic magic. When Hrutr goes to Norway to take care of inheritance problems, their queen Gunnhildur becomes intrigued with him and makes him her lover. She takes care of his inheritance problems. Hrutr is engaged to Unn who is bound to wait for him for three years. When he leaves for Iceland to marry Unn before the three years pass, Gunnhildur escorts him to his ship. She asks if he has a fiancée in Iceland but he denies, daring not to admit this to her. The queen knew he was lying and was angered that he wanted to go to the arms of another woman. She placed a spell on him and told him he would be never enjoy the woman he loved in Iceland, that he should suffer as she did. Gunnhildur's spell worked. Hrutr and his love Unn could never consummate their love, but Hrutr was able to have intercourse with other women; he is said to have had 30 children (Magnusson, 1960).

About 90% of Icelanders now belong to the national Evangelical Lutheran church, yet a strong supernatural tradition persists. Icelanders remain fascinated with and seek advice from medians and fortune-tellers. The idea of a predetermined destiny is reflected in the idea that God will place only the amount of sorrow on individuals that they can bear. Some individuals and/or families will thus endure more pain and sorrow then others. If this pain and sorrow is then evidence of God's belief in the strength of the individual or the family entity then it will not be alleviated with therapy. It is to be endured with dignity.

Stoicism and Pride

The Sagas told of women of strength and men of pride. A man's greatest attribute was his pride, and keeping face was preferable to death (Kristjansson, 1988, 1993). In one of the masterpieces of Icelandic literature, Njalssaga, written in the late-1200s, one of the most memorable passages in the Sagas portrays the pride and strength of a man, Gunnar, and the stoic strength and wrath of his wife Hallgerd. The Saga takes place at the close of the 10th century. The scene is one in which Gunnar's enemies are threatening him in his home. Gunnar puts up a heroic fight but the string of his bow breaks. He asks Hallgerd for a lock of her hair to mend the bow and she refuses. Gunnar had slapped Hallgerd once, and she avenged the slap by refusing to help him. Gunnar knows he cannot win the battle without his bow yet he accepts Hallgerd's decision. He remarks that he shall not ask her again. Gunnar is killed (Kristjansson, 1988, 1993).

Dignity and Strength

Hallgerd has never mentioned the slap; instead, she waited for the perfect moment to avenge it. That this will cause Gunnar's death is of no consequence. What mattered was her loss of pride. The condescension that her husband had shown her would finally be avenged. Gunnar was Hallgerd's third husband; the others had offended her as well and both died. A few good sessions with a family therapist might have prevented the disaster. The silent revenge of one partner and the unwillingness of both to confront the issue remain with us. A stoic and dignified demeanor are respected and respect is important. Emotional strength and individuality are encouraged in both men and women. Not showing emotion, even at a loved one's funeral, is praised as a show of endurance and strength.

THE GROUNDWORK FOR FAMILY THERAPY

The hospital for the mentally ill was founded in 1907. In 1929 Helgi Tomasson, a specialist in nerve and psychiatric medicine, began work there and revolutionized the treatment of the mentally ill. Patients were given appropriate medicine and restraining was abandoned. He became director of the hospital in 1940 and worked there throughout his life. His son, Tomas Helgason, took over his position and, like his father, worked tirelessly for the welfare of the mentally ill in Iceland. Despite great resistance from his colleagues, he lobbied for a new and modern psychiatric facility that was finally built within the main area of the National University Hospital in 1979-80. This gave the mentally ill equal access to the main facility and greatly reduced prejudice against them (Gudlaugsdottir, 2003; Juliusdottir, 2003).

In the 1960s Sigurjon Bjornsson, a respected psychologist, analyst, and trainer, published his survey on the care of children in the infant unit at the Thorvaldsen association. He found that children were left in their cribs without touch or contact for long periods. His controversial findings revolutionized the care of hospitalised children (Juliusdottir, 2003). As in many other countries, individual therapy with children and/or adolescents led to an interest in interdisciplinary and family work. Much of the pioneering work in family therapy was within social rehabilitation in the Division of Mental Health Protection for Children.

Tomas Helgason was a broadminded leader and psychiatrist. The zeitgeist of the 1970-1980s was favourable toward family work, yet it was in large part due to Helgason that families and the social milieu of patients were brought into the rehabilitation process. He supported the pioneering ideas of social workers on group homes and halfway houses at the beginning of the 1970s as well as working closely with the social services in Reykjavik. He participated with professionals in conscious-raising groups and took an active role in developing community work, ideology, and techniques in the wards in accordance with social medicine theories in that decade (Juliusdottir, 2003).

Sigrun Juliusdottir, the country's primary pioneer in family therapy, formed an interdisciplinary team at the time, "the family team." The team used half a day a week to watch videos of family therapy sessions and use the reflecting team method as well to find new professional material. The team worked mostly with families of hospitalised schizophrenic patients. It worked together for 10 years and introduced its work at the First Nordic Family Therapy Congress in Linkoping, Sweden, in 1984 as well as in Helsinki, Finland.

Through the initiative of Gylfi Asmundsson, psychologist, the Tavistock Group was contacted and a contact created between Tavistock and these forerunners in Iceland. Tomas Helgason avidly supported such initiatives, which made it possible to form projects to incorporate and develop new methods such as those of the Milan-group in the 1980s. Without his support, family therapy as a method of therapy would not have been as easily accepted by Icelandic professionals as it was (Juliusdottir, 2003).

THE PRIMARY PIONEERS AND TRAINING PROGRAMS

Sigrun Juliusdottir and Kristin Gustavsdottir are the primary pioneers in family therapy as well as supervision in Iceland. Kristin Gustavsdottir practiced family therapy at the Psychiatric Hospital from 1965-1970. She went to Smith College in 1969 and interned at the Eastern Pennsylvania Psychiatric Institute in Philadelphia. Ivan Bosnormenyi-Nagy, David Rubenstein, and Gerald Zuk were there at the time. She visited Nathan Ackerman in New York and Murray Bowen as well as Salvador Minuchin and Jay Haley at the Philadelphia Child Guidance Clinic. She observed these pioneers at work and introducing their theories to the staff at the Psychiatric Hospital in Iceland. From 1970-1972 she held regular staff workshops and courses for beginners as well as for the more advanced, introducing them in addition to Virginia Satir, Norman Paul, and to Theodor Lidz's research into schizophrenia. Another forerunner, Ingibjorg Pala Jonsdottir, took part in the workshops and family therapy sessions with her. Professionals from all professions showed interest in this new way of working. Gustavsdottir felt, however, that social workers had the background and education to be in the forefront.

In 1972, Gustavsdottir left for Sweden with her husband, Karl Gustaf Piltz, and she established the IFT, "Institute for Familjeterapi" (Institute for Family Therapy), although they continued traveling to Iceland to train. Her contribution to family therapy in Iceland was to introduce colleagues to it in these early stages through a series of seminars on theory, group training, supervision, and lectures (Gustavsdottir, 2003).

Dr. Sigrun Juliusdottir has been especially influential in Iceland. In the Department of Social Work at the University of Iceland, she has been in a position to influence the training of social workers and to incorporate family work into the training, to an even greater extent than occurs in other Northern countries. She started practicing as a chief social worker at the psychiatric division of the state hospital in Iceland in 1972. She was later trained in marital and family therapy as well as in supervision and psychotherapy, in the United States and in Europe. She completed a PhD at The University of Gothenburg in 1993. Her dissertation built on a study of interactional patterns and adjustment strategies of Icelandic families analysed in a historical-sociocultural perspective. She now heads the Department of Social Work at the University of Iceland.

Juliusdottir completed a master's degree in clinical social work with focus on training and supervision in marital and family therapy from the University of Michigan in 1978, and subsequently started groups for professionals at the psychiatric hospital. The goal of one of these groups was to train participants in supervision. She collaborated with Inga Sylvander, a Swedish psychologist who is highly respected for her pioneering work in teaching and training supervision. Sylvander held seminars for the Icelandic study/training group in supervision. The IFT, "Institute for Familjeterapi" (Institute for Family Therapy), in Sweden conducted a year of seminars in supervision as well for these forerunners, who worked together from 1981-1985. The supervision study group arranged for themselves a one-year psychoanalytically oriented training in therapy. Hogni Oskarsson, a psychiatrist who had recently returned to Iceland after finishing his training in the USA, led the group. Another group practiced family sessions at the Children Psychiatric Ward; in part, the same people belonged to both groups. Professionals from other countries were contacted to train the groups. People such as Kirschenbaum, Boszormenyi-Nagy, Minuchin, and Satir, for instance, came to Iceland to train them (Juliusdottir, 2003). Their influence is certainly still with us.

The 1980s and 1990s, were marked by substantial development as well as the 1970s. The IPF, "Institut fur Paar und Familietherapie" (Institute for Couple and Family Therapy) in Germany, under Hakon Oen's leadership, trained three groups of professionals for three consecutive years each. Sigrun Juliusdottir supervised the first three-year training program in 1983-1985 but subsequently withdrew due to differing professional views and emphasis. Johann Loftsson and Andres Ragnarsson, both psychologists and graduates of IPF, took over the supervision for the IPF. The major difference between the training at the Continuing Education Center at the University of Iceland and the IPF was a difference in emphasis. Sigrun Juliusdottir, a scholar and academician, placed a heavier emphasis on theory; Hakon Oen placed heavier emphasis on self-work and practice. More than 50 people trained at the IPF, and despite a host of controversy, the institute had a substantial impact on the profession in Iceland. Many students excelled and became excellent therapists, some went on to pursue masters and doctorates, and others became leaders in everything from nursing to management and politics.

Sigrun Juliusdottir, together with Nanna K. Sigurdardottir, social worker and family therapist, started a two-year training program in family therapy at the Institute for Continuing Education at the University of Iceland that ran from 1990-1992 and another from 1994-1996. Kristin Gustavsdottir and Karl Gustaf Piltz acted as external experts and consultants. The training had great impact on the profession in Iceland as well.

The pioneers Jonsdottir, Juliusdottir and Sigurdardottir are the first generation in Iceland to practice family therapy (Gustavsdottir, 2003). Juliusdottir and Sigurdardottir founded a private practice (TENGSL) in 1983. In addition to the two-year training programs in family therapy mentioned above, they offered a variety of training courses in therapy and supervision for interdisciplinary groups of professionals. Together they have conducted extensive research on the upbringing conditions of children in different family types and on divorced families and custody arrangements. Furthermore, Juliusdottir implemented the first Icelandic interdisciplinary program, in supervision at the Institute of Continuing Education. The program, as others that Juliusdottir has led, was renowned for its quality. Her students, including this author, subsequently formed the Icelandic Association of Supervision.

Dr. Florence Kaslow of the USA is among the excellent trainers that came to Iceland. Her work on supervision, divorced parents, and mediation and her emphasis on safeguarding the rights of the children are well known, and certainly in the spirit of the Icelandic pioneers. In 1989, she spent four days with the last group of trainees at the IPF. This vibrant woman caught the attention of the students in her seminar with ease. She conducted it in a spirit of respect and openness that undoubtedly contributed to the depth of learning that took place and contributed to a new perspective of professionalism. She demonstrated with grace how to enter the system and dance within it. She demonstrated how to assist the members, with understanding and respect, find new ways of caring. The family therapy students were at times doubtful that it was possible to work with stoic Icelanders in the ways which Kaslow demonstrated. She stressed that all human systems tend to work best when subsystem boundaries are clear, interactions are clear, lines of authority are visible, rules are overt and flexible, and stressors are confronted instead of silenced. She emphasized that the self-knowledge of the therapist and nonjudgmental attitudes are foundations for successful family therapy.

Kaslow emphasized that family therapy is a unique form of therapy to be contrasted with others. This is in line with the EAP, the European Association of Psychotherapy (EAP), the European Association of Family Therapy (EFTA), and the American Association for Marriage and Family Therapy (AAMFT). Family therapy was practiced as a tool and primarily by social workers. Kaslow contributed to the participants' continued development within a unique psychotherapeutic modality for which there is no direct substitute in other modalities.

Kaslow intuitively homed in on the major issue facing Icelandic therapists at the time. She, as well as Oen, noticed the weak boundaries between subsystems. It is only four years ago that the age of childhood was extended to 18 from 16, in line with the European Union; until then children of 16 were considered adult. Parents were financially responsible for their youngsters but had no legal authority to obtain information on their grades or school attendance, for example.

Children had been accustomed to more freedom then in other countries, due to less danger, a tight-knit community, and the closeness of the extended family. When women turned to the workplace it was not uncommon for school children to remain unattended, before and after school, while their parents were working. These children were referred to as "key children" because some of them wore chains with keys to their homes around their necks and could let themselves in after school. The system was not prepared for the effect on children resulting from the transition of mothers and grandmothers from the homes to the workplace.

After completing training at the IPF in 1990 and inspired by our training with Oen as well as Kaslow's seminar, the author along with Rosa Thorsteinsdottir and Solveig Gudlaugsdottir visited the Bishop of Iceland. The purpose was to inquire about the possibility of churches providing shelters for children ages five to 10. The Bishop approved a pilot project that included two shelters, which we designed and ran. Two forces made the center unique: (a) family therapy was offered to the children's families, and (b) we encouraged senior citizens to volunteer and be with the children. Many of the children had only experienced a one-generation culture, children with and taking care of each other. They had never experienced what Eugenijus Laruinaitis of the Lithuanian Psychotherapeutic Society calls the "kitchen culture," a situation in which the generations gather around the kitchen table to enjoy conversation over coffee and sweets. Many of the senior citizen volunteers had known only this kitchen culture and thus benefited from the shelters as well. They found new meaning in being with the children and relief from the loneliness and the fast, instant culture that was so alien to them. The center answered a dire need and in 1994, the city of Reykjavik took over its management and began to offer care for children in grammar schools. Unfortunately, the two forces that had made the centers unique, i.e., the family therapy and the senior citizen volunteers were not used further.

During an AAMFT conference in Baltimore, the author, along with four other participants in Kaslow's seminar in Iceland, met her by chance. Her warmth and interest in us and the professional development in Iceland touched us. She encouraged us to join the International Family Therapy Association and with this renewed contact began a professional collaboration that later helped change the isolation of the Association of Professionals Working in Family Therapy (FFF). This fruitful alliance and sincere friendship that Florence Kaslow developed with Icelanders will hopefully climax with her return to Iceland and an IFTA congress in Reykjavik in the not too distant future.

THE ASSOCIATION OF PROFESSIONALS WORKING IN FAMILY THERAPY IN ICELAND (FFF)

This association in Iceland was formed by students of the first two-year training program in family therapy conducted by Dr. Sigrun Juliusdottir at the Continuing Education Center. Hrefna Olafsdottir, social worker and family therapist, was the first president of FFF, serving until 2000, when Ludvig Larusson, psychologist and family therapist, became president.

In 2000, during the V Nordic Congress in Finland, Olafsdottir accepted the challenge for Iceland to hold the 2002 Nordic Congress. When she became ill and resigned, the new president, Ludvig Larusson, along with the other members of the Board of Directors, Helga Thordardottir, Bjorg Karlsdottir, and the author, brought the Congress to fruition. The Norwegian chapter avidly supported Iceland in this endeavor with both advice and a generous financial contribution. Kirsti Haaland and Pal Abrahamson were on the advisory board and were especially helpful. William Nichols, president of IFTA from 1999-2001 and a member of the advisory board for the VI Nordic Congress, gave selflessly of his time and wisdom. With their never-ending willingness to help, these people helped place the FFF firmly within the Nordic alliance.

The FFF board of directors has also taken the initiative to become members of IFTA as well as EFTA, the European Family Therapy Association, which is developing credentialing across countries and setting precedent for the possibility of professionals moving across borders to work. This is in line with the European Association of Psychotherapy, the European Commission and the European Union.

THE VI NORDIC CONGRESS IN FAMILY THERAPY

The VI Nordic Congress in Family Therapy was in Reykjavik in August of 2002. The theme was "Fire and Ice," meant to illuminate the resemblance and paradoxes between the people and the environment of the Nordic countries. What is similar and dissimilar between our cultures in the Northern countries, all with their distinctive environments, identity, as well as cultural and family traditions? Has this facilitated or hindered the functioning of the individual, the family and its wider network? How can we as family therapists in the

Northern countries learn from and support each other and how can we best serve our clients?

The protector of the Congress, Olafur Ragnar Grimsson, President of Iceland, formally opened the Congress. The attendance was beyond expectation and many of the pioneers from other Nordic countries attended, for example, Gunnar and Bente Oberg, Magnus Ringborg, member of the IFTA Board of Directors from Sweden, distinguished trainer and authority on family therapy, Kristin Gustavsdottir, Karl Gustaf Piltz, and many more. FFF was honored that they attended the Congress and shared their professional knowledge and expertise. Gustavsdottir and Piltz spoke of working with stress and burnout in couple therapy. Ringborg conducted a brilliant lecture on the culturally incompetent family therapy teacher. Mia Andersson (Sweden) lectured on long-term anorexia. Soren Hertz (Denmark), former chair of STOK (Systemic Association of Therapy and Consultation), explored the idea of "working systemically in a diagnostic field," discussing two central systemic ideas: the position of family therapists marginalizing to a limited therapeutic room, and the ideas of the not-knowing position marginalizing from the crucial issue of how to define the problems people are struggling with; and asked the poignant question, "How can I remain systemic in a diagnostic world?" Allen Holmgren (Denmark) asked why we place such high emphasis on feeling, noting that feelings change, they come and go. Jan-Christer Wahlbeck (Finland) lectured on uniting opposites. Wahlbeck was captivated by the mystique of Iceland: In summer, the nights are bright and run into the day; in winter, the sun shines for a few hours a day; the nights are never-ending. Wencke Seltzer (Norway), former president of IFTA, spoke of the propensity of the profession to idealize a certain mode of working according to the prevailing style of the moment, noting that each mode of working has its pros and cons and that as therapists we must not fall into a trap of cultism in practice. Kirsti Haaland (Norway), chair of the IFTA Congress in Oslo, reminded us to consider the silent voices of the children and to include them in our work with families.

Iceland's primary pioneer, Dr. Sigrun Juliusdottir, lectured on family therapy and postmodernity, as well as the concepts of change, globalization, and diversity. She emphasized that life today is about change. The changed family concept is from obligations to individualization and globalization. For better or for worse it is here to stay, i.e., with the emergent flexible, multiple selves. She spoke also of the instant society in which it is no longer possible to require students to sit for long periods and listen to a lecture that takes thought and attention. The preference is for instant, quick solutions in life and in learning. She asked if solidarity was lost, and referred to recent Nordic research offering hope that it was not.

Elena Smith, chair of STOK, accepted the responsibility for the VII Nordic Congress in 2004 in Denmark.

CONCLUSION

Family therapy is increasingly accessible and accepted and a sought-after resource. The national church of Iceland, for example, offers family therapy in their family service center. Akureyri, a city in the north, and an increasing number of towns employ professionals in family therapy. Counselors are employed by schools with grades eight to 10 as well as in upper secondary, vocational schools, and universities. Counselors serve on student protection committees and are often the first professionals that students go to if they need help. They are in a prime position to intervene quickly and are increasingly working with families and/or referring to family therapists.

The development of family therapy has perhaps been similar as in other countries. It began with work with children and adolescents and grew from individual therapy. Due to different professional views and emphasis of trainers, trainees, and professions, it has taken time to come to the point to where the profession is today. The preference has been to keep family therapy a specialty of certain professions. Utilized as a tool and practiced by a wide range of professionals, there has been resistance to developing it as a separate discipline. The spirit of working together to evolve family therapy with a multiplicity of ideas and towards a tradition specific to Iceland is finally upon us. Credentialing issues arise in this new arena, and FFF is now concentrating on making FFF an association of credentialed professionals. Questions that will finally be faced relate to ethical standards of practice and what requirements should be set for credentialing individuals.

The university offers courses in family therapy in their social science department and next fall an MSW with emphasis on family work will be offered for the first time. This program is only for social workers, however. FFF's goal is to establish an interdisciplinary training program within the university. The Septum's Leonardo program is a collaborative cross-modality initiative developed by the Institute for Creative Counseling and Psychotherapy and Clan-William Institute in conjunction with the University of Sheffield. The program is a one-year stand-alone program or one that can be integrated into a diploma in humanistic and integrative psychotherapy or a diploma in systemic family therapy. Both fulfill the training requirements for registration with, for example, the Irish Council for Psychotherapy, which then fulfill the standards of EFTA and the EAP. Ed McHale, the director of the program in Ireland, contacted the author with a proposal to conduct such a program in Iceland, certainly an interesting possibility.

Whatever the future holds, therapists in Iceland have their share of work as elsewhere. As we have seen, a depth and breath of history and culture needs be taken into account in order to understand the larger picture. The Sagas offer insight into the cultural atmosphere in Iceland and other Northern countries. Other atmospheric factors prevail in other cultures. Therapists will fare better if they have tasted, smelled the culture and how the environment, the history, the pride, and pain of its people have influenced it. It is our past that shapes our present and the present our future. We can enrich our own cultures by learning about the cultures of our brothers and sisters in other cultures and together work toward a collective future of peace, with respect and dignity for all.

REFERENCES

Aðalsteinsson, J. H. (1978). *Under the cloak: The acceptance of Christianity in Iceland with particular reference to the religious attitudes prevailing at the time.* Uppsala: Acta Universitatis Upsaliensis.

Einarsson, S. (1957). *A history of Icelandic literature.* New York: Johns Hopkins Press.

Ellis-Davidson, H. R. (1973). Hostile magic in the Icelandic sagas. In V. Newall (Ed.), *The witch figure: Folklore essays by a group of scholars in England honouring the 75th Birthday of Katharine M. Briggs* (pp. 20-41). Boston: Routledge & Kegan Paul.

Gislason, G. Þ. (1990). *The challenge of being an Icelander. Past, present and future.* Reykjavik: Almenna Bokafelagid.

Gudmundsson, A. T., & Kjartansson K. (1996). *Earth in action. The essential guide to the geology of Iceland.* Reykjavik: Vaka-Helgafell.

Herman, T. S. (2002). Iceland. In A. Pritz (Ed.), *Globalized psychotherapy* (pp. 169-173). Vienna: Facultas AG.

Hollander, L. M. (1989). *The saga of the Jomvikings.* Trans. Reprinted. Austin: University of Texas Press.

Juliusdottir S. (1993). *Den kapabla familjen i det islandska samhallet. En studie om lojalitet, aktenskapsdynamik och psykosocial anpassning* (Interactional patterns and adjustment strategies of Icelandic families analyzed in a historical-psychosocial cultural perspective). Doctoral Dissertation. Gothenberg/Reykjavik: Gothenberg University.

Kokelaar, B. P., & Durant, G. P. (1983). The submarine eruption and erosion of Surtla (Surtsey). *Iceland: Journal of Volcanology and Geothermal Research, 19*, 239-246.

Kristjansson, J. (1993). *Icelandic manuscripts: Sagas, history and art.* Reykjavík: Hid Islenska Bokmenntafelag.

Kristjansson, J. (1988). *Eddas and sagas; Iceland's medieval literature.* P. Foote, trans. Reykjavík: Hid Islenska Bokmenntafelag.

Njáls saga. (1960). Trans. Magnus Magnusson and Herman Pálsson. In: *Njáls saga.* Harmondsworth: Penguin.

Page, R. I. (1995). *Chronicles of the Vikings: Records, memorials and myths.*

Roberts, J. M. (2000). *The Penguin history of twentieth century.* London: Penguin, Toronto: Univ. of Toronto Press.

INTERVIEWS

Bjorg Karlsdottir, Social Worker, Family Therapist and Supervisor, Department of Psychiatry University Hospital.

Kristin Gusafsson, MA, Social Worker, Family Therapist, Supervisor and Director of the Institute for Familjeterapi.

Nanna K. Sigurdardottir, Social Worker, Family Therapist, and Supervisor.

Rosa Thorsteinsdottir, Family Therapist and Teacher.

Solveig Gudlaugsdottir, MA, Psychiatric Nurse and Family Therapist, Department of Child and Adolescent Psychiatry.

Sigrun Juliusdottir, PhD, Social Worker, Family Therapist, Supervisor and Director of the Department of Social Work, University of Iceland.

INTERNET REFERENCES

CIA World Factbook (2002). http://www.cia.gov/cia/publications/factbook/geos/ic.html

DeCode Genetics. http://www.decode.com/

Department of Child and Adolescent Psychiatry. http://www2.landspitali.is/bugl/index.htm

Directorate of Health. http://www.landlaeknir.is

Government Offices of Iceland. http://raduneyti.is/interpro/stjr/stjr.nsf/pages/index.html

Iceland Organization. http://www.iceland.org

The National Statistical Institute of Iceland. http://www.hagstofa.is

The National University Hospital. http://www4.landspitali.is/

A Treatise on Doors and Bridges

Carol L. Philpot

SUMMARY. In 1987, Florence Kaslow, president of the Division of Family Psychology of the American Psychological Association, appointed Carol L. Philpot and Gary Brooks co-chairs of a newly formed Gender Issues Committee. They were given a mandate to open a positive dialogue between the genders that would diminish the animosity that had developed in the wake of the feminist movement of the 1970s. The synergy between the co-chairs resulted in a decade of research, writing, and clinical practice designed to achieve that mandate, culminating in the APA publication of *Bridging Separate Gender Worlds: Why Men and Women Clash and How Therapists Can Bring Them Together* in 1997. This article discusses the main tenets of that book. *[Article copies available for a fee from The Haworth Document Delivery Service: 1-800-HAWORTH. E-mail address: <docdelivery@haworthpress.com> Website: <http://www.HaworthPress.com> © 2004 by The Haworth Press, Inc. All rights reserved.]*

KEYWORDS. Gender, gender roles, communication, gender-sensitive psychotherapy, Florence Kaslow

I have done a great deal more with my life than I ever anticipated. Although I was both a good student and an athlete in high school and college, I grew up

---

Carol L. Philpot is Professor Emeritus and former Dean, School of Psychology, Florida Institute of Technology, Melbourne, FL.

[Haworth co-indexing entry note]: "A Treatise on Doors and Bridges." Philpot, Carol L. Co-published simultaneously in *Journal of Family Psychotherapy* (The Haworth Press, Inc.) Vol. 15, No. 1/2, 2004, pp. 71-86; and: *Family Therapy Around the World: A Festschrift for Florence W. Kaslow* (ed: William C. Nichols) The Haworth Press, Inc., 2004, pp. 71-86. Single or multiple copies of this article are available for a fee from The Haworth Document Delivery Service [1-800-HAWORTH, 9:00 a.m. - 5:00 p.m. (EST). E-mail address: docdelivery@haworthpress.com].

in a time when women were expected to marry, have children, and be content "keeping the home fires burning." I secretly dreamed of writing Nancy Drew mysteries for little girls, but I knew that I would be perfectly satisfied ironing shirts, changing diapers, cooking meals, and making a cozy home for a loving husband and children. Nevertheless, life seems to have beckoned me through a number of open doors that greatly altered that domestic fantasy. When opportunity knocked, I answered. And, to quote Robert Frost, "That has made all the difference" (Frost, 1969).

On one occasion the knocker at the door was Florence W. Kaslow. Late in the fall of 1984, I attended a divorce mediation workshop presented by Dr. Kaslow in Orlando, Florida. In all honesty, I did not really know her international reputation at the time. I merely thought divorce mediation was a good idea and it would be a potentially profitable addition to my part-time private practice in family and couples therapy. Little did I know the influence Dr. Kaslow would have on the direction of my career and my level of achievement. I simply wanted to learn how to do divorce mediation. At the end of the very informative five-day workshop, during which I was impressed with Dr. Kaslow's ability to talk intelligently without notes for 40 hours, she announced that she was doing an advanced family therapy workshop in Cancun in December. Quite frankly, I thought Cancun would be a great place to go for continuing education credits as a vacation at the end of a busy semester. Since I was the faculty member who taught family therapy at the School of Psychology of Florida Tech in Melbourne, I could even justify the trip to my dean. It was in Cancun that I began a friendship with Florrie that has enriched my life both professionally and personally for two decades.

When I returned to work for the spring semester, I was able to convince my dean that Dr. Kaslow should be brought in as adjunct faculty to supplement the marriage and family program I had developed at the School of Psychology. While guest lecturing, Florrie observed that as one of two females on a 14 member faculty, I served as a mentor and role model for the many female students we had in our Doctor of Psychology (PsyD) program. I was very familiar with the struggle of combining career and family, having done so myself for many years. Therefore, I was understanding and supportive of their efforts to do it all, while many male faculty just "didn't get it." I became the advocate of female students in faculty discussions and influenced department policy-making in a female-friendly direction.

Florrie's observation of my role led her to offer me two opportunities, which were the genesis of my research, writing, and political career in family psychology. She asked me to write an article entitled "When Mother Is a Family Therapist" for the *Journal of Psychotherapy and the Family*, which was the first of many professional articles to come. She also asked me to serve as co-chair of the Gender Concerns Committee of the American Psychological Association's Division of Family Psychology (Division 43). (She was incoming president of the division at that time.) My service in this position led to other board positions, culminating in the presidency of Division 43 in 1992. But more importantly, while serving as co-chair of the Gender Concerns Committee, I developed professional relationships with Gary Brooks, Roberta Nutt, and Don-David Lusterman, who were eventually to become my co-authors on the most important contribution I have made to the field of psychology.

Before Florence Kaslow became president of Division 43, the Gender Issues Committee did not exist. Due to the influence of Division 35 (Psychology of Women), there was a Women's Issues Committee, but no equivalent Men's Issues Committee. Florrie's personal philosophy was that there was too much conflict between the genders. Her vision was that a Gender Issues Committee, co-chaired by a male and female, would open a positive dialogue between the genders that would diminish the animosity. She deliberately selected co-chairs (Gary Brooks and myself) who had a great deal of empathy and respect for the other gender and who were knowledgeable about both men's and women's issues. The synergy that developed between us far exceeded her expectations.

As partial fulfillment of our duties as co-chairs, Gary and I invited Roberta Nutt and Don-David Lusterman to join us in a panel presentation at APA. The plan was to have one expert on women's issues (Roberta), one on men's issues (Gary), and both a man and woman (Don-David and myself) to present a more conciliatory, interactive approach to gender issues. Our original goal was to present concurrently the problems men and women suffered as a result of the rigid gender roles they had been assigned in a patriarchal society. The presentation was well-attended and dynamic. As it turned out, the Zeitgeist was right for a decade of future presentations on gender, essentially variations on a theme.

During the next 10 years, we had the opportunity to further develop our ideas. As systemic therapists, we already used a paradigm that considered the interactions among the parts of a system within a particular context, which was an approach that led to our endorsement of such concepts as the gender ecosystem, gender socialization, androgyny, and the gender role journey. We developed guidelines for conducting gender-sensitive psychotherapy that emphasized the systemic nature of gender socialization. We also began to see clearly how men and women participated in the process of socializing one another, a process that could have either negative, rigidifying effects or produce positive, growth-enhancing co-evolution. We worked with our clients and students in ways that educated them about the effects of gender socialization and their own participation in the process with the idea of creating more than just a cognitive understanding of gender socialization. Our goal was empathic knowing: that is, an emotional understanding of the other gender's experience gained by "walking in the shoes of the other." Once empathic knowing had been achieved, we found that our clients were able to resolve their differences in constructive ways. To that end, we independently developed a variety of techniques and approaches to therapy that appeared to be effective with the diverse populations we each served. We began to share these ideas with each other and our audiences. We developed a "passion" for helping others overcome the mutual misunderstandings and blame between the genders that we often saw, not only in our patient or student populations, but among colleagues in professional organizations as well. This passion led to the publication of *Bridging Separate Gender Worlds: Why Men and Women Clash and How Therapists Can Bring Them Together* in 1997. The remainder of this article will summarize the main tenets of that book.

GENDER-SENSITIVE PSYCHOTHERAPY

During the 1970s, feminist scholars began to question the theories and techniques of psychological practice. By now all therapists are familiar with the feminist critique which essentially pointed out that what appeared to be psychological "truths" from a male perspective did not hold true for women. Thus normative female behavior was pathologized while many of the established therapeutic treatments for women basically supported the patriarchal status quo. Family psychology did not escape that critique. Such concepts as hierarchy, enmeshment and disengagement, circularity and neutrality came under fire. Therapists were encouraged to recognize that the structure of the family unit in which the woman was seen as responsible for the home and childcare while the man was expected to be the provider and protector perpetuated a power differential based on gender that was detrimental to women. As Goodrich pointed out:

> It is the knowledge that (the woman) is the unilateral provider of the experience of family for others–and the necessary years and years of thinking of others first and continually (because he will not)–that robs women of power. (Goodrich, 1991, pp. 18-19)

Now we recognize that the same structure is detrimental to men as well, producing such problems as psychosomatic illnesses, early death, alexithymia, defensive autonomy, alienation, and destructive entitlement. We are aware that psychotherapy that is insensitive to gender can be harmful to men too.

Today when we speak of gender-sensitive psychotherapy, we mean that therapists must be aware of both men's and women's issues that might influence the outcome of psychotherapy. A gender-sensitive psychotherapist is knowledgeable about the differing perceptions of reality for men and women due to biology, socialization, role assignments, and power differentials in the political, economic and legal arenas. She or he views the often predictable dichotomies of distancer/pursuer, expressive/instrumental, logic/emotion as inevitable, although exaggerated, results of socialization rather than intrapsychic pathology. The gender-sensitive therapist imposes no limits on the roles to be played by either gender and is familiar with the theories and research on gender differences, including their limitations.

GENDER SOCIALIZATION: PROCESS AND OUTCOMES

Through a process of modeling, reward and punishment, labeling and cognition, expectations, and self-fulfilling prophecies, men and women learn to act and think like men and women. From birth girls and boys are treated differently (Huston, 1983). Parental and societal expectations for boys are not the same as they are for girls. Certain behavior is labeled female; other behavior is labeled male. Children, particularly boys, are punished for deviating from this behavior and rewarded for emulating it. Children learn quickly to do what gets them the reward, which perpetuates the stereotypes (i.e., the self-fulfilling prophecy). Research shows that people ignore and deny the existence of evidence that does not fit the stereotype. We place different labels on the same behavior dependent on gender; for example, a sensitive woman is caring, while a sensitive man is a wimp. By doing so, we force people into the stereotypical mold of male or female despite individual differences. Positive self-concept for sex-typed individuals is dependent on conforming to the norm. There is a large body of research that demonstrates the effects of language, play, media, books, religion, school, parents, teachers, peers, and extended family on an individual's concept of what is male and female (Beall & Sternberg, 1993; Crawford & Unger, 2000; Hyde, 1996; Philpot, Brooks, Lusterman, & Nutt, 1997; Wood, 1994).

Research in the 1970s through the 1990s clearly established the existence of the gender ecosystem. That is, gender socialization affects the value systems, communication styles, behavior patterns, personality characteristics, roles, problem-solving styles, and sexuality of individuals such that most men and women live in different worlds. Of course there are always exceptions, and men and women are more alike than different. But for a majority of men and women, certain differences will hold true.

Males tend to value autonomy over affiliation whereas the opposite is true of women. Males are more often characterized by self-reliance, competitiveness, emotional repression, and achievement-orientation (Doyle, 1989). Women generally endorse the values of nurturance, cooperation, emotionality, and dependency (French, 1985). For women, family is a priority. Men focus on work and the external world. Men live in a hierarchical world where weakness is deplored. They prefer action to words; they use communication to give information or to establish their position on the pecking order. Women use communication to connect with and empower others. They prefer to talk out their problems and get a consensus from their confidantes (Tannen, 1990). Men are raised to protect and provide for women and children. Women are raised to be the caretaker, to nurture and to put others first. Women are desired for their beauty; men for their money and power. Sexually, men are more visual, focusing on the appearance of their partner. They are taught to take the initiative and are concerned with performance. They like variety in sexual partners (Zilbergeld, 1992). Women look for an emotional connection and are more content with monogamy. Most of these differences are due to a combination of biology and socialization, with a heavy emphasis on the latter (Philpot et al., 1997).

There are negative consequences of rigid gender socialization for both men and women. Men suffer psychosomatic illnesses due to the repression of emotion and the pressure to control and achieve. They are taught to be risk takers, to defend their honor, to be macho. Furthermore, they are placed in dangerous situations due to their protector role (i.e., firemen, policemen, soldiers, and so forth). Due to the above, men die 10 years younger than women (Waldron, 1976). Men define themselves through their careers, a factor which becomes negative when their career fails to give satisfaction or when they are no longer working. The breadwinner role dominates a man's life, which does not allow him to pursue and develop other aspects of himself. Men are prone to be emotionally repressed and alexithymic; that is, they cannot put words to their feelings. They suffer from destructive entitlement, believing they are entitled to special treatment and service because they protect and provide. They also demonstrate defensive autonomy; they resist suggestions and requests because they do not want to appear controlled by others. Finally, many males experience homophobia, which prevents them from developing close relationships with other men. Therefore, they are often isolated and lonely, particularly if their wives leave them (Levant & Kopecky, 1995/1996).

Women suffer depression twice as much as men worldwide. Research (McGrath, Keita, Strickland, & Russo, 1990) indicates multiple causes, but among them are women's lack of power and autonomy, tendency to put family before self, and vulnerability to physical and sexual abuse. A traditional woman follows her husband to wherever he wants to live, defers to her husband's opinions and wishes, serves her husband and children, has no time for herself or her interests, and loses her self-respect because she is basically a servant. Women also lose self-respect because the values that are typically considered feminine are held in lower esteem in our culture than are male values. Therefore, women must choose between feeling unfeminine or inferior. Women make 75 cents on the dollar when compared to men, even when education, occupation, experience, and skill are taken into account. Women's traditional work is considered less valuable than men's, and, furthermore, when women become dominant in a formerly male occupation, its value diminishes. Women are given the role of childcare and housework in our society, the second shift (Hochschild, 1989) which does not contribute to the Gross National Product, and therefore has no monetary value. Their role assignment interferes with their ability to be economically independent and thus reduces their power in a relationship.

Therefore, women often stay in an abusive or unsatisfying relationship to provide for themselves and their children. Furthermore, women are taught to define themselves through their relationships. Because being married is so vital to their identity, women will monitor the relationship, take the blame, accommodate their spouse, and try to change themselves, clearly demonstrating an imbalance of power in marriage. Women who choose to have a career and no marriage frequently feel unsuccessful because "without a man they are nothing" (Dowling, 1982). Traditional women were taught not to express anger, assert themselves, or be selfish in any way. Even today, women who defy those rules are given derogatory names and demeaned.

Although women have always focused on their ability to attract men, in the last several decades, they have been influenced by the media to attain an unrealistic weight level, a fact that has led to an upsurge of eating disorders such as anorexia and bulimia (Nichter & Vuckovic, 1994). Even when they do not fall victim to body distortion and eating disorders, they spend inordinate amounts of time and money trying to make themselves beautiful, a phenomenon now know as the third shift (Wolf, 1991). Finally, because our society sexually objectifies the female body and in spite of cultural changes some people still think of women as male property, women are very vulnerable to sexual harassment and abuse as well as physical abuse. All of these problems are related to gender socialization.

THE GENDER ECOSYSTEM: CLASH OF THE GENDERS

In family systems theory, a system refers to a group of interrelated individuals that has a boundary, like a family, a place of employment, or a school. When we speak of ecosystems, we are referring to large systems, such as major religious, ethnic, or cultural groups that share beliefs, attitudes, expectations, and behaviors. The gender ecosystems are the largest and most basic of all ecosystems, because every individual belongs to one or the other. Gender is the first classification into which people are divided; it comes before age, ethnicity, religion or socioeconomic status. Male and female gender ecosystems indoctrinate their members with values, expectations, and behaviors, many of which transcend even ethnic or national cultures. When the male and female gender cultures interact, whether in the workplace or in an intimate relationship, there is considerable opportunity for misunderstanding and conflict. A few examples may help to illustrate.

Because males perceive the world to be a hierarchical system, where autonomy and self-reliance is highly valued, they will resist any appearance that others, especially women, are telling them what to do. A gentle request to take out the garbage or pick up his socks can create resentment and defiance in some men, a phenomenon known as defensive autonomy. Men joke about their "honey-do lists" and refer to the "marital yoke," but the negative implication is clear. Complying with the wishes of a woman puts a man on a lower rung of the power ladder and is unmanly. Complicating matters is the fact that certain work (cleaning house, changing diapers) has been labeled female and thus devalued for so long that many men consider it demeaning. Therefore, marital therapists frequently see couples who have perpetual arguments regarding sharing the housework and childcare, in which men who clearly recognize their wives carry a disproportionate share of the burden still find it difficult to take on their fair share.

Closely related is the male emphasis on self-reliance. A man who asks for help is lower on the hierarchy than the one who offers assistance. The oft-repeated joke about the man who will not ask for directions is an excellent example of this. A woman, on the other hand, is accustomed to asking for assistance and sees no shame in it. Conflicts between spouses on consulting a professional or seeking advice from family and friends can arise because of gender differences in the perception of seeking help.

Women have been taught to value relationships above all else. They have also absorbed the notion that they are responsible for the health of the relationship. Due to this, they tend to monitor relationships, looking for ways to tweak and improve even minor flaws. Insecure women seek constant verbal reassurance that the relationship is satisfying and strong and that their spouses love them. Men, however, view discussions about the relationship as a laundry-list of failings and things that need fixing, or worse yet, potential traps they may fall into. Men are not taught to talk about feelings; indeed, they are taught to suppress them (Levant & Kopecky, 1995/1996). At the same time, women use conversation to connect with others and feel closer when they have heart-to-heart talks (Tannen, 1990). The woman may very well be attempting to develop more intimacy through conversation about the relationship, but the man is anxious, uncomfortable, and avoidant. The combination results in very unsatisfying relationship discussions between spouses and often sets up a pursuer/distancer cycle of interaction.

Other gender differences in conversational styles set the stage for further conflict. Women use conversation to connect and therefore will talk about everyday details of their lives that men find boring and inane. Men, on the other hand, use conversation to impart information, to establish their authority, and to impress others with their knowledge (Tannen, 1990). When women talk about their problems, they look for commiseration, validation, acceptance. But males offer solutions. The result is that while males establish themselves as higher on the hierarchy by providing the needed advice, women feel put down and devalued rather than connected. Women therefore turn to other women who know how to support them and men are bewildered by the lack of appreciation for their attempts to provide answers.

Men and women also emphasize different problem-solving techniques. Valuing self-reliance and wishing to appear strong and competent, men do not readily share their concerns and dilemmas with their wives. They do not wish to appear vulnerable. Women believe that they would feel closer to their husbands if the men would only open up and share their innermost thoughts. But in reality, wives are often frightened or repulsed by their husbands' insecurities. Therefore, most men think their problems through in solitary, maintaining the illusion of having it all together, but simultaneously distancing themselves from their wives. Meanwhile, women like to talk through their problems, often seeking a consensus from valued friends and acquaintances. Men see this behavior as "airing their dirty linen in public" and are annoyed. Men also tend to distract themselves from problems by involving themselves in activity. Women tend to revisit problems until they are resolved and even seem to enjoy the process. Men are much less process-oriented and more goal-directed. These differences tend to cause strain in a relationship.

In terms of sexuality, males are more able to enjoy non-relational sex while most females want an emotional connection. This difference can cause confusion and pain during the courtship years. Nevertheless, both genders value a committed, emotionally intimate, and sexually satisfying relationship (Zilbergeld, 1992). Indeed, some males find sex to be the only way they can express intimacy with women.

Due to gender socialization, most men prioritize work and economic success, putting most of their time and attention into the job. In the process they often neglect the relationship, minimizing problems and taking it for granted. They are often surprised and baffled when a relationship ends, because they have not been paying attention. Women prioritize relationships, making sacrifices in careers and other personal interests to put their husbands and children first. They also take on the burden of nurturance in the family, thus overloading themselves and becoming exhausted. They can become resentful and angry, leading to conflict and eventually separation.

Since men value autonomy and self-reliance and are homophobic, they tend to avoid close relationships with other men who are perceived as competitors or worse (i.e., potential partners), thus leaving them overly dependent on their wives for emotional support. Although they overtly deny such dependency, when a relationship fails, men suffer isolation and depression. Women generally have a larger support system and their dependency on their spouses is more likely to be financial rather than emotional.

Since the women's movement of the 1970s and the men's movement of the 90s, the roles of men and women have become blurred. Although the goal of these movements has been to release individuals from rigid gender rules and allow them to live more fully, some of the centuries-old values have not changed. The result is that the new expectations are overlaid on top of the old.

For women this means that not only must she meet all of the criteria of the old wife (housekeeper, cook, laundress, mother, family nurturer, decorator, chauffeur, counselor, sex kitten, companion, social secretary, seamstress, referee, and tutor), but also must have a successful full-time career and always look beautiful as well–the superwoman syndrome.

For men, it means they must be sensitive, gentle, emotionally expressive, sexually adept, good housekeepers and cooks, excellent fathers, and continue to be great providers and protectors as well. In some cases there are conflicting skills required by the various roles each gender is expected to play, while often there simply is not enough time and energy to do it all. Thus, both men and women suffer a type of gender role strain, a sense of inadequacy due to their inability to meet all the requirements for their gender.

GENDER ROLE STRAIN

Pleck (1981) identified three types of gender role strain. The first, discrepancy strain, refers to the above-mentioned situation. It occurs when a man or woman feels that he or she does not measure up to society's definition of what makes a good man or woman. For example, a woman does not look like a Barbie doll or fit into size 2 clothing. A man does not make an adequate living to support his family.

The second type of strain is dysfunction strain: that is, when a man or woman does actually fulfill the gender mandate, but its very fulfillment is detrimental to his or her health. For example, the woman who suffers eating disorders while accomplishing the beauty mandate or the man who has a heart attack working 18 hour days in order to be financially successful.

Finally, both genders suffer trauma strain in the process of gender socialization. This is the trauma experienced when they discover the pain of unfair gender rules. For example, little boys learn that they must go back out and face the bully in order to be a man. Little girls learn that they must curtail their intellectual or athletic abilities in front of males or they will be ostracized socially by both genders.

GENDER ROLE JOURNEY

In our therapeutic work with couples who struggle under the yoke of rigid gender socialization, we have found the gender role journey (O'Neil & Egan, 1992) to be another useful concept. O'Neil identified the stages of moving from unconscious compliance with gender programming received in childhood, with all of its egocentricity and unrealistic expectations (Stage 1), to a state of gender-role freedom in personal and professional relationships (Stage 5). This journey is not a smooth one that a couple makes together. Most often, one partner has surged forward and is literally dragging a reluctant and somewhat recalcitrant spouse behind. The stages, however, are fairly predictable. The process begins with the totally enculturated male or female (Stage 1) and then moves to vague dissatisfaction with the gender role on the part of one spouse or another (Stage 2). The dissatisfied spouse begins a questioning process and accompanying consciousness-raising that results in anger and a tendency to blame the other gender (Stage 3). In Stage 4, individuals move beyond blame and take responsibility for their own happiness, making appropriate and often unilateral changes in attitude and behavior. Finally, they reach a point where they gain an understanding of the other as well and see the entire system in which they both play a part. At this final stage, empathy for the struggle of the other spouse can facilitate the growth of the partner (Stage 5). As therapists, it is our responsibility to help our clients move along this journey through a successful co-evolutionary process.

ANDROGYNY/EMPATHIC KNOWING/CO-EVOLUTION

Although the research clearly shows that gender differences exist, men and women have the capacity to adopt all human values and attributes, whether they have been socially defined as masculine or feminine (androgyny). Despite gender socialization, men and women are more alike than different. In other words, there is common ground for understanding and accepting one another without blame and criticism. The universal human needs to be understood, validated, respected, valued, and supported form the bridge between the genders as they struggle with marital issues.

At the core of our gender-sensitive work with couples is the concept of empathic knowing. Empathic knowing consists of two ingredients: (a) a knowledge of gender socialization, including its systemic nature, and (b) empathy for the plight of both genders. It is a cognitive/affective shift from a position of angry blaming to mutual understanding. The goal of our therapy is to create an environment in which the clients can discharge their own sense of entitlement and defensiveness long enough to walk in the shoes of their partner with true empathy. They learn to respect and value the differences in the other gender and participate in a cooperative effort to meet their individual and mutual needs.

It is also vital for our clients to understand that they have participated in the molding of the other over a lifetime. By modeling what previous generations have done and what they see in the world around them, women and men have automatically placed gender expectations on one another and either subtly or overtly discouraged what does not fit the model. Thus, they have participated in perpetuating the very characteristics and behaviors they now complain about. They cannot be blamed for this, however, because they are only doing what comes naturally. When they understand this, they can begin to listen to the experience of the other without feeling the need to defend themselves or counterattack. Understanding the co-evolution process has a liberating effect, because once one realizes that one's responses to one's spouse can have either a rigidifying or growth-enhancing result, one can put aside defensiveness and cooperate in finding solutions to the mutual gender binds. The result is mutual growth and satisfaction.

INTERVENTIONS

To facilitate a positive co-evolutionary process, we have accumulated a number of techniques that I will describe briefly below.

Validation

Both spouses must be simultaneously validated. This is a tricky process, when each is rigidly defending his or her position as the right way of being and blaming the other. However, family systems therapists are adept at presenting issues in a systemic manner that avoids taking sides. The therapist can validate the experience of each partner caught up in the gender system without accusing or blaming the other partner. For example, it is frustrating when a man offers advice to his wife in dealing with a problem and she dismisses it. It is simultaneously demeaning to a woman to be told how she should handle something when she already knows what to do, but just wants sympathy and understanding. Both points of view can co-exist. It's simply that the male and female come to this situation with different expectations and desires.

Normalization

Equally important is the therapist's reassurance that many men and women suffer the same misunderstandings because of our gender ecosystems. Some of the media's most popular cartoons and sitcoms derive their popularity from their portrayal of stereotypical gender conflicts. The problems the clients are having are due to having been raised in separate cultures, not because of some personal deficiency. It is normal for them to view situations as they do.

Psychoeducation

As clients bring up issues that have clear roots in gender socialization, the therapist can identify this fact and educate the couple regarding the gender ecosystem, the process of gender socialization, and stereotypical gendered behaviors. In the above example, for instance, the therapist can explain how men and women use conversation differently. He can interpret for the husband that his wife wants sympathy and understanding, not advice. He can explain to the wife that her husband believes he is helping by providing a solution, essentially fixing the problem. He can help them learn to give the other what they need in any given situation rather than responding unconsciously in a stereotypical male or female manner. As an adjunct to couples therapy, bibliotherapy and psychoeducational workshops about gender can be used to speed up this learning process.

Scapegoating the Ecosystem

I have found it particularly useful to blame the gender ecosystem and unite the couple against it (Philpot, 1992). Instead of being angry with each other or with the other gender in general, I direct their anger toward the rigid rules of behavior that they learned in their gender ecosystems. They have both been victimized. They can support one another in making new rules for their relationship that do not necessarily follow the dictates of the gender ecosystem.

Reframing and Translating

Brooks (1991) has developed a process of interpreting male behavior to females and vice versa which he calls reframing and translating. Essentially, the therapist is a gender broker who acts like an interpreter in international negotiations. After receiving input from one partner, the therapist decodes the message by placing it in the context of that person's value system. Then before sending it to the intended receiver, the therapist reframes the message into the spouse's language, emphasizing the positive intention of the sender. Today we might call the therapist a "spin doctor." Using the example above, the therapist would indicate to the wife that her husband is showing his love by fixing her problem and ask her if it is working. After she indicated that it was not, he would then turn to the husband and explain that she would prefer that he just be a good listener and commiserate with her as a way of showing his love. He might even recognize that the husband will feel like this is an ineffective waste of time when compared to offering a solution, but that this is what his wife wants at this time. In this way the therapist helps the couple negotiate new arrangements that more closely meet each other's needs.

Empathic Interviewing

Lusterman (1993) uses basic communication skills training to help the couple break their patterns of accuse and counter-accuse. He teaches them to ask open-ended questions, to use active listening and reflection, to avoid interruption, and to validate the needs and concerns of the other. I find it helpful to have clients pretend they are interviewing a stranger for a newspaper article and are really trying to present that person's point of view. This technique is helpful in eliminating the "but what about me?" response that is so often in the forefront of their minds.

The Gender Inquiry

The gender inquiry, developed by Lusterman and honed and polished by Philpot and associates (1997) is a list of questions about gender to be used to stimulate conversation about an individual's personal experience of gender socialization. The questions are arranged in chronological order from early childhood through adulthood, but are intended to be used as a guide rather than as a questionnaire. The purpose of these questions is threefold: (a) They teach, through personal example, that the gender ecosystem is at the core of many of the misunderstandings and dissatisfactions the spouses are experiencing and therefore depersonalize much of the conflict between spouses; (b) they demonstrate how the sexes influence and mold one another within the family of origin and pass on similar destructive messages to future generations; (c) they expand cognitive maps and offer the possibility of change in the present to bring about change in future generations. The gender inquiry can structure a discussion about gender when the context of therapy raises gender conflicts. The gender inquiry can be conducted by the therapist in the presence of the other spouse, or alone. Both spouses should be given the opportunity to tell their socialization story. The gender inquiry is an effective means to bring about empathic knowing.

CONCLUSION:
THE ROLE OF THE THERAPIST IN SOCIAL REVOLUTION

As we enter the 21st century, western society continues to experience the drama of a social revolution. Men and women are struggling to redefine themselves in relationship to one another. The people who have been caught in this transitional stage lack role models and rulebooks that can guide their interpersonal relationships. As therapists, we can help women and men explore their gender socialization, eliminate what is harmful, and retrieve and revitalize what is good. We can facilitate the sharing of their gender-role journeys, providing a therapeutic environment in which parity, respect, and mutual appreciation are priorities. In effect, we can bridge separate gender worlds.

ON DOORS AND BRIDGES

The gender work that I have done in teaching, writing, research, and my practice has been an attempt to help men and women break out of the rigid gender roles of a patriarchal society without blaming one another and creating a divide neither gender really wants. But the bridge-building efforts of my colleagues and I might never have reached a broad audience without the assistance of Florence Kaslow. It was she who put us in a position where our influence could make a difference. It was she who had the idea from which our vision grew. It was she who opened the door so that we could begin to build bridges.

REFERENCES

Beall, A. E., & Sternberg, R. J. (1993). *The psychology of gender.* New York: Guilford Press.

Brooks, G. R. (1991). Traditional men in marital and family therapy. In M. Bograd (Ed.), *Feminist approaches for men in family therapy* (pp. 51-74). New York: The Haworth Press, Inc.

Crawford, M., & Unger, R. (2000). *Women and gender: A feminist psychology (3rd ed.).* New York: McGraw-Hill.

Dowling, C. (1982). *The Cinderella complex.* New York: Pocket Books.

Doyle, J. A. (1994). *The male experience (3rd ed.).* Dubuque, IA: William C. Brown.

French, M. (1985). *Beyond power: On women, men and morals*. New York: Ballantine Books.

Frost, R. (1969). The road not taken. In E. C. Lathem (Ed.), *Poetry of Robert Frost: Collected poems & unabridged*. New York: Henry Holt.

Goodrich, T. (1991). *Women and power: Perspectives for family therapy*. New York: Norton.

Hochschild, A. (1989). *The second shift: Working parents and the revolution at home*. New York: Viking Penguin.

Huston, A. C. (1983). Sex-typing. In P. H. Mussen (Ed.), *Handbook of child psychology (Vol. 4, 4th ed.)* (pp. 387-467). New York: Wiley.

Hyde, J. S. (1996). *Half the human experience (5th ed.)*. Lexington, MA: D. C. Heath & Co.

Levant, R. F., & Kopecky, O. (1995/1996). *Masculinity reconstructed: Changing the rules of manhood–at work, in relationships and in family life*. New York: Dutton/Plume.

Lusterman, D.-D. (1993). *How to train for empathic interviewing*. Unpublished manuscript.

McGrath, E., Keita, G., Strickland, B., & Russo, N. (1990). *Women and depression: Risk factors and treatment issues*. Final report of the American Psychological Association's National Task Force on Women and Depression. Washington, DC: American Psychological Association.

Nichter, M., & Vuckovic, N. (1994). Fat talk: Body image among adolescent girls. In N. Sault (Ed.), *Many mirrors: Body image and social relations* (pp. 109-131). New Brunswick, NJ: Rutgers University Press.

O'Neil, J. M., & Egan, J. (1992). Men's and women's gender role journeys: A metaphor for healing, transition and transformation. In B. R. Wainrib (Ed.), *Gender issues across the life cycle* (pp. 107-123). New York: Springer.

Philpot, C. L. (1992). Gender-sensitive couples therapy: A systemic definition. *Journal of Family Psychotherapy, 2 (3)*, 19-40.

Philpot, C. L., Brooks, G. R., Lusterman, D.-D., & Nutt, R. L. (1997). *Bridging separate gender worlds: Why men and women clash and how therapists can bring them together*. Washington, DC: American Psychological Association.

Pleck, J. H. (1981). *The myth of masculinity*. Cambridge, MA: MIT Press.

Tannen, D. (1990). *You just don't understand: Women and men in conversation*. New York: Ballantine Books.

Waldron, I. (1976). Why do women live longer than men? *Journal of Human Stress, 2*, 1-13.

Wolf, N. (1991). *The beauty myth*. New York: Morrow.

Wood, J. T. (1994). *Gendered lives: Communication, gender and culture*. Belmont, CA: Wadsworth Publishing Company.

Zilbergeld, B. (1992). *The new male sexuality: The truth about men, sex, and pleasure*. New York: Bantam Books.

Exploring Culture in Practice:
A Few Facets of a Training Course

Reenee Singh

SUMMARY. While recent literature has reflected an interest in incorporating diversity and multiculturalism in the course design of existing marriage and family therapy training programmes in the United States, correspondingly little has been written about similar attempts in the United Kingdom. This paper reviews the literature on training in cultural competency and then describes an introductory systemic training course entitled "Exploring Culture in Practice." The course was organised by the Marlborough Family Service and Tavistock Clinic in London and was attended by mental health workers. The paper focuses on three central areas in multicultural training: constructions of the family; the concepts of "race," culture, gender, and power; and the family life cycle. It offers a theoretical background, possible experiential exercises and participant feedback for each of these three areas. *[Article copies available for a fee from The Haworth Document Delivery Service: 1-800-HAWORTH. E-mail address: <docdelivery@haworthpress.com> Website: <http://www.HaworthPress.com> © 2004 by The Haworth Press, Inc. All rights reserved.]*

Reenee Singh is a systemic psychotherapist, Asian Service, Tavistock and Portman NHS Trust, London, UK, and Project Leader of the Refugee Project, Institute of Family Therapy, London, UK (E-mail: rsingh@tavi-port.nhs.uk).

The author would like to acknowledge Jenny Altschuler, Sara Barratt, Grania Clarke, Raina Fateh, and Ann Miller.

[Haworth co-indexing entry note]: "Exploring Culture in Practice: A Few Facets of a Training Course." Singh, Reenee. Co-published simultaneously in *Journal of Family Psychotherapy* (The Haworth Press, Inc.) Vol. 15, No. 1/2, 2004, pp. 87-104; and: *Family Therapy Around the World: A Festschrift for Florence W. Kaslow* (ed: William C. Nichols) The Haworth Press, Inc., 2004, pp. 87-104. Single or multiple copies of this article are available for a fee from The Haworth Document Delivery Service [1-800-HAWORTH, 9:00 a.m. - 5:00 p.m. (EST). E-mail address: docdelivery@haworthpress.com].

http://www.haworthpress.com/web/JFP
Digital Object Identifier: 10.1300/J085v15n01_07

KEYWORDS. Culture, multiculturalism, family, cultural genogram, family life cycle

FOREWORD

I felt privileged when I was asked to write for the Kaslow Festschrift, and thought that an article on multicultural training would be a fitting contribution, as Florence Kaslow has been a prominent influence on training in many different cultural contexts. As a systemic psychotherapist of Indian origin, trained in the United Kingdom (UK), I have struggled with issues in my own training where I would feel marginalized, misunderstood, or confused, unable to make the links between taught theoretical concepts and my own experiences of clinical practice with Asian families. My desire to contribute this particular paper was thus also prompted by a commitment to designing and providing training that equips the practitioner to work with diverse family forms in varied cultural contexts.

OVERVIEW

In my mind, there are two main reasons why family therapy training programmes, traditionally located in the Western world, should incorporate cultural awareness and sensitivity in their course design.

First, the number of people from ethnic minorities living in the west is increasing at a rapid rate. According to the United States Bureau of the Census, 1998 (cited in Bean, Perry, & Bedell, 2002), African Americans constitute the largest ethnic group in the United States, with current populations estimated at 33 million, and projections of more than 60 million by the year 2050. In the United Kingdom (UK), South Asians make up the largest ethnic minority of 1.7 million (Centre for Social Markets, 2001). There are also a vast numbers of refugee families who present with a range of mental health needs. The kinds of families who seek mental health services are increasingly likely to be from varied cultural backgrounds, pointing to the need for family therapists to be culturally sensitive.

While ethnic-specific services–that is, services which have been operationally defined as those in which a majority of the staff are of the same ethnicity as their clients (Takeuchi, Sue, & Yeh, 1995)–are one possible answer to working with clients from ethnic minorities, there is no conclusive evidence that ethnic matching affects therapeutic outcomes (Atkinson, 1983). Further, ethnic-specific services need to go beyond a bilingual/bicultural matching of therapist and client into the realm of constant negotiations between therapist and client and flexibility in the services provided.

As Ito and Maramba (2002) state: "It is clear that ethnic-specific services are not merely a laundry list of attributes but a process of constant cultural negotiations and modifications between clients and therapists" (p. 64). Another difficulty inherent in providing an ethnic-specific service within a mainstream service is that it tends to locate problems of ethnic minorities in that particular service, rather than attempting to integrate them into the entire multidisciplinary team. This is not to suggest that ethnic-specific mental health services are not useful in improving ethnic minority use and retention, but rather to argue the case for all family therapists to be trained to think about and work with those from cultures other than their own, given that we live in a multicultural society.

Second, family therapy's theories and practices are based on white, Eurocentric, middle class, male notions of "the family," normative child-rearing practices, and gender, which may be entirely inconsistent with other cultures or socioeconomic classes. Although the tenets of family therapy have been challenged over the years, beginning with feminist critiques of employing cybernetic metaphors of abuse (Taggart, 1985; Goldner, 1985; MacKinnon & Miller, 1987; Luepnitz, 1988), it is only in the last decade that educators in the field of family therapy have been grappling with the issues of racial and cultural sensitivity in training programmes (McDowell, Fang, Brownlee, Young, & Khanna, 2002). Simultaneously, white multicultural educators have been fighting for social justice, equality, and unpacking white privilege and racism in training programmes (Clark & O'Donnell, 2000).

It is beyond the scope of this paper to review the entire literature in the field of training in family therapy, so I will focus on a few studies that are particularly relevant to the training course that I will describe in the next section.

Falicov (1995) and Hardy and Laszloffy (1995) developed helpful frameworks and tools for training. Falicov's (1995) multidimensional framework integrates culture with all other aspects of family therapy. She uses the term ecological niche to describe how the multiple contexts in which a family is located–such as culture, class, and family positions–converge. This idea, she argues, helps therapists to conceptualize the multiple contexts in which families exist and also how their own ecological niche may be similar or different from that of other families within and outside their ethnic and cultural group. Hardy and Laszloffy (1995) extend the use of a traditional genogram to the cultural genogram as a training tool to promote cultural awareness and sensitivity by helping trainees to understand their cultural identities. They outline a detailed sequential explanation of how the cultural genogram can be constructed and used in training, with a list of questions to facilitate the trainee and the trainer.

Watts-Jones (1997) suggests that the standard genogram is inadequate for African American families and proposes a genogram based on the assumptions that kinship must be recognised as construed by the particular ethnic/racial group of the family and that functional relationships are as important to represent as biological ones. The African American genogram may be useful with other families in cultures where functional kin relationships are considered significant. In a recent qualitative research study, Keiley and associates (2002) demonstrate the use of the cultural genogram in a graduate-level course in gender and culture for family therapists-in-training at an accredited programme in family therapy in the United States. They suggest changes to Hardy and Laszloffy's (1995) facilitating questions to take into account the experiences of international students who are not necessarily migrants to the United States and those whose cultural journeys are affected by other factors such as having biethnic, biracial and bicultural parents, adoption, or foster care experiences or clashes between one culture and another.

In another interesting research study within the North American literature, Bean, Perry, and Bedell (2002) carry out a content analysis of the relevant treatment literature in order to examine the most common expert recommendations for family therapy with African Americans. The 15 specific guidelines that were generated include: orient the family to therapy, do not assume familiarity, address issues of racism, intervene multisystemically, do home visits, use problem-solving focus, involve a religious leader, incorporate the father, and acknowledge strengths. I was struck by how similar the guidelines are to those that somebody working with Asian families in the UK might recommend!

Going beyond incorporating multicultural awareness and sensitivity in existing trainings, McDowell and associates (2002) propose a model for transforming graduate programmes to reflect the principles of diversity and social justice. They argue that such a model must address not only the typical practices of recruiting and retaining students of colour but also examine readiness, assessment, and professional development. Readiness exists at the levels of faculty, organizational, and programme readiness. The process of recruitment and admissions involves identifying potential students, building relationships, and reviewing admissions process. Retention takes place at the levels of academic support, faculty support, university/academic environment, social and cultural environment, supervision, and financial support. Assessment incorporates feedback and includes a student of colour advisory board, and professional development includes professional mentoring and matched job placements. I was particularly impressed by the way in which the authors employ non-Western pedagogy focusing on group work, including group tests in their methods of assessment, as, in my experience, these are often far more suited to Asian students. Although their model may sound somewhat utopian, they describe admirable work in progress in a marriage and family therapy programme within an established Midwestern university in the United States.

There is relatively little written in this area in the UK. Remarking on the paucity of articles on training in family therapy journals in the UK, the editor of the *Journal of Family Therapy*, Ivan Eisler, suggests that one possible reason may be that for most family therapists, teaching and training is not a normal expectation of their job, and is seen more as an "add-on" to their clinical responsibilities (Eisler, 2003). Another related reason could be that while most marriage and family therapy programmes in the United States are based in university settings, this is not the case in the UK.

Bringing issues of multiculturalism in training into contemporary UK systemic literature, Guanipa (2003) describes a prototype curriculum of an introductory course in multiculturalism for marriage and family therapy students. The course was relevant to this paper as it was a semester-length course (for a duration of 16 weeks). The course content focused on the five areas of cultural self-awareness, marriage and family therapy multicultural knowledge base, developing multicultural clinical skills, multicultural mission, and altruism and multicultural research. Some of the instructional strategies used were weekly diaries, class presentations, guest speakers, video presentations, and post-observation discussions and community visits. Guanipa's (2003) paper contains useful ideas to all those who wish to design systemic courses in multiculturalism.

Of notable exception to the lack of literature on training in multiculturalism in the UK is Dwivedi's (1999) report of the CONFETTI (Confederation of Family Therapy Training Institutions) working party on "race," "ethnicity," and "culture" in family therapy training. This report, which spans the entire issue of the Association of Family Therapy journal, *Context*, includes a rationale for such training, theoretical issues, practice issues, organisations for training and service delivery, personal development, and an extensive bibliography. Much of the course, "Exploring Culture in Practice," was based on the ideas presented in this report, which is indeed a landmark in family therapy training in the UK.

Following on from the CONFETTI report, the BPS (British Psychological Society) published a training manual on "race" and culture, which contains both introductory and specialized modules, on a range of topics such as learning disabilities, adult mental health, and substance misuse (Patel, 2000).

EXPLORING CULTURE IN PRACTICE: A BRIEF DESCRIPTION OF THE COURSE

A requirement of the master of science degree in systemic psychotherapy at the Tavistock Clinic is for trainees to design and teach an introductory course.

As part of our training, Raina Fateh (a colleague at the Marlborough Family Service) and I decided to facilitate a course which would employ systemic thinking in working with ethnic minority families. The course grew from a realization during our work in the Brent, Kensington, Chelsea, and Westminster (BKCW) NHS Trust–which the Marlborough Family Service is a part of–that mental health professionals often felt stuck when working with ethnic minority families. We decided to name our course "Exploring Culture in Practice," as we did not wish to position ourselves as "experts" teaching about culture, but envisaged that the course would be a space where professionals could explore together some of the dilemmas of working within and across culture. We were fortunate to receive guidance, supervision, and support from Jenny Altschuler at the Tavistock Clinic and Ann Miller at the Marlborough Family Service.

The intended learning outcomes of our course (adapted from the CONFETTI report) were for participants to:

- Think critically about issues of race, culture and ethnicity, both theoretically and practically, through the use of questions, vignettes, exercises, and references.
- Think critically about the way in which ideas of connectedness and autonomy differ across life cycle stages in different cultures.
- Hold and contain multiple perspectives rather than be pulled toward a universalist or essentialist position.
- Think about the effect of the similarity and difference of their culture from their clients.
- Do some work in relation to their family of origin, using a cultural genogram.
- Be able to think about the meaning of power and inversions of power in their work with their clients as well as within the agency settings.
- Be able to think about the meaning of pathology in a particular culture and the repercussions of diagnosis.
- Widen the definition of the family to include different family forms across different cultural groupings.

The course ran for 10 fortnightly sessions between January and July 2001. It was attended by 15 professionals within the BKCW Trust, many of whom were community psychiatric nurses, working in adult mental health settings. The participants, who defined themselves ethnically as African, Afro-Caribbean, Asian, and white British, were all interested in becoming more competent when working with clients from another culture. The sessions, each for a duration of three hours, included theoretical presentations, experiential exercises, the use of clinical video and film clips, and group discussions. We devoted one session to a discussion of cases from the participants' agency settings and invited two renowned guest speakers to another session. Although the course was non-assessed, we gave participants papers and books to read between one session and the next. We helped participants to develop core systemic practice skills, to critically examine issues of race and culture, and to make connections between their personal and professional lives. It was a pleasure to co-facilitate the course, as the participants was engaging, lively, and insightful, constantly contributing to our learning. Feedback from the participants was overwhelming, pointing to the need to develop and facilitate such courses in the future.

For the purposes of this paper, I am using my experience of teaching, both on "Exploring Culture in Practice," and subsequently on other short- and long-term courses, to present three areas or topics in the course design that, with hindsight, I believe are central to the design of a course that encourages practitioners to be more culturally competent. They are: constructions of a family; the concepts of "race," culture, gender, and power; and the family life cycle. Each area is vast and could comprise an introductory course in its own right, or be used as a thread that weaves through the entire design of a course. As my own ideas about training develop, partly through participant feedback, the timing of each one of these three areas within a course and the content of each area inevitably changes. Further, there is much overlap between the three areas, and they are not intended to be watertight topics. Thus, I am presenting these ideas not as a blueprint for developing similar training, but rather as one perspective, which may be used in conjunction with others. In this paper, I will provide a brief theoretical outline for each area, one possible experiential exercise for each and feedback from the participants on "Exploring Culture in Practice" with relation to each area.

CONSTRUCTIONS OF "THE FAMILY"

It may be helpful to start a course on multicultural family therapy by critiquing notions of "the family." In thinking about the family as socially, culturally, and historically constructed, I like to start with a brief presentation on the broader area of social constructionism, which has influenced much current thinking and research in family therapy. The key assumptions of social constructionism are a critical stance toward taken-for-granted knowledge, historical and cultural specificity, and the connection between knowledge, arising from social processes and social action (Burr, 1995).

Constructions of the family include constructions of kinship, family structures, maps and genograms. Although the area also includes gender, marriage, and ideas of normative child development, I usually focus on constructions of kinship and genograms in this topic, as other areas are covered under the topics of the family life cycle and the concepts of "race," culture, gender, and power.

Theoretical Outline

Krause (1998) highlights the idea that Anglo-American ideas of kinship, based on genealogies of lineal descent, do not take into account collateral relationships (relationships between people in parallel lines, such as between children of two siblings) and affinal relationships (that is, relationships through marriage). She illustrates her argument with family maps of a hypothetical matrilineage and patrilineage, both of which appear to be very different from a traditional genogram. The implication for systemic psychotherapy is that kinship is culturally constructed and that it is important for the cross-cultural therapist to enter into and become familiar with the family's meaning of family structure and relationships.

Perelberg (1992) employs the concept of "family map" as a level that mediates between culture and patterns of interaction within a family. She defines a family map as a "set of ideas which guide behaviour and emotion in everyday life" (p. 134). The map includes ideas about gender, parenting, and the connections maintained within the network of friends and relatives. Perelberg's concept of "the family map" facilitates the cross-cultural therapist's thinking about specific aspects of cultural difference, while acknowledging the agency of the individual of family in mediating these differences.

Luepnitz (1988) emphasizes the relevance for family therapists of studying the historical context of "the family" in order to avoid making assumptions about the "normal" family. She illustrates changing family structures and the social organization of gender by discussing five different kinds of families: the upper-class family of the Roman Republic, the aristocratic family of sixteenth and seventeenth century Europe, the peasant family of sixteenth and seventeenth century Europe, the modern family, and the American Black family. She points out that current ideology about the family is based on the bourgeois Western family of the eighteenth and nineteenth centuries. Luepnitz (1988) provides an interesting feminist analysis of motherhood, the cult of domesticity and romantic love, and sexuality in the modern day Western family.

Exercise

An exercise that fits well with a theoretical presentation of constructions of "the family" is the cultural genogram. To my mind, it is useful at the beginning of a course, especially in conjunction with thinking about diverse family forms, to help participants think about how their culture affects their own families of origin. It introduces participants to a variation of a basic tool used in family therapy, and could help them begin to think about the diverse family forms, informed by culture, that exist within their own group of participants. On the other hand, especially if the participants do not know each other well, it may be more useful to introduce it after the participants have come to know each other a little. One possibility is to first have two or three theoretical sessions on the key ideas of systemic thinking, social constructionism, constructions of a family, and family of origin issues, leading to the experiential exercise of a cultural genogram.

Hardy and Laszloffy (1995) offer a step-by-step description of how to construct a cultural genogram. During a training course, participants can be asked to break into pairs and help each other to construct a cultural genogram, with the help of the facilitators. In a smaller group, cultural genograms can be mapped together with the help of a facilitator. Participants are asked to identify the issues of pride and shame in their families and to answer the questions, modifications to which have been suggested by Keiley and associates (2002), as reviewed earlier in this paper. Facilitators should allow at least 45 minutes per person to answer the questions and construct the genogram.

Feedback from Participants

Consistent with a course designed on the principles of systemic thinking for the course "Exploring Culture in Practice," we asked for informal feedback after each session, asked the participants to fill in feedback forms after the fourth (approximately the middle of the course), and the tenth sessions (the end of the course).

At the end of the course, we asked two participants to write a position paper about what they had learned. Feedback on the constructions of "the family" was that it was "a reminder of the existence of different family forms in different cultures," that it was interesting, relevant, and useful, although some participants found it too theoretical. Interestingly, one of the position papers focused entirely on the cultural genogram and the way in which it can be used to challenge Western constructions of "the family." Extracts from the paper, reproduced with the consent of the participant author, follow:

> When I started the Ethnicity and Diversity Training I had an extremely limited and third hand understanding of the Genogram and how and where to apply it in clinical practice. Unfortunately I also had a philosophical and theoretical stand point to validate my position of not knowing, which, in retrospect, I now think may have been naïve and a bit pre-emptive. . . .

Whilst learning about the genogram from a cultural perspective I was able to review my position and I realised that my thinking had previously led me clinically, to be "painted into a corner." In creating my own map of my own family I was able to identify, more clearly, the cultural influences that had played a role in my family context. I was also able to reconstruct certain "flattened out" perspectives regarding my family and see particular patterns that emerged from a generation perspective. Add onto this map other information and influencing factors such as religious beliefs, important family values or sayings and/or sociological factors (". . . A woman's place is in the home . . ." "Those that say they are bored have usually done nothing to deserve it . . ." "Don't wash your dirty linen in public . . . ," etc.) and the contextual tapestry would weave an even richer picture. . . .

I can now see that the use of a Genogram, particularly that which offers a multi-dimensional exploration can aid the client in their own reflexivity. I can see how it can be useful in eliciting a client's meaning and act as a starting point for further discussion. I would like to think that the Genogram would extend to challenging a western view of the family structure. Not only through the acknowledgement of both matriarchal or patriarchal lineage, but in recognising the validity of other non-genetically linked, but significant relationships that constitute "family" to some of our clients.

THE CONCEPTS OF "RACE," CULTURE, GENDER, AND POWER

Although, for the purposes of this paper, I have grouped the concepts of "race," culture, gender, and power under one heading, I am aware that this is a vast topic that could extend over several training sessions. Indeed, for the short (10-session) training course "Exploring Culture in Practice," we broke the subject matter into two sessions, one on "race, culture, and power" and the other on "gender and power."

Theoretical Outline

Race is a term that has largely been discredited in biological science, but was particularly prevalent in the 19th and 20th centuries. The term assumed that humans could be clearly divided into populations based on biological characteristics and that these characteristics determined behaviour and institutions (Littlewood, 2001). Osborne (1971), cited in Fernando (1991), summarizes the scientific findings:

- Differences within races are greater than the differences between races on important physical characteristics apart from those used to define race.
- There is no evidence for designating any race as "superior" or "inferior" in terms of ability in any particular sphere or in adaptability to the environment.
- There are no "pure" races that have genetic characteristics and that are unique.
- "Primitive" physical characteristics such as thin lips, flat noses, and straight hair are found in all races.

Littlewood and Lipsedge (1989) make a distinction between ethnicity and culture, as the former is a static and the latter a dynamic concept. An ethnic group:

> may be a nation, a people, a language group, or so called race or group bound together in a coherent cultural entity through a shared religion, belief in a common descent, or through the recognition of particular shared physical characteristics which are selected for remark or identity by the group or others. (p. 25)

Brah (1996) argues against an essentialist definition of ethnicity, as ethnicities are fluid rather than fixed, and because the boundaries of ethnicity could be drawn around a number of different criteria and are dependent on fluctuating political, economic, and cultural contingencies She views culture as "the symbolic construction of the vast array of a social group's life experiences. Culture is the embodiment, the chronicle of a group's history" (p. 18).

Krause and Miller (1995) pose a "double definition of culture." Thus culture is both a blueprint for behaviour, thoughts, and feelings as well as a changing body of ideas, which is open to individual interpretation. A dual definition, according to Krause and Miller (1995), incorporates the continuity of cultural themes, or the generative aspect and the interactive aspect, that is, the redefinition or change of these themes through interaction. Krause (1998, 2002) cautions that "culture is a complex illusion"; difficult to define as it is both inside and outside persons; in that cultural conventions influence those that live within them, but that the ways in which cultural conventions affect persons varies from one situation to another.

When working with ethnic minority families, while it is important to think about their similarity and difference from us (mental health professionals) in terms of their ethnicity and culture, it is equally important to think about the context of powerlessness and racism in which they live. Power operates at both the level of enforcing sanctions as well as the level of defining and constructing reality. Recent thinking about power, couched within a postmodern view, "states that power grants privilege—the privilege to have one's truth prevail" (Paré, 1995, p. 9). Western convention defines mental health and 'normal' functioning and behaviour. Linking to the last section of this paper, notions of the normative family, child rearing and gender draw on Western dominant societal discourses.

Feminist critiques of systemic thinking (see, for example, Goldner, 1985), while important to present in a systemic course that includes thinking about gender, have their limitations when thinking about the experiences of coloured women. In the words of Almeida (1998):

> Gender oppression must be viewed in the context of other oppressions with which it is embedded: racism, colonization, classism, heterosexim and homophobia. . . . Thus we need to illuminate multiple levels of oppression, including the privileging and power of some men over other men, some women over other women, and heterosexuals over homosexuals. (p. 417)

Exercise on Identifying Gender Beliefs

These are adapted from Burck and Daniel (1995). Approximate time is one and a half hours.

Part 1

The group divides into pairs:

  A. They are asked to identify four beliefs that they have received from their families of origin and/or community and culture about how men and women should be and then compare which ones are similar or different (20 minutes).
  B. They are asked to identify one way in which they have tried to do something different and think about the effect of one or more of the beliefs on this change and the effect of the change on the belief (15 minutes).
  C. Larger group feedback (15 minutes).

Part 2

  A. The participants break into pairs to think about how some of these common gendered beliefs would affect their women and men clients from the same and different cultural backgrounds (20 minutes).
  B. Larger group feedback and discussion (15 minutes).

Feedback from Participants

Feedback from the two sessions on "Race, Culture, and Power" and "Gender and Power" was very positive. It included the following comments:

- Very, very useful. It was tremendous that the students came from such varied cultural backgrounds.
- Very interesting session, especially the "power" component.
- Educative and inspiring.
- Such an eye-opener. Especially on different cultural perspectives of power and gender.
- Overall, the most useful sessions were on culture, gender, and genograms.
- The session on gender made me more sympathetic towards the male perspective!

THE FAMILY LIFE CYCLE

Theoretical Outline

The interdisciplinary family development approach originated in the pioneering work of Evelyn Duvall and Rueben Hill in the late 1940s (Duvall, 1957). Over a period of time, the family development approach drew on a number of different theoretical models; the idea of family stages came from rural sociology, the notions of human developmental needs and tasks from human development research and child psychology, and conceptualizing the family as a system of interacting actors from structure-functional and symbolic-interactional theory (Hill & Rodgers, 1964, cited in Nichols & Pace, 2000).

Although the family life cycle was widely used in the social work discipline, it was not until 1973 that the family development framework became generally known to family therapists (Falicov, 1988). Solomon (1973) and Haley (1973) were the first to introduce family development ideas to the field of family therapy. Solomon's (1973) schema of the family life cycle, influenced by Erikson (1963), included the stages of marriage, the birth of the first child and subsequent childbearing, the individuation of family members, the actual departure of the children and the integration of loss (Falicov, 1988). Haley's (1973) model of the life cycle focused on transitions from one stage of the family life cycle to another, and he viewed symptoms in an individual family member as indications that the family was "stuck," that they could not progress from one family life cycle stage to the next.

The family life cycle is based on ideas from models of individual development, e.g., Erik Erikson (1968). In the field of sociology, Duvall (1971) defined the family life cycle as "the sequence of characteristic stages beginning with the family formation and continuing through the life of the family to its dissolution." He proposed the stages: Beginning families, Childbearing families, Childrearing families, Families with teenagers, Families as launching centres, Families in middle years, and Ageing families. Each stage was characterised by its particular developmental tasks.

The concept of the family life cycle was later adopted and adapted in systemic thinking by clinicians and researchers, for example, Palazzoli, Boscolo, Cecchin, and Prata (1978) and Minuchin (1974). The original family development schemas have been extended to include a three-generational perspective and the transitions of divorce and remarriage (Carter & McGoldrick, 1980), single-parent families (Hill, 1986), and to take into account the sociopolitical contexts in which families are located (Aldous, 1990).

Falicov (1988) makes a distinction between the concepts of "family development" and "family life cycle," as the former is a broader, more overarching concept. While the family life cycle refers to the events that are connected to the entries, exits, and major changes in the life of a family, family development includes psychological processes, migration, acculturation, and any "set of events that significantly alters the texture of family life" (Falicov, 1988, p. 13).

According to Burnham (1986), families progress from one developmental stage to another through triggers, i.e., events or issues that can prompt a family system to change its current patterns of relating. Triggers could be exits, formations, or entries. In terms of timing, the trigger points may be expected or unexpected. Expected triggers are physiological development, cultural patterns or family scripts, which are idiosyncratic rules and rituals that govern transitions in the life cycle of relationships. Unexpected triggers are those that are not in the family's schedule of anticipated events, examples of which are divorce and migration.

Of particular relevance to this paper, Falicov (1988) argues that the family life cycle framework does pay sufficient attention to the sociocultural contexts in which families are located. She emphasizes the importance of introducing cultural relativity with regard to issues of cultural development in the training of family therapists. In an attempt to raise awareness of cultural variations of family life cycles, we (Nath, Singh, & Craig, 1999) developed a framework based on the family life cycle prescribed in Hindu religious epics and on our clinical experiences. Our framework incorporated the prominence of the stage of marriage and the importance of collateral and affinal family relationships in a multigenerational Indian family of "kul."

In the "Exploring Culture in Practice" forum, I used our thinking about the Indiana family life cycle to illustrate one way in which family development can assume different forms. I also highlighted the point that adolescence as a family life cycle does not have a place in many cultures, and discussed the issues for second generational adolescents growing up in Western nations.

Another way in which thinking about the family life cycle is relevant to training in cross-cultural practice is to examine the effects of migration/relocation on the family life cycle. How does migrating at a particular stage of the family life cycle affect the developmental stages/tasks of the family? Would the family life cycle have unfolded in a different way if the family had re-mained in its own country/within its own culture?

Exercise on the Family Life Cycle and Geographical Relocation

This exercise is adapted from Dwivedi (1999, the CONFETTI report). Ap-proximate time is 1 hour and 15 minutes.

Aim: For trainees to understand how their current model of practice can be used to encompass the therapeutic needs of refugee families. Facilitators should note that this is a powerful exercise and make certain they feel safe to lead it and leave plenty of time for discussion of the issues that arise.

Number of participants: minimum 8, maximum 20.

1. The facilitators will provide a brief explanation of sculpting as the ex-ercise is in the format of a sculpt (5 minutes).
2. Ask for volunteers for two groups of five family members. The roles assigned will be a grandmother, a mother, a father, a 15-year-old boy and a 10-year-old girl (5 minutes).
3. One group of five family members will be asked to sculpt while the other observes from an outside circle (in role).
4. The "inside" family group is asked to sculpt the following scenario: "This is a family who has just found out that there is a sudden crisis in their country and they have to leave the next morning, taking the bare minimum with them" (3 minutes).
5. The inside group is then asked to talk about their experiences in role (15 minutes).
6. The inside group is de-roled and changes place with the "outside" group (3 minutes).
7. The "outside" (now inside) group is asked for their experiences of ob-serving (10 minutes).
8. A new scenario is presented to the inside group: "Six months after their migration, the same family is gathered together, discussing their new family life." They are asked to sculpt the new scene (5 minutes).
9. The inside group talks about their experiences during the sculpt (10 minutes).
10. The inside group de-roles (3 minutes).
11. The outside group talks about their experiences of observing and then de-roles (10 minutes).

Feedback

The participants appeared to find the session on the family life cycle and the sculpt very helpful. The feedback included the following comments.

- The sculpt about refugee families was particularly enjoyable.
- I found the discussion on the family life cycle, especially adolescence and culture most enjoyable and practical as well. We, those from different cultures living in Western cultures, face lots of problems with our adolescent children.
- The sculpting exercise on the family life cycle was enjoyable, powerful, and enlightening.
- This session was very interesting, particularly when considering how different cultures view the various life cycle stages (for example, old age, respect given, or not given).
- An eye-opener to people's different expectations of the family. I found the sculpt especially useful.
- I enjoyed the sculpt and found it very interesting. It made me look at refugee experiences in a different light.

CONCLUSIONS

While I believe that it is essential to critique the received knowledge of concepts from Western family therapy in a multicultural training course, it is important to emphasise that this process is more effective when grounded in developing core systemic skills, such as hypothesizing and circularity. Another important consideration is the group process and power differentials that take place in any training course, but which may be used as a vital part of the training in a multicultural group. Teaching methods and materials that are culturally isomorphic is yet another area for facilitators to consider carefully in their design.

"Family therapy" is taught, both formally and informally, in countries all over the world, with different contexts shaping the structure of each course design. This paper has focused only on training programmes developed in the Western world; it is in itself a comment on the "dominant discourse" of training in systemic psychotherapy as traditionally located in North America and the UK. Thinking about systemic trainings in countries where family therapy is a relatively new field could open up a fascinating area for discussion.

REFERENCES

Aldous, J. (1990). Family development and the life course: Two perspectives on family change. *Journal of Marriage and the Family, 52*, 571-583.
Almeida, R. (1998). The dislocation of women's experience in family therapy. *Journal of Feminist Family Therapy, 10 (1)*, 1-22.
Atkinson, D. R. (1983). Ethnic similarity in counselling psychology: A review of research. *Counselling Psychologist, 11*, 97-92.

Bean, R. A., Perry, B. J., & Bedell, T. M. (2002). Developing culturally competent marriage and family therapists: Treatment guidelines for non-African-American therapists working with African American families. *Journal of Marital and Family Therapy, 28,* 153-164.

Brah, A. (1996). *The cartographies of disaspore: Contesting identities.* London: Routledge.

Burck, C., & Daniel, G. (1995). *Gender and family therapy.* London: Karnac.

Burnham, J. B. (1988). *Family therapy. First steps towards a systemic approach.* London: Routledge.

Burr, V. (1995). *An introduction to social constructionism.* London: Routledge.

Carter, E., & McGoldrick, M. (Eds.) (1980). *The family life cycle: A framework for family therapy .* New York: Gardner Press.

Centre for Social Markets (July 2001). British Asians today: A statistical overview.

Clark, C., & O'Donnell, J. (2000). Rearticulating a racial identity: Creating oppositional spaces to fight for equality and social justice. In C. Clark & J. O'Donnell (Eds.), *Becoming and unbecoming white: Owning and disowning a racial identity* (pp. 1-9). London: Bergin and Garvey.

Duvall, E. M. (1957). *Family development.* Philadelphia: J. B. Lippincott.

Dwivedi, K. N. (1999) Sowing the seeds of cultural competence: Family therapy training for a multi-ethnic society. The report of the CONFETTI working party on "race," "ethnicity" and "culture" in family therapy training. *Context, 44.*

Eisler, I. (2003). Editorial. *Journal of Family Therapy, 25 (1),* 1-3.

Erikson, E. H. (1963). *Childhood and society.* New York: Norton.

Falicov, C. J. (1988). Family sociology and family therapy contributions to the family development framework: A comparative analysis and thoughts on future trends. In C. J. Falicov (Ed.), *Family transitions* (pp. 3-55). London: Guilford Press.

Falicov, C. J. (1995). Training to think culturally: A multi-dimensional comparative framework. *Family Process, 34,* 373-388.

Fernando, S. (1991). *Mental health, race and culture.* London: MacMillan.

Goldner, V. (1985). Feminism and family therapy. *Family Process, 24,* 31-47.

Guanipa, C. (2003). Sharing a multicultural course design for a marriage and family therapy programme: One perspective. *Journal of Family Therapy, 25 (1),* 86-106.

Haley, J. (1973). *Uncommon therapy. The psychiatric techniques of Milton Erickson.* New York: Norton.

Hardy, K. V., & Laszloffy, T. A. (1995). The cultural genogram: Key to training culturally competent family therapists. *Journal of Marital and Family Therapy, 21,* 227-237.

Hill, R. (1986). Life cycle stages for types of single parent families: On family development theory. *Family Relations, 35,* 19-30.

Hill, R., & Rodgers, R. H. (1964). The developmental approach. In H. T. Christenson (Ed.), *Handbook of marriage and the family* (pp. 171-211). Chicago: McNally. Cited in Nichols, W. C., & Pace Nichols, M. A. (2000). In W. C. Nichols, M. A. Pace-Nichols, D. S. Becvar, & A. Y. Napier (Eds.), *Handbook of family development and intervention* (pp. 1-19). New York: John Wiley and Sons.

Ito, K. L., & Maramba, G. G. (2002). Therapeutic beliefs of Asian American therapists: Views from an ethnic-specific clinic. *Transcultural Psychiatry, 39 (1),* 33-73.

Keiley, M. K., Dolbin, M., Hill, J., Karuppaswamy, N., Liu, T., Natranjan, R., Poulsen, S., Robbins, N., & Robinson, P. (2002). The cultural genogram: Experiences within an MFT training program. *Journal of Marital and Family Therapy, 28,* 165-177.

Krause, I. B. (1998). *Therapy across culture*. London: Sage.

Krause, I. B. (2002). *Culture and system in family therapy*. London: Karnac.

Krause, I. B., & Miller, A. C. (1995). Culture and family therapy. In S. Fernando (Ed.), *Mental health in a multi-ethnic society: A multi-disciplinary handbook* (pp. 149-171). London: Routledge.

Littlewood, R., & Lipsedge, M. (1989). Ethnic minorities and the psychiatrist. In R. Littlewood & M. Lipsedge (Eds.), *Alients and alienists: Ethnic minorities and psychiatry* (pp. 2-26). London: Unwin Hyman.

Luepnitz, D. A. (1998). *The family interpreted*. New York: Basic Books.

MacKinnon, L. K., & Miller, D. (1987). The new epistemology and the Milan approach: Feminist sociopolitical considerations. *Journal of Marital and Family Therapy, 13*, 139-155.

McDowell, T., Fang, S-R., Brownlee, K., Gomex Young, C., & Khanna, A. (2002). Transforming an MFT program: A model for enhancing diversity. *Journal of Marital and Family Therapy, 28*, 179-191.

Minuchin, S. (1974). *Families and family therapy*. London: Tavistock Publications.

Nath, R., Singh, R., & Craig, J. (April 1999). *A life-cycle for a multi-generational Indian family*. Paper presented at the International Family Therapy Association Congress. Akron, Ohio.

Nichols, W. C., & Pace-Nichols, M. A. (2000). Family development and family therapy. In W. C. Nichols, M. A. Pace-Nichols, D. S. Becvar, & A. Y. Napier (Eds.), *Handbook of family development and intervention* (pp. 1-19). New York: John Wiley and Sons.

Olson, D. H. (1986). Circumplex model, VII: Validation rules and FACES III. *Family Process, 25*, 337-351.

Osborne, R. H. (1971). Races and the future of man. In R. H. Osborne (Ed.), *The biological and social meaning of race* (pp. 147-157). San Francisco: Freeman. Cited in S. Fernando (1991) *Mental health, race and culture*. London: MacMillan.

Palazzoli, M. S., Boscolo, L., Cecchin, G., & Prata, G. (1978). *Paradox and counter-paradox: A new model in the therapy of the family in schizophrenic transactions*. London: Jason Aronson.

Paré, D. A. (1996). Culture and meaning: Expanding the metaphorical repertoire of family therapy. *Family Process, 35*, 21-42.

Patel, N. (2000). *Clinical psychology, race and culture. A training manual*. London: BPS Books.

Perelberg, R. J. (2000). Familiar and unfamiliar types of family structure: Towards a conceptual framework. In J. Kareem & R. Littlewood (Eds.), *Intercultural therapy* (pp. 7-21). London: Blackwell.

Taggart, M. (1985). The feminist critique in epistemological perspective: Questions of context in family therapy. *Journal of Marital and Family Therapy, 11*, 113-126.

Takeuchi, D. T., Sue, S., & Yeh, M. (1995). Return rates and outcomes from ethnicity-specific mental health programs in Los Angeles. *American Journal of Public Health, 85*, 638-643.

Watt-Jones, D. (1997). Toward an African American genogram. *Family Process, 36*, 375-383.

Toward Triadic Communication:
A Crisis in Japanese Family Relationships

Etsuko Sato Vosburg

SUMMARY. Like any industrialized nation, Japanese socioeconomic change has influenced the people's way of life. Since 1960, the number of psychosocially disturbed youngsters has steadily increased. Their symptoms vary according to their ages and circumstances, but the common denominator is "social withdrawal." They withdraw from self, family, friends, and from becoming self-supporting. Parents feel disappointed and angry, but mostly guilty. Not knowing how to deal with these youngsters, the parents keep on overprotecting or underprotecting them. Consequently, meaningful communication in the family disappears. To help the parents, especially the mother, we run the family support group at Tokyo Youth Center. This paper is a report on our efforts to help the families. *[Article copies available for a fee from The Haworth Document Delivery Service: 1-800-HAWORTH. E-mail address: <docdelivery@haworthpress. com> Website: <http://www.HaworthPress.com> © 2004 by The Haworth Press, Inc. All rights reserved.]*

Etsuko Sato Vosburg is Professor Emeritus, St. Paul's (Rikkyo) University, Tokyo, Japan.

Address correspondence to: Etsuko Sato Vosburg, 1-13-16-201, Narimasu, Itabashi-Ku, Tokyo, Japan 175-0094.

The author expresses deep appreciation to Carolyn Vosburg Hall for editorial and proofreading assistance.

[Haworth co-indexing entry note]: "Toward Triadic Communication: A Crisis in Japanese Family Relationships." Vosburg, Etsuko Sato. Co-published simultaneously in *Journal of Family Psychotherapy* (The Haworth Press, Inc.) Vol. 15, No. 1/2, 2004, pp. 105-117; and: *Family Therapy Around the World: A Festschrift for Florence W. Kaslow* (ed: William C. Nichols) The Haworth Press, Inc., 2004, pp. 105-117. Single or multiple copies of this article are available for a fee from The Haworth Document Delivery Service [1-800-HAWORTH, 9:00 a.m. - 5:00 p.m. (EST). E-mail address: docdelivery@haworthpress.com].

KEYWORDS. Symbolic interaction, utterances/meanings, triadic communication, group therapy and Japanese culture

FOREWORD

I have known Florence Kaslow for more than 13 years. I met her for the first time at the International Congress of Psychology in Kyoto, Japan, in 1990. What an exuberant and intelligent person she was. She also was cute. (Sorry, Florence, but you still are!)

That was a memorable year for Japanese family psychologists because the International Academy of Family Psychology was formed and its first congress was held. Florence was one of the keynote speakers, and I translated her speech into Japanese. It was a wonderful experience to get to know her.

After that year, Florence visited Japan a few more times to give talks and workshops on divorce therapy, family development, and supervision. She made quite an impact on Japanese family psychology researchers and clinicians with her logical but passionate presentations.

After that, my late husband Bob and I met Florence and her husband Sol in Padova, Italy, and Athens, Georgia, and developed a warm bond. Since we lived in Sarasota, Florida, we drove over to West Palm Beach twice to see them at home. I still remember a happy Florence surrounded by her family. In March 2003, Florence and Sol visited Sarasota to cheer me up while I was mourning my husband's death.

I deeply appreciate your love and care, Florence.

INTRODUCTION: THE FAMILY AND TRIADIC COMMUNICATION

According to Mead (1938), our feelings and thoughts become clear and reachable to oneself and others only when they are expressed verbally. As we all know, he calls this process "Symbolic Interaction" (Mead, 1938). We commonly think that our feelings and thoughts preexist in our minds but Mead's message is contrary. He emphasizes that the meaning of utterance cannot be established unless it is confirmed by both the speaker and the listener at a given moment. He gives a vital role to the reaction of the listener. If I push Mead's intention one step further, I may say the listener's feedback determines the meaning of utterance.

In a conversation between two people, the direction of utterance is restricted by the nature of the relationship. Since each is busy asserting or defending his or her point of view, it is difficult to objectify the self in the relationship and relationship itself. We need the third eye which is the view from outside.

Okamoto (Okamoto, 1982) once observed the mother-infant relationship and reported "a triadic relationship as an early form of dialogue." The summary of his observations is as follows:

a. A mother and infant (several months old) gaze at each other.
b. The mother shifts her eyes to the toy hanging from the ceiling.
c. The infant follows the mother's line of sight (sharing the line of sight).
d. The infant moves its eyesight toward the toy the mother is watching (sharing the object).
e. After infants develop language ability, they exchange words about the toy (sharing the meaning of object). (Mother) Isn't that pretty? (Infant) Pitty, pitty. (Mother) Moving round and round. (Infant) Aound, aound.

Okamoto thus concluded that the structure of dialogue is triadic, and the triadic relationship proceeds from the first stage of sharing the line of sight, to the second stage of sharing the object, and finally to the third stage of sharing the meaning of the object.

The following is another example of family interaction, which is completed by triadic communication:

There is a boy who is expressing his vexation by crying. When his mother sees him crying she responds, "Crying is not for boys." By her response, we know from the meaning or intent of the boy's crying that vexation is not accepted by her. He, therefore, will continue to cry. Mother, on the other hand, will be hurt because her intent–to avoid his sissyness and raise him to be a strong and sound male–is not being heard. Both of them feel frustrated and unhappy. Whose fault? Nobody's.

What will happen if a third party (i.e., father) intervenes between mother and boy here by pointing out their respective sense of frustration and helping them verbalize their feelings? If the mother and boy do that, they definitely will feel better and may understand each other better.

Their exchange of words and body language becomes true communication. As a result, each family member (mother, father, boy) raises his or her own self-esteem and increases in intimacy as a team. Since we believe that triadic communication can contribute to the betterment of family relations, we organized and have run family support groups for the last 15 years at the Tokyo Youth Center. Before I go into reporting one of these group's experiences, let me briefly sketch the way social-economic conditions in Japan affected the Japanese family.

JAPANESE SOCIO-ECONOMICS AND FAMILY RELATIONS
(SATO, 1993)

The 1960s

Until 1955, the number of average family members had stayed at five (two parents and three children), more or less. Between 1955 and 1965, however, it reduced to 4.5. An 0.5% decrease in only 10 years is a serious matter. The combination of increase in aging population and decrease in the number of offspring resulted in the change in population structure. A so-called "Old Age Society" emerged. In terms of economic activity, the country went into "the higher growth period" which brought us the days of "conspicuous consumption" for the first time in the history of Japan. Three Cs—color television, air conditioning, and cars—were mass-produced and started to penetrate the average household. Though the Japanese family enjoyed this affluence, it had to pay the price.

A consuming society encourages an endless desire for material fulfillment among its people. For example, many housewives who used to be content with domestic activity began taking part-time semiskilled jobs to supplement the family budget. We might say the Japanese family forced itself to be included in the market economy as a unit of consumption. As a result, the division of labor in the family necessary to maintain an active interaction among its members had decreased. The children were deprived of an opportunity to learn how to connect selves to others, that is, socialization. Without an affirmation of self through cooperative, triadic communication, which derives from the division of labor, the family bond is bound to be weak. Primary interest of each family member, especially that of children, shifts to the relationships they form outside the home.

The 1970s

During the 1970s, isolation from each other in the family worsened as a result of "Oil Shock" in 1973. Since business enterprise was forced to tighten its management, the fathers were pressured to devote more time and energy with less money to do business as "Company Soldiers." Home for the fathers became the place to rest and sleep for the next day's struggle. Even though the fathers were with their wives and children physically, they were absent-minded or too tired to engage or involve themselves with the wives and children. The fathers' participation in family chores and child rearing suffered tremendously. Working mothers were an unhappy bunch. In addition to their part-time job, they had to take responsibility for child-rearing and household chores unaided. Naturally their fatigue and anger toward the husband increased.

The situation was especially difficult for the young mothers. They developed a gloomy outlook for the future. Many young couples came to the big city (i.e., Tokyo, Osaka, Nagoya) seeking economic opportunity but their living conditions were not good. Most of them rented a small apartment where young mothers raised their babies without help from the husbands, in-laws, or other relatives. A lack of proper information and interpersonal support, plus the flood of information through mass media, all contributed toward the panic, loneliness, and confusion of young mothers. Some became neurotic and/or suicidal. An overall picture of the Japanese family, however, presented a false sense of stability during this period.

The 1980s

During this decade, conflict within the family surfaced. The main problem was the breaking up of the employment-for-life and the seniority system in the business world. Many companies faced the dilemma of an aging society where an extension of retirement age resulted in the shortage of posts and money on the one hand, and on the other, an average life expectancy that was too long to retire at 55. They tried to deal with this dilemma by adjusting a payment structure and creating new temporary positions. Let's look at how these social-economic trends affected family life.

The security of the middle-aged fathers' positions in the company was threatened by a series of rationalizations of management policy such as demotion, early retirement, and relocation. Their health problems (psychosomatic complaints such as headache, diarrhea, phobia) increased to the extent that they became a "social problem." Compared to the fathers, the mothers became more energetic. Since the introduction of the Equal Opportunity Law in 1981, the employment opportunities greatly improved, which in turn contributed to the breakdown of sexual roles in domestic and business scenes. Mothers gained power.

How about children? They were the unfortunate group affected most by this social change. Within the family they had to live in the cocoon of the mother-child relationship without the physical and emotional presence and support of the fathers. They were also exposed to marital tension. In school, they had to endure competition among friends and classmates. As a result the youngsters suffered from emotional and behavioral disturbances, which were manifested by school refusal, social withdrawal, school violence (toward teachers), bullying (from classmates), and family violence (toward mothers and sometimes fathers).

1990 to the Present

Work situations had worsened steadily due to a low economic growth rate during this decade. Employment-for-life and the seniority system kept changing. Work ethics, which had supported these systems, also changed from work-centered to leisure and family-oriented. Since most companies could not pay for overtime work any longer, the fathers were forced to come home earlier than formerly with less money. Even so, the fathers hoped to have quality time with wives and children. The home, however, had become a different place than they anticipated. Wives had given up on husbands as partners a long time ago and had developed their own world (i.e., wives stopped sharing the bedroom). The children who were lucky enough to avoid becoming "Identified Patients" were eager to make connections with friends outside of home. They now spent long hours in their own rooms communicating with friends using new media such as PCs (personal computers), e-mail, cell phones, dial services, and so on.

Today, the family members in Japan are not talking to each other meaningfully in a triadic manner. Even when they talk, it is usually a task-oriented matter. The quality of relationships, as a result, is not that of self-esteem and intimacy enhancing.

REPORT ON A FAMILY SUPPORT GROUP (SATO, 1999)

I have been involved in helping families with psychosocially disturbed offspring, as I mentioned earlier. Their symptoms vary according to their ages and circumstances, but the common denominator is "social withdrawal." They withdraw from self, family, friends, getting jobs, becoming self-supporting, falling in love, being married, and having babies. Parents feel disappointed, angry, and mostly fatigued. They, however, cannot stop calling their child a "school refusal kid" as one could 20 years ago. After getting professional help, some parents withdraw from their children altogether. This all or nothing attitude leaves the kids in the lurch and creates an increase of tension in the family.

Our job is to let the parents accept the offspring's unusual but unique lifestyle, yet not to give up involvement with them, and to start to live for themselves. To help the parents, especially the mother, to reach the goal, we run the family support group. Because we believe that only when the mothers regain self-esteem and intimacy with their spouse can they find a new way to communicate with their children who are in pain.

Standard of Analysis (Sato, 1986-1991)

	Level of communication	Quality of communication
1st stage	content-oriented	instrumental communication
	(need for digital information)	(monologue)
2nd stage	relations-oriented	expressive communication
	(demand emotional affirmation)	(dyadic exchange)
3rd stage	content-relation-oriented	empathetic communication
	(integration of both levels)	(triadic connection)

Hypothesis

Through the group process, level of communication shifts from the content-oriented to the relation-oriented, to content-relation-oriented. As a result, the quality of communication changes from instrumental to expressive to empathetic.

The Goal of the Group

Participants are to increase their self-esteem as an individual and increase intimacy with their family members (especially with the Identified Patient and the spouse).

Participants

Eight members (seven mothers and one father)

1 therapist

1 co-therapist

Profile of participants

Family role	Age	Occupation	IP (age and sex)
Mother	40	part-time clerk	male, 30
Father	60	retired CEO	male, 40
Mother	50	part-time teacher	male, 26
Mother	50	housewife	male, 31
Mother	40	school nurse	female, 24
Mother	50	radio announcer	female, 28
Mother	40	housewife	female, 23
Mother	40	housewife	male, 27

Logistics

Once a month, two hours per session

12 sessions total

Summary of the 12 Sessions

See Table 1.

Analysis of the Group Process

The First Stage (April to July)

During this phase, content-oriented utterances on actions (i.e., so and so did so and so) were observed. Though this kind of utterance repeated, there were few responses from the others, especially in a way they want to hear. Each person uses the words according to his or her own habitual usage and expects to be understood and responded to immediately. This is because of the premise that the self and others are the same. In reality, the speakers and listeners don't share the situation or experiences. Moreover, the listeners have a tendency to hear the content of utterances and respond accordingly, therefore, they cannot respond to the speaker's plea: "Please love me who is trying very hard." The speaker might experience the catalytic pleasure of spilling out distresses, but these feelings do not last long. A catalytic pleasure only gives a temporary outlet but leaves the speaker with the emptiness that comes with a premature and unrewarded self-exposure.

What is happening here is the separation of self and words. The words do not connect people but rather alienate them from each other. In this phase, the group members use the words as tools to appeal and by so doing, they turn themselves into the instrument of utterance. Since the instrumental communications leave the group members up in the air with unfinished feelings, they soon loose confidence in utterance. As the group moved on, the most talkative members became silent.

The Second Stage (September to November)

In this phase, the group members became aware of themselves in relation to their family members and spoke about their feelings such as, "I feel anxious" or "I am afraid of my son."

An expression of their straight feelings, however, did not get affirmation from the listeners. After several attempts, the speakers came to feel that they were not understood by anybody. Since the need for emotional connection and

TABLE 1. Summary

	Group member utterances	Pre-position of self and others	Level of communication	Quality of communication	Therapist's utterances
1st stage, April to July	Is it okay to just watch him time like this? Is it okay to do so and so? My son cannot live without me. My husband does not help me at all. You have to graduate from high school at least. It's like being in Hell every day. I wonder if it's too late?	You and me are the same (no realization of the differences between self and others).	Content level (exchange of factual information)	Instrumental communication (monologue)	What bothers you most *right now?* What do you feel about it? Did your daughter actually say so? You did say it to your son directly? I didn't get what you just said. What do you think about that?
2nd stage, September to November	Just listening to you makes me tired. I feel anxious. I am fearful of schizophrenia. I am afraid of my son. I am fearful of my son's violence. My heart pounds when I hear the phone ring. I told my husband how I felt. Our relations are worse than ever.	Nobody understood me. I am the hardest hit (absence of others).	Relation level (demanding emotional confirmation)	Expressive communication (didactic)	In your case . . . . Your son is not capable, but does not want to. It is your feelings but not your daughter's. What's happening between you and John's . . . . Why don't you try . . . . I think that's fine.
3rd stage, December to March	What you said makes me feel good. I realize I judged my son by my own yardstick. You try hard but your husband too. You have changed a lot and I respect you. I understand what you say. I'd like to be a mother with a big heart. I came to realize that the good times and bad times circulate. your comment makes me feel good.	I am I. You are you, but we can share a moment (the difference exists, but we can reach).	Content-relation coincided	Empathetic communication (triadic)	Please help her, anybody? You seem nodding . . . . What do you think she just said? What you just said is very important. It's wonderful! I completely agree with you.

affirmation remains so strong, they resort to expressing themselves in body language (i.e., to cry) and acting out (i.e., be late for the meeting time).

Why could the speaker's feelings not get affirmation from the listeners? That is because the feelings expressed were separated from "here and now" experiences that were shared by others in the group at that moment. The best thing the listeners could do when they heard the speaker's moving experiences at "there and then" was to project their own "there and then" experiences onto the speaker. There was no immediacy of sharing, therefore, they were a long way from empathy.

It is interesting that the pattern of communication and interpersonal attitude in the "there and then" repeats itself in the "here and now." When the individual laments constantly that she has not been understood by her husband, for example, her communication of lamentation alienates other group members. Her pain does not reach the others because her tone of voice sounds oppressive and accusatory. Only after she gets feedback from the therapist and the other members and learns to utter and change the way she expresses her pain can she communicate her pain to the group and thus to her husband.

The therapist, at this stage, spent most of her time (1) clarifying the source of feelings (i.e., "That's not your daughter's feelings but yours"), (2) calling attention to the content (situation and/or action) from which the feelings arose (i.e., "What were you doing when you felt angry?"), and (3) giving direct advice (i.e., "Why don't you try . . ."). Her aim is to help the group members clarify the meaning of utterance and calm the escalation of feelings due to overexposure.

The Third Stage (December to March)

During this stage, the group members became interested in each other. This interest moved from what the individual utters to his or her existence, so to speak. As a result of triadic interaction, the group members collectively established the meaning of utterances, which led to the affirmation of self and others in a given moment (i.e., "I came to realize what you are trying to say," "What you said made me feel good").

When the group members stick with the "here" and "now," they can exchange empathetic responses (i.e., "I feel your pain now," "Your comment makes me feel good"). Upon realizing the situational and personal differences between the self, the other group members and the family members, they now say, "I realize I judge my son by my yardstick."

By the end of the third stage, the group members' utterances moved beyond instrumental and became communal activity itself. Since the verbalized language (content level) and the body language (relation level) came together, the contents and feelings of the speaker reached the listener simultaneously, as intended. Empathetic (triadic communication) communication thus was achieved.

To make clear the meaning of change of the level and quality of communication through the group process, specifically, an effect on the family members, I present the case of Akiko next.

AKIKO'S EXPERIENCES: A CASE REPORT (SATO, 1999)

A Profile

Akiko is a 45-year-old school nurse who lives with her husband (48 years old) and a daughter, Tomiko (24 years old). Tomiko has been "socially withdrawn," mostly staying in her room all day, fighting Akiko, and throwing things whenever things do not go the way she wants. Akiko is moderately built with a fair complexion.

Since her daughter stopped attending high school, Akiko has felt guilty for her career-centered life. So as Tomiko's withdrawal escalated into family violence, she quit her job as school nurse. But deep down, Akiko resented Tomiko for that. These ambivalent feelings toward her daughter drained her energy mentally and physically, and led her into a state of chronic depression.

Akiko in the Group

The First Stage (April to July)

The characteristics of Akiko's utterances are a disjunction between the verbal language and body language. Whatever the topic, including fights with her daughter, she maintained a faint smile when she uttered. Since she has a fair complexion and classical features, she looked like a Japanese "Noh" mask. She covered her mouth with her hands frequently. During this phases, her utterances centered on complaints toward her husband's behavior, "He is psycho." "He is not cooperative." "He criticizes me all the time." At times she complained about the daughter also: "Tomiko throws her food at me." "She abuses me." "She prevents me from leaving the house." Though she could complain a lot, she could not express her feelings toward these ferocious behaviors. Besides, utterances were not made spontaneously but as a result of encouragement from the therapist. She remained tense through most sessions without any eye contact with other members.

The Second Stage (September to November)

At the beginning of this stage, in fact at the first session, Akiko announced to the group that she had gone back to her job as school nurse. When she told her daughter about her intention of returning to her job, the daughter first threw things. Akiko, however, did not take back her words and kept saying that this was important to do so for the sake of her sanity and well-being. The daughter stopped talking to Akiko for the next few days but later told her it was all right for her mother to go back to her job. Everybody in the group was happily surprised and congratulated Akiko. Though she did not respond to the group's congratulations, she started to talk more about her daughter. The more she talked about her daughter, the more it became apparent that she had been treating her 24-year-old daughter as if she were a three-year-old. Faced with the members' criticism, she just repeated "Yes, but . . ." The therapist defended Akiko's defense.

At the October meeting, Akiko reported spontaneously that she felt more tolerant toward her daughter and that her relationship with her daughter felt more intimate. Responding to the other members' comments, she showed a different range of emotions. Akiko, however, did not give in to the pressure from the group to stop overprotecting her daughter by saying, "It had to be done."

During November in a session Akiko reported that her relationship with her daughter had suffered a setback. When Tomiko began to show irritability again, Akiko felt a surge of anger. (She later admitted to the group that her anger was the result of disappointment.) Akiko could not control her anger and lost her temper. Mother and daughter had several big fights. The difference this time was the fact that her husband came to her rescue. Akiko said, "I could save my face." Being asked by the therapist how it felt "saving face," she said it felt good. Akiko also felt warm toward her husband at that moment. The group members made her promise to let her husband know how she felt the next time when she experienced warmth toward him. The group was very supportive through the whole session. At the end of the session, Akiko thanked everybody and added that she felt really disappointed with herself for not having been able to keep her cool. Her sense of disappointment was accepted by the therapist.

The Third Stage (December to March)

At first, Akiko's utterances were mostly about her husband: "I hate him." "I cannot stand him." "I dislike him." Since her remarks were general and all feelings expressed were sweeping in nature, the therapist helped her to specify when and what situation in which she felt angry. Feelings are about something all the time. At one point, she suddenly started to cry and became silent. Akiko did not come to the next meeting.

At the beginning of the February meeting, she thanked the group for helping her and told them the reason she was absent from the January meeting was due to her sense of shame for having cried in front of everybody. Akiko looked very happy when she said that her daughter had found a part-time job two days a week. When one of the group members commented, "Things were hard for you but it's the same with your husband." Akiko nodded deeply and muttered, "I've never thought of my husband's feelings."

At the final session, in response to the therapist's request to make a reflection on the year's work, Akiko said that she is able to speak out about how she feels right at the moment without holding grudges. She also became able to empathize with her daughter and husband.

CONCLUSION

There is no question that today's families who try to survive in an aging, low-growth and overstimulated society have to live in protective shells. However, the shields which protect the family from outside pressures eat up intimacy between family members. To liberate the individual from mutual isolation, we need a meaningful interaction–a triadic communication–within the family.

I hope I was able to show you that the group process encourages the group members to move from instrumental communication to triadic communication. This change also helps the individual members of the group to learn the mode of communication which will enhance his or her self-esteem and develop an intimacy with others. However, the resources, which nourish the individual, have to be found beyond the home. We need to enlarge the concept of family beyond a blood connection. In today's complex society, only when individual family members bring back energy from outside into the nuclear family does the family become a secure base and a source of strength to its members.

REFERENCES

Mead, G. H. (1938). *The philosophy of the act.* (C. W. Morris, in collaboration with J. M. Brewster, A. M. Dunham, and D. L. Miller, eds.). Chicago: University of Chicago Press.

Okamoto, N. (1980). *Children and language.* Japan: Iwanami Publishing, Ltd.

Sato, E. (1993). Recovery of family community. *Journal of Japanese Social Psychology 9(3).*

Sato, E. (1999). *Change of communication in the family support group in couples therapy.* Japan: Kongo Publishing, Ltd.

Sato, E. (1999). Youth and family. In *Modern Esprit No. 388.* Japan: Shibundo Publishing, Ltd.

Working with Abusing Families:
General Issues and a Systemic Perspective

Arnon Bentovim

SUMMARY. Growing up in a context of violence has pervasive effects on children and young people's development, causing significant deleterious effects to the capacities to attach, to manage and regulate emotional lives, and to develop a sense of self and capacity to relate. The intergenerational effects of abuse have been shown to be extensive. The question is how best to intervene with abusive families. A model is presented which distinguishes between "family work," an integrated systems approach which links protective and therapeutic work for individuals, groups, and families, where the courts and community are the client, and "family therapy" where the family itself is the client. The assessment of prognosis for work is outlined as well as the stages of therapeutic work including the stage of disclosure, work in a context of protection, rehabilitation, and a new family placement when rehabilitation cannot be achieved. *[Article copies available for a fee from The Haworth Document Delivery Service: 1-800-HAWORTH. E-mail address: <docdelivery@haworthpress.com> Website: <http://www.HaworthPress.com> © 2004 by The Haworth Press, Inc. All rights reserved.]*

Arnon Bentovim is Director, London Child and Family Consultation Service. He is an Honorary Consultant Psychiatrist, Great Ormond Street Children's Hospital and the Tavistock Clinic London, and University College London. He is President, International Family Therapy Association, 2003-2005.

Address correspondence to: Arnon Bentovim, 97 Harley Street, London W1G 6AG, UK (E-mail: bentovim@lcfcs.co.uk).

[Haworth co-indexing entry note]: "Working with Abusing Families: General Issues and a Systemic Perspective." Bentovim, Arnon. Co-published simultaneously in *Journal of Family Psychotherapy* (The Haworth Press, Inc.) Vol. 15, No. 1/2, 2004, pp. 119-135; and: *Family Therapy Around the World: A Festschrift for Florence W. Kaslow* (ed: William C. Nichols) The Haworth Press, Inc., 2004, pp. 119-135. Single or multiple copies of this article are available for a fee from The Haworth Document Delivery Service [1-800-HAWORTH, 9:00 a.m. - 5:00 p.m. (EST). E-mail address: docdelivery@haworthpress.com].

Digital Object Identifier: 10.1300/J085v15n01_09

KEYWORDS. Violence, child abuse, family work, family therapy

Growing up in a climate of violence has a pervasive effect on a child's development extending to adult life, and to parenting and partnering. It is essential that we develop a broad-based approach if we hope to ameliorate the effects. The recent world report from the World Health Organisation on violence and health concludes that "understanding the context of violence is vital in designing interventions" (World Health Organization, 2002). A systemic approach takes into account all aspects of the child's context in finding successful ways of working. The impetus to preparing this chapter came from a seminar conducted with Florence Kaslow at the International World Family Therapy Congress in Dusseldorf in 2000. The theme was 'Family Violence–Therapeutic Approaches.' I spoke about family violence involving children, whilst she addressed the complimentary theme of violence against partners: complimentary themes, interlocking principles. I have continued to develop my thinking, and this paper represents developments facilitated through working with Florence Kaslow, celebrating the role of a colleague who has contributed a great deal to our multifaceted field.

The initial recognition of child abuse as an entity followed the publication of Henry Kempe's seminal paper on the battered child in 1962 (Kempe, Silverman, & Steele, 1962). This formulation had the effect of defining the situation, and helping people conceptualise and understand and bring together many disparate observations to the entity which we now recognise as child abuse in all its forms. This process of social construction has gradually helped professionals find a way of conceptualising the process to understand the true extent of abusive actions perpetrated against children in its many different forms and in many different contexts.

This paper explores a development of the thinking on working with abusive families. Family work with abusive families has started to differentiate between families with physical abuse and neglect, and families where sexual abuse has occurred (Kolko, 1996; Crittenden, 1988; Stratton, 1991; Hanks, 1993). Given the fact that a much clearer concept of family work has developed in the field of sexual abuse, this paper will deal essentially with family work where physical abuse and neglect occur. Work with families where children have been emotionally abused is less developed, and the focus is largely still on defining the core concepts involved (Crittenden & Ainsworth, 1989; Erickson, Egeland, & Pianta, 1989; Glaser, 1993; Hobbs, Hanks, & Wynne, 1993). Specifically, this paper explores the role of family work and family therapy with families where child abuse has taken place and addresses a number of conceptual, planning and practice issues relevant to working with families where physical or emotional abuse or neglect has taken place.

In considering family work with abusive families, there has been a major critique by feminist thinkers such as Bograd (1988) who pointed to the potential dangers in attempting to work conjointly with families where an abusive family member was organising family life and grooming children to become victims of their perverse interest and abusive action. Addressing such issues within a family context, it was feared, could result in secondary victimisation, retaliation, increased silencing and fear, all of which would be against the interests of children.

Restructuring the relationship between an abusive father and a terrified child seemed inappropriate when the approach used ordinarily relies on the fact that the family context is assumed to be providing adequate care for family members, but negative aspects of family character were hindering development for a particular child or the family as a whole. Thus, it became essential to focus on the traumatic reality caused by abuse and its impact on individual functioning and relationships. In introducing the theme of Trauma Organised Systems (Bentovim, 1995), it was pointed out that abusive events have traumatic effects on the lives of children, and repeated cumulative traumatic events cause increasingly severe effects on the emotional lives of those who are involved. Those who were traumatising the child were part of a system that allowed them to maintain abusive action in secrecy. Other adults in the children's world were also caught in the process and involved in a system of secrecy, denial, and blame. In the growing area of trauma therapy, Eth and Pynoos (1985), Figley (1990), and Herman (1992) stressed the need to work with the facts of abuse, the objective reality of traumatising events. Therapeutic work required the tracking of such details for each individual before there could be the possible integration for the family as a whole.

Different strands in the field of family therapy, with an emphasis on constructed reality and solution-focused therapy on the one hand, and on trauma and trauma work on the other, produce tensions and dilemmas in terms of practice for the clinician or practitioner working with abusing families. Experiences of authors over some years shows that an integrated approach which brings together both aspects of therapeutic work is crucial to effective work with abusing families. Therapists need to help families and individuals deal with the trauma they have experienced. Families also need to look at the relationship between the traumatic experiences they have had as individual family members and the solutions they have evolved as families, and at the impact of both on the way family members now relate.

Nevertheless, while the objective reality of the trauma of abuse is an essential focus for therapeutic work with abused children and other family members, it is also the case that the individuals concerned have had to make sense of their own experience, and they have constructed their own psychic sense of causality–the meaning they give to that traumatic experience. This "constructed reality" of individual family members or the family as a whole (e.g., that abuse is harmless, the child's action evoked an abusive response, silence is best) may hinder the growth and development or recovery of the family members, and therefore require therapeutic intervention.

New developments in family therapy have given rise to other significant tensions and dilemmas for practitioners working with abusing families. The psychologically and developmentally damaging effects of child abuse fuel the responsibility of social service and legal systems to evaluate the risk to the child and the actual harm resulting from child abuse and neglect and to act on that assessment in their work with abusing families. It informs the need for them either to bring about change in the relevant patterns of family relationships, or to provide alternative care outside the family for the abused or at-risk child. The relationship between therapeutic work and statutory contexts–a significant factor in dealing with physical abuse and neglect–has been clarified and developed in the work at the Hospital for Sick Children, Great Ormond Street, London, in Rochdale and elsewhere (Dale et al., 1986a, 1986b; Bentovim et al., 1988; Furniss, 1990), through the work of multisystemic approaches (Henggeler, 1999).

This linear relationship between the family and the statutory agencies responsible for child protection work is, however, sometimes seen as incompatible with the therapeutic relationship between therapist and family in family therapy. There is a greater emphasis on the need for the therapist to remain neutral and adhere to the concept of circular rather than linear causality, which some see as inevitably blurring the issue of individual responsibility. Thus, professionals have been concerned about using a family therapeutic intervention with abusing families because of these apparent tensions. Furniss introduced an integrated therapeutic and legal framework for working with abusing families (Furniss, 1990; Bentovim et al., 1988; Trepper & Barrett, 1989; Sheinberg, 1992; Sheinberg et al., 1994; Bentovim, 1995). In this paper an approach to working with abusing families is described which allows therapeutic work to progress within the legal framework of child protection without denying the reality of the abuse, splitting the professional network, or cutting across the work of the various professionals who form the child protection network or team around an abused child.

CONCEPTUAL AND PLANNING ISSUES

Family Therapy and Consultation

The increased understanding of the context and greater clarity of aims of family work with abusive families has led to a clear distinction between family therapy which occurs as a result of a free contract between the family and the therapist and conditional family work in the context of statutory decision making. Family work with abusing families does not constitute therapy in the traditional sense. Family members do not come to therapy of their own free will, and the basic contract is not between therapist and family, but between therapist and the statutory agency on the one hand, and between the statutory agency and the family on the other.

This means that the basic rules of confidentiality do not apply, and therapists therefore need to distinguish carefully between therapy where these rules can apply and therapeutic work with abusive families as part of consultation to statutory agencies. Family work in child-abusing families can therefore only take place with close and open cooperation between therapist and statutory worker. Family therapists should not accept abusing families for "therapy" independently of the professional child protection system, because this creates the danger of inducing damaging splits in the professional network between the therapist as the "good person" and the statutory worker as the "source of all bad things."

All therapeutic work which therapists undertake with abusing families needs to relate to the requirements of decision-making processes by statutory agencies regarding the future of the family concerned. In that sense, family work with abusive families is part of a consultation process to social services departments or courts, in which the social services department or the court is the client rather than the family. All therapeutic work needs to take place in the context of consultation with these institutions.

The nature of the therapeutic family work as part of consultation to social services and courts needs to be made explicit to the family, either by having the social worker present during family sessions or by referring explicitly to the link between therapist and statutory agencies. In a family session, we might therefore say, "What would the social worker/the court say about the change you have achieved so far in these sessions? Do you think they would feel it is safe for your child to live with you again or not?" This not only reminds the family of the context of consultation, it also helps therapists to remind themselves that any family work with abusive families is part of consultation and not traditional family therapy.

A family approach and a family therapy approach to working with abusing families. A family approach uses a family systems theory framework to conceptualise the dysfunctional aspects of abuse at a family level and in the context of family relationships. Using a family systems perspective helps to keep the central family process and the child's need for carers in mind, while opening up the options for different, concurrent forms of therapy in addition to family sessions. It also provides a unifying rationale for a range of protection, care planning and therapeutic tasks which need to take place when attending to the welfare of the abused child and family.

Thus, a family approach to working with abusing families, in contrast to a family therapy approach, encompasses work on different levels using concurrent forms of therapy, including individual, group and family sessions as well as family-professional network sessions. For example, with physical abuse and neglect, and even perhaps emotional abuse, in some less serious abusive situations conjoint family sessions may be the appropriate sole form of therapy; with sexual abuse, concurrent forms of therapy are always required. Abusers always need individual and/or group work focussed on their abusive behaviour and cycles of abuse. Mothers, as non-abusing parents, need individual help with the crisis of emotional turmoil, loss and practical problems that come with disclosure (Hooper, 1992). The support of a group counteracts the isolation, disempowerment, and low self-esteem associated with living in a family system shaped by the abuser's enactment of child sexual abuse as a syndrome of secrecy and addiction (Hildebrand, 1988). Research on outcomes of treatment (Hyde et al., 1996; Monck et al., 1996) demonstrates the effectiveness of group intervention with women.

Issues of Motivation

Our skill needs to lie in knowing why abusing families are not motivated to be helped, and how we can motivate them to feel that they want help. The distinction between therapy and consultation in family work with child abuse underlines the fact that families are not primarily self-motivated to seek help as a result of emerging family problems. They are motivated to cooperate because of the danger of family break-up, and because of the openly stated preconditions for rehabilitation or for keeping their children at home.

The basically negative contextual framework of coercion in family work in cases of child abuse needs to be positively reframed by an explicit therapeutic contract which states openly the required aims and goals of family work. Some systemic approaches already make the development of the required aims and goals of treatment part of the treatment process itself. Questions are asked, such as "What do you think needs to change in your attitude and behaviour toward your child in order for social services/the court to be satisfied that it is safe for you to continue living with your child?" and "What do you think social services/the court needs to know from you for them to trust your word when you say you are able to understand and satisfy the needs of your child without abusing him or her?" A systemic approach to family work can help to link issues of statutory responsibility and control with therapeutic aspects of required family functioning. The process of defining the aims for family work can help to motivate family members towards a wish for therapeutic change if we create a context where families take part and are co-responsible for the development of explicit, understandable, operationalised and detailed goals for therapy.

Indicators for or Against Involving the Whole Family

Family work needs to be considered in all forms of treatment of child abuse where rehabilitation is being contemplated. Rehabilitation can only be considered when there is a reasonable prospect for change which emerges following an initial phase of assessment.

A hopeful prognosis requires that parents take adequate responsibility for abusive action where appropriate, there is a protective capacity within the family, e.g., a non-abusive parent who recognises that his or her partner has abused the child, and is prepared to protect the child over and above their relationship with their partner. There needs to be the possibility of a capacity for change in parents who have been abusive, with a willingness to work reasonably cooperatively with child care professionals, and to accept the need for change even if it is with the motivation of maintaining children within the family context rather than them being removed, or removed permanently. There needs to be the potential for the development of a reasonable attachment and relationship between the parents and children, and appropriate therapeutic settings need to be available, whether on an outpatient basis, a day-care setting, or residential resource depending on the severity of abuse, and the nature of family difficulties and strengths.

A hopeless prognosis for family work exists when none of these criteria are fulfilled: where there is rejection of the child, a failure to take responsibility, the needs of parents take primacy over the needs of the children, a combative oppositional stance to professionals emerges, or psychopathology in parents, e.g., drug abuse, serious marital violence, or longstanding personality problems which may not be amenable to therapeutic work, or where there is complete inability or unwillingness to accept that there are problems. In such situations family work has no place since the child will be persuaded to withdraw his or her statements or to become part of a process of maintenance of secrecy and denial.

Doubtful prognosis situations prevail where professionals are not yet clear from the original work with the family whether the situation is hopeful or hopeless. There is uncertainty whether there is adequate taking of responsibility, whether parental pathology is changeable, whether there is going to be willingness to work with care authorities and therapeutic agencies, or whether resources will be available to meet the extensiveness of the problem.

As a result of such an assessment in the initial stage of work when disclosure of abuse has occurred, it becomes possible to be clear about which family member will be able to participate in family work, and at which stage. A good deal also depends on the assessment of the child. Children who are severely traumatised by abuse may be retraumatised through contact with an abusive parent, even when that parent is taking responsibility for his or her abusive action. In such situations it is often essential for the majority of work to be carried out either with the child individually, in groups, or with a protective parent, before any question of contact with the abusive parent is considered. Family work needs to be at its most intensive when rehabilitation is considered following parental involvement in individual and group work either as a protective parent or as an abuser dealing with abusive and violent action. Work involving the whole family then becomes far more of a possibility.

PRACTICE ISSUES

It is helpful to think of therapeutic work occurring in stages with different forms of family work being required at each phase.

The Phase of Disclosure

Work in this phase needs to focus on the following main issues:

1. The extensiveness of abuse which has been perpetrated against the child or children must be clarified, and details established concerning the nature of abuse, its length, severity, context, and who is responsible. Very often the initial presentation of abuse is a tip of an iceberg, and it is essential to ensure that sufficient time is given in a context of safety to ascertain how extensive the abuse has been; otherwise, the nature of therapeutic work of the individual and the family will be underestimated.
2. There needs to be an assessment of the effect of abuse on the child or children, and the impact on the children's capacity to attach themselves and on their relationships. The traumatic impact of abuse, post-traumatic disorder and the effect on the sense of self and self-esteem as a result of traumagenic and dynamic effects needs to be considered. Again, without such an assessment it is not possible to embark on the family aspect of the work as it would be very easy to underestimate the impact of abuse and the extensiveness of therapeutic work required.
3. The degree of responsibility taken by the perpetrator of abuse needs to be assessed, and the fit between the perpetrator's explanation and the victim's account. Does this make sense, is it possible to draw together the strands of what has happened to be able to plan a rational approach to work?
4. What is the attitude of the non-abusing caretaker, the degree of sympathy and belief in the victim's statement, the attitude towards the perpetrator, whether that perpetrator is a partner or a young person within the family context who has abused a younger child? Is it possible for the

parent to hold their own need for a partner separately from the needs of the child?

5. What is the relevant family history of parents as individuals, do they have a history of abuse themselves, what is their relationship history, the nature of present and past marital and parenting relationships with siblings and general functioning?

6. Is it possible to assess the level of family health (Bentovim & Kinston, 1991) by looking at family competence, the capacity to provide adequate care for children, the nature of discipline, the management of conflict and decision making? These basic functions are underpinned by characterological factors such as identity, sense of family togetherness, the quality of communication, listening, hearing, and the alliances between family members both within the same generation and across generational boundaries. Assessments can be made both qualitatively and quantitatively, and a profile of family strengths and difficulties can be constructed (Bentovim & Bingley-Miller, 2000). A variety of approaches are used to stimulate family interaction (e.g., tasks and interviews) to help professionals make judgements which then help to act as a focus for therapeutic work.

7. It may well be that such family information can only be gathered through meetings with subsystems of the family. In the absence of full knowledge and understanding of the extensiveness of abuse, responsibilities and protective capacities, it may not be appropriate to involve the abused child in family meetings at this stage. Motivation for help both by the child who has been victimised and family members needs to be assessed at this stage, and a balance between protection and therapeutic work achieved.

The Phase of Treatment in a Context of Safety

During this phase there needs to be work where the victim is separated from the abusive context, whether living with a protective parent/family member, the perpetrator living separately, or the child living in alternative care. A good deal of the work during this phase is inevitably focussed on the individual. Abuse-focussed therapeutic work for victims whether individually or within group contexts is required to repair attachments, manage emotional dysregulation, and develop a healing sense of self.

Disruptions of a child's attachment can be repaired through individual and group work. Individual therapists need to create a working alliance with the child or young person, to be consistent and reliably available, and to create a sense of safety. Group work fosters cohesion, belonging and identity, and provides a sense of safety in the group to reverse the fears inherent in family life and share support substituting pleasure for pain. Family work can foster the development of secure attachments both in the phase of separateness or as the situation moves to the next phase of rehabilitation. Connections may be made through a caring parent, sharing and comparing their own experiences in their family with the child's experience. It is important that family therapy techniques such as reframing negative behaviour and positive connotation (giving apparently negative behaviour a positive meaning) connect children with family scripts and the experiences that parents have had growing up themselves. The process of "externalising" distances abusive experiences from self and relationships, and strengthens and promotes bonds within the family with a protective parent. Later the sharing of experiences with the abusing parent which have been learnt from their own therapeutic work can help the child or young person feel part of the family context, rather than being blamed, excluded and scapegoated.

Therapeutic work with emotional dysregulation is aimed at reducing anxiety, developing a capacity to cope with emotional problems, and becoming able to effectively process experiences of abuse by sharing and exposing them either with an individual therapist or the group context and eventually with family members. A variety of approaches are helpful to monitor arousal and foster containment. To be involved in such work, a protective parent needs to be able to be open to the experiences of the child, to be able to listen and share, and contain what may have been an extreme sense of terror, fear, and powerlessness at the hands of the abusive parent. There needs to be the development of safe family care rituals to cope with sleeping difficulties, ways of coping with excitement, anger, sexualised behaviour, and a modulation of the process to avoid retraumatisation.

For the child to develop a more satisfactory sense of themselves, he or she has to be helped to realise that what is defined as problematic (e.g., switching off angry oppositional behaviour, fear, and avoidance) is part of a survival strategy and a strength not a weakness. Family work needs to be absolutely clear about the origins of blame, to help the child understand the way in which the abuser attributes abusive action to the victim rather than taking responsibility themselves. Where rehabilitation is a possibility, family work requires a carefully planned apology and taking of responsibility for abusive action. This must be more than the often brief acknowledgement which is possible in the earlier phases of work.

The Phase of Rehabilitation

Rehabilitation requires that parents themselves confront their abusive behaviour. When both parents have taken part in abusive action, they need to take on board the extensiveness of their abusive actions, to understand their origins and the process of abuse, and the damaging effect that this has had on the child.

The apology session is a valuable component of part of a rehabilitation process. Questions that the child has about what has happened to him or her can be put to the abusive parent. Responses can be worked out with the therapists, and a joint meeting established where responsibility can be taken and victims freed from their own sense of confusion and guilt and attribution of abuse to their own actions.

Often intensive couple therapy is going to be required because of the secrecy and often-associated violence between parents, before meetings involving the victim and siblings can be initiated. Permanent family structures are required where protection is uppermost. Asen, Cheetman, and Small (1989) indicate that in severe physical abuse, in 30% of cases, rehabilitation is not possible because of a failure to progress through such a process.

The New Family Phase

When a child cannot return home, intensive family work with a new family context is required, including planning long-term care and preparation of a family for a child who has experienced extensive abuse. There needs to be planning of a protective context within the foster family and careful consideration of the appropriate mode of contact with the original family. Work with the foster family or alternative adoptive family is essential to maintain an appropriate supportive stance and to incorporate the victim into a new family context.

Extensive grooming of the child and, indeed, of the family context occurs as part of the process of abuse so that the protective parent's capacity to care is undermined, the child feels blamed and responsible for abuse perpetrated against himself or herself, and is therefore silenced and adapts to the role attributed to them—a "corrupting process." Professionals who learn of inappropriate activities with a family are perceived as misinformed and prejudiced against the family rather than seeing abusive reality for what it is.

The first stage of work, disclosure, is therefore often a prolonged and extensive piece of work requiring collaboration between social work, police, and specialist interviewers with children and with adults. The complexity of legal contexts mean that difficult decisions have to be taken about child protection action, about criminal action, the likelihood of success of such processes, and the role of potential therapeutic work. The cost of taking responsibility often seems extremely high to the abuser. The state of the child–mental health indices, anxiety, depression, post-traumatic stress–are affected by the severity of abuse, and also whether the child perceives him or herself to be supported. To be an older female is often associated with being disbelieved by a mother who puts her need for her partner above the protection of the child, and parents come together in opposition to authorities who are perceived as putting ideas in their child's head. The young person is thus doubly rejected.

ASSESSMENT AND AIMS FOR TREATMENT

Aims for Treatment

The aims for treatment work where it is possible to involve the whole family or part of the family include the following: [Note: The following involves a suggested adaptation of sexual abuse research/treatment materials to general abuse.]

1. Assigning responsibility for the abuse. It is felt that, given the considerable variability in responsibility which was expressed by family members at the outset, children blaming themselves, mothers blaming the child, and parent abuser often denying the abuse, the following treatment aims needed to be achieved:

    a. Father/mother/children need to acknowledge that abuse was the responsibility of the perpetrator, not the child.
    b. Mother/father acknowledge their own responsibility for abuse or for lack of availability to the child to be protective when applicable.
    c. There is evidence of the child's resolution of conflicted feelings toward the perpetrator and parents, that is, instead of justifying the abuse through various distortions and rationalisations, the appropriate attribution of responsibility is taken.

2. Treatment focused on family relationships.

    a. Family members are able to express reasonable anger to each other in an appropriate non-destructive and non-scapegoating manner.
    b. Family members can develop relationships sufficiently open for painful issues to be confided and shared between child and parents, and between the parents themselves.
    c. Family allows all members space to speak and listen to each other without scapegoating.
    d. There is recognition of individual needs, appropriate to age.
    e. Recognition of appropriate qualities in all family members, including each member recognising positive aspects of themselves.
    f. Establishment and maintenance of appropriate generational boundaries.
    g. Provision of adequate protection from further abuse to children.

3. Treatment focussed on origins and effects of abuse.

a. Recognition of potential and actual damage which might be the result of abuse. Parents show a capacity to help child with actual behavioural effects of abuse. Recognition of damage caused to adults by abusive experiences in their own youth where relevant.
b. Recognition by adults of need for help on an individual and couple basis.
c. Ability of family and professionals to work together cooperatively.

Many of these treatment goals needed to be achieved in the first two stages through individual and group work whether with victims, protective parents, or abusers, either young people or parental figures. (See Bentovim et al., 1988; Monck et al., 1996, for details of individual/group work.)

We have noted three different family contexts where treatment is offered:

1. Those families where there is no change of membership because the abuser had left it forever prior to disclosure, and where the fact that the abuser had left the family had enabled the child to disclose abuse perpetrated against them.
2. Families which hoped to reintegrate the offender or the victim if she had been moved out.
3. Families which were new where there was no intention to reunite with the offender.

Specific areas of work included the following:

The Process of Clarification and Taking Appropriate Responsibility

The process of clarifying exactly what abuse has occurred, to whom, and how extensively and who is responsible needs to be a theme kept in mind throughout therapeutic work. The work with the abused child begins at the point of disclosure, needs to be extended both during the initial diagnostic phase and the phase of exposure in the individual/group therapeutic phase.

Perpetrators in treatment also need to acknowledge and share the extensiveness of their abusive action, using victim statements as a key to their work. Both victims and perpetrators need to share with protective parents, with victims acknowledging and attributing responsibility for abuse and failure to protect, and giving appropriate apologies. In work with perpetrators who do take adequate responsibility, acknowledging appropriate responsibility and apologising for harm caused to a victim can be a key moment in therapeutic work for the whole family whenever it occurs.

The structure of current child protective action usually means that police/social work professionals carry out initial investigation and assessments. The necessity for memorandum interviews and police statements means that early clarification/responsibility work is not feasible and needs to take place once such processes have occurred. Referral to therapeutic services is made at a later stage. By the time of such referral, there may be a high level of denial by alleged perpetrators that abuse had occurred, disbelief by mothers, and children in alternative care. The scope for family clarification, taking adequate responsibility, and apologising is more limited in such instances and needs to take place at a later stage of treatment, when possible.

Working on Denial, Minimisation, and Projection of Blame

One of the continuing processes of family work at all stages is the constant revisiting of the issue of who is responsible for abusive action, resisting the desire to blame the victim, and minimising the extent of abusive action and its impact. A most helpful therapeutic approach to dealing with denial, minimisation and projection of blame is to constantly ask the question, what would happen if there was no denial, if there was no minimisation, if the victim was not blamed. What would the consequence be for a mother who is a non-abusing parent if the abuser fully took responsibility for his/her action? Would there be any possibility of maintaining a relationship, or is there a necessary degree of denial for parents to maintain a relationship and function as parents? If the victim was not blamed, what would be the consequences? What would be the responses if a mother who is a non-abusing parent, instead of contending that she had no knowledge or information that abuse was going on, were to acknowledge that she had seen, that she was aware peripherally of abusive action? What would be the consequences, would there be depressive, suicidal behaviour? An approach which positively connotes denial as a means of self-protection and sees dissociation as a defence which is necessary before full acceptance makes it possible to work with denial, minimisation, and blame, even if this results in stress on the potential to relate, say, between a mother and her children, or between parents in the early stages of work.

A sequence of hypothetical questions may need to be used to clarify the function of denial when abusive action is denied by a perpetrator. For instance, a parent or an older sibling who is alleged to have abused within the family context, and who is denying this, may be asked what the consequences would be if they did recall that abuse had occurred. For instance, if they woke up one morning and became aware that the allegations made were true, that their own "protective" dissociation had lifted, and they discovered that they had indeed been responsible for abuse. They may be asked what their partners would say/think, what extended family members would say, what they themselves might do with such a realisation. Do they think they might be able to live with themselves, might there be a risk of suicide? Did they feel that this sort of behaviour was one which could be treated adequately? If responses are such that there may indeed be serious suicidal attempts, then again denial can be positively connoted. If there is a feeling that neither they nor any other family member believe that treatment is possible, then denial can be positively connoted because it means that if the court believes the child has been abused then he or she will be protected. If no treatment was possible then this would be the best outcome for the child. Perhaps at some level this is what the parents want professionals to do to protect their children from themselves.

Addressing Abuse of Power, Powerlessness, and Empowerment

Research on factors which trigger abusive behaviour and intense traumatic responses (e.g., flashbacks, visualisations) demonstrates the pervasive effects of the sense of powerlessness experienced by both perpetrators, victims, and other family members. Powerlessness may result in the use of oppressive and violent strategies to resolve differences between parents, and between children and parents. A belief in powerlessness leads to an abdication of responsibility on the part of family members or to constant power struggles to gain control. It is essential that work with individuals and in family contexts offers opportunities to develop appropriate non-coercive self-management, anger management, different ways of assertiveness, and a contract of non-violence. There is often a need to track intergenerational patterns of abuse, coercive strategies, power-oriented approaches through genograms and through helping parents see that they have survived themselves and that strategies of inappropriate power use are part of the same scenario they have been subject to and have adopted as a dysfunctional coping strategy.

Loss and Bereavement

In situations in which there is no proposal by the family to reunite with the offender and in which the family has become a single-parent family without wishing to do so, therapeutic attention needs to be paid to issues of loss and bereavement. It is important to try and involve all family members dealing with the loss and with the grief reactions since all children experience the change. Non-abused siblings sometimes feel the loss very differently from the victims, and there needs to be an acceptance of difference. Mothers need support often in these situations, and in some families there may need to be some active involvement of extended family members who might be supportive in a session. Mothers can be encouraged and helped to share openly, either with extended family or friends in order to gain some social support.

Meeting of Individual Needs

Helping parents understand the impact of abuse on their children–regressed behaviour, the aggression associated with powerlessness, the dissociation associated with traumatic phenomena such as flashbacks, reenactments, depressed affect, fears, and phobias–is an essential aspect of family work. Promoting communication, seeking solutions to problem behaviour, offering support, and constantly linking the care professionals with the therapeutic needs of the family is an essential therapeutic task.

There is no one set of techniques which are useful in every context. Techniques from structural family therapy may be used, getting parents and children to work through a problem to a solution. Apparently difficult behaviour may need to be connoted positively as examples of healing, frustrations understood as necessary processes towards change. Children need help to repair disrupted attachments, develop more satisfactory emotional dysregulation, and reverse their negative sense of self. Abusive parents need help to face the nature of their abusive action, to understand its origins, the factors which maintain it, and how to prevent relapse and recurrence. Protective parents need to understand how the addictive needs of a partner can distort and destroy family life. These are all important elements which need to be confronted to create a healthy family life for those who are willing to undertake the long journey to health.

REFERENCES

Asen, G. E., Piper, R., & Stevens, A. (1989). A systems approach to child abuse. *Child Abuse and Neglect, 13,* 45-58.

Bentovim, A. (1995). *Trauma organised systems: Physical and sexual abuse in families.* London and New York: Karnac.

Bentovim, A., & Bingley-Miller, L. (2000). *The assessment of family competence, strength and difficulties.* Brighton: Pavillion.

Bentovim, A., & Kinston, W. (1991). Focal family therapy: Joining systems theory and psychodynamic understanding. In A. S. Gurman, & D. P. Kniskerm (Eds.), *Handbook of family therapy* (pp. 284-324). New York: Brunner-Mazel.

Bentovim, A., Elton, A., Hildebrand, J., Tranter, M., & Vizard, E. (Eds.) (1988). *Child sexual abuse within the family.* London: Wright.

Bograd, M. (1988) *Power, gender and the family: Feminist perspectives on family systems therapy.* In M. A. Dutton-Douglas, & L. A. Walker (Eds.), *Feminist psychotherapies: Integration of therapeutic and feminist systems* (pp. 80-88). Norwood, NJ: Ablex.

Crittenden, P. (1988). Family and dyadic patterns of functioning in maltreating families. In K. Browne, C. Davies, & P. Stratton (Eds.), *Early prediction and prevention of child abuse* (pp. 110-116). Chichester: John Wiley and Sons.

Crittenden, P., & Ainsworth, M. (1989). Child maltreatment and attachment theory. In D. Cicchetti, & V. Carlson (Eds.), *Child maltreatment: Theory and research on the causes and consequences of child abuse and neglect* (pp. 126-140). Cambridge: Cambridge University Press.

Dale, P., Davies, M., Morrison, T., & Waters, J. (1986a). *Dangerous families: Assessment and treatment of child abuse.* London: Tavistock.

Dale, P., Waters, J., Davies, M., Roberts, W., & Morrison, T. (1986b). The towers of silence: Creative and destructive issues for therapeutic teams dealing with sexual abuse. *Journal of Family Therapy, 8,* 1-25.

Erikson, M., Egelend, B., & Pianta, R. (1989). The effects of maltreatment on development of young children. In D. Cicchetti, & V. Carlson (Eds.), *Child maltreatment: Theory and research on the causes and consequences of child abuse and neglect* (pp. 211-234). Cambridge: Cambridge University Press.

Eth, S., & Pynoos, R. S. (Eds.) (1985). *Post-traumatic stress disorder in children.* Washington, DC: American Psychiatric Association.

Figley, C. (Ed.) (1990). *Treating stress in families.* New York: Brunner/Mazel.

Furniss, T. (1990). *The multi-professional handbook of child sexual abuse: Integrated management, therapy and legal interventions.* London and New York: Routledge.

Glaser, D. (1993). Emotional abuse. In *Bailliere's clinical paediatrics,* Vol. 1(1), (pp. 251-265). London: Bailliere Tindall.

Hanks, H. (1993). Failure to thrive: A model for treatment. In C. Hobbs & J. Wynne (Eds.), *Bailliere's clinical paediatrics* (pp. 275-291). London: Bailliere Tindall.

Henggeler, S. W. (1999). Multisystemic therapy: An overview of clinic procedures, outcomes and policy implications. *Child Psychology Psychiatry Review, 4,* 2-10.

Herman, J. (1992). *Trauma and recovery: From domestic violence to political terror.* New York and London: HarperCollins.

Hildebrand, J. (1988). The use of group work in treating child sexual abuse. In A. Bentovim, A. Elton, J. Hildebrand, M. Tranter, & E. Vizard (Eds.), *Child sexual abuse within the family* (pp. 150-168). London: Wright.

Hobbs, C., Hanks, H., & Wynne, J. (1993). *Child abuse and neglect: A clinician's handbook.* London: Churchill Livingstone.

Hooper, C. A. (1992). *Mothers surviving child sexual abuse.* London: Routledge.

Hyde, C., Bentovim, A., & Monck, E. (1996). Treatment outcome study of sexually abused children. *Child Abuse and Neglect, 19,* 1387-1397.

Kempe, H., Silverman, F. H., & Steele, B. F. (1962). The battered child syndrome. *Journal of the American Medical Association, 181,* 17-24.

Kolko, D. J. (1996). Individual cognitive behavioural treatment and family therapy for physically abused children and their offending parents: The comparison of clinical outcomes. *Journal of Child Maltreatment, 1,* 322-342.

Monck, E., Bentovim, A., Goodall, G., Hyde, C., Lewin, R., Sharland, E., & Elton, A. (1996). *Studies in child protection.* London: HMSO.

Stratton, P. (1991). Incorporating circularity in defining and classifying child maltreatment. Human systems. *Journal of Systemic Consultation and Management, 2(3/4),* 145-296.

Trepper, T. S., & Barrett, M. J. (1989). *Systemic treatment of incest: A therapeutic handbook.* New York: Brunner/Mazel.

World Health Organization. Krug, E. G., Dahlberg, L. L., Mercy, J. A., Zwi, A. B., & Lozano, R. (Eds.) (2002). *World report on violence and health.* Geneva: WHO.

Fathers Who Make a Difference

Pedro Herscovici

SUMMARY. This article is a presentation of our work experience in helping separated and divorced fathers to go through this transition while retaining their parental identity. Our approach is based on the review of the significations of the role of the father, searching for descriptions that highlight parental relationships so as to produce a model that is useful in resolving the post-divorce family reorganization. Thus, different family members are reconciled by contextualizing distinct role ideologies. In view of the need of both parents and offspring of a new familial solidarity, the importance of the narratives related to shared parental commitment is emphasized.

KEYWORDS. Fathers, Argentina, divorce, post-divorce, therapy

FOREWORD

Florence Kaslow, PhD, has been a pioneer and continues to be an authoritative reference in Argentina in the field of divorce therapy and family mediation. Over the years Dr. Kaslow has traveled to various cities lecturing on the

Pedro Herscovici is Co-Director, TESIS Center of Systems Therapies, and Professor, School of Psychology, Universidad del Salvador, Buenos Aires.

Address correspondence to: Pedro Herscovici, J. Salguero 2745, Piso 1 Of. 13, (1425) Buenos Aires, Argentina (E-mail: hersco@ciudad.com.ar).

This article was originally published in *Sistemas Familiares, 18* (3), 57-66, 2002. This material is used by permission of Sistemas Familiares.

[Haworth co-indexing entry note]: "Fathers Who Make a Difference." Herscovici, Pedro. Co-published simultaneously in *Journal of Family Psychotherapy* (The Haworth Press, Inc.) Vol. 15, No. 1/2, 2004, pp. 137-148; and: *Family Therapy Around the World: A Festschrift for Florence W. Kaslow* (ed: William C. Nichols) The Haworth Press, Inc., 2004, pp. 137-148.

http://www.haworthpress.com/web/JFP
Digital Object Identifier: 10.1300/J085v15n01_10

foundations of such family practices and contributing to keeping us on the cutting edge.

Dr. Kaslow has made an outstanding impact in the field on many counts, but one of special value is the *Handbook of Relational Diagnosis*, of which she is editor and an author. The ecologic focus on interpersonal relationships and family dynamics of this volume is a crucial tool for clinical therapists in Argentina. I dedicate this article to Dr. Kaslow who has always welcomed unusual opinions on all sorts of topics. Moreover, Florence has helped me to strive to aim for greater honesty, patience, and inclusiveness, as well as to transcend my local cultural milieu, thus enabling me to construct better discussion contexts.

INTRODUCTION

Some time ago I interviewed the mother of two girls, two and four years old. They were referred to me by a Family Civil Court. This woman had a problem with her former husband: He did not abide by their signed agreement on visitation rights. The father argued he had no time to fulfill this obligation. I interviewed him, and, after gaining his trust and acceptance, we agreed that he should commence practicing visitation right away. However, he requested that he be allowed to start out with only one of his daughters–the eldest. He argued that visiting with both daughters at the same time and following the court agreed-upon schedule would be too difficult for him to manage. As it was a reasonable request I promised to tell his ex-wife about it. At our next meeting with her, however, this news was not welcomed. The mother argued that the two sisters should not be separated during visitation, adding that once and for all the father should assume responsibility and not manipulate matters subject to whim. She also demanded that during visitation neither the father's mother nor girlfriend should be present. I could only argue that it would be positive to allow the father time, in order to establish visitation gradually, giving him the opportunity to learn his parental role.

As is often the case, this man was probably willing to deploy his dormant or undeveloped parenting skills. Nevertheless, for this to happen he needed not only a therapist, but the support, patience and understanding of his parenting partner. In other words, so that the girls could have a father, the mother would have to let go of her post-divorce resentment. She should also allow him sufficient time and adapt the circumstances surrounding the visits, in order to ensure the success of the process. (I would like to point out the fact that it was hard for her to consent to the presence of another woman next to him who could "coach" him at this stage of adapting to his fathering role.)

Summing up this case, after divorce the family system began a reorganization process. This happened as soon as the father was able to take advantage of his own learning potential and to discover his fathering sensitivity. A sustained and effective bond was attained with his two daughters. This brought about a significant difference in their lives and, incidentally, in that of his ex-wife as well.

Arrangements and agreements by gender at a family level are currently not the same as in the past. That is to say, they abide neither by tradition nor by automatic rules. Being a father nowadays often implies a certain level of confusion. Beyond idealizing a model and its imperfections, and well beyond the decline of the patriarchal male role model, the importance of male parents is decisive in children's lives: Children need them, in order to identify the adult world and to prepare to occupy a place in it, developing a sense of responsibility (Pittman, 1993).

Maintaining the father's identity is an endless task, and the parental partnership is the appropriate context for establishing this identity. What do we mean by this? That joint decisions are more relevant than any unilateral decision. Fortunately, there are at present multiple options for both men and women. As regards the issue currently concerning us–male behavior–men may give up the heavy burden of pretending to be *macho* heroes and devote themselves instead to developing that particular sensitivity involved in being a father.

We are aware that the work environment, the family structure and social gender expectations have changed significantly over the past years and that the focus on males has grown accordingly. New parenting involves changes in family practices and in the significance of such practices. Divorce, remarriage and fertility patterns all relate to this new situation. To reflect on being a father means to think about it within the framework of such changes, which vary according to the population segment. Different socioeconomic and educational levels involve differing family practices and therefore distinct ideologies concerning the role of the father.

The context of male parenthood has changed and so has the number of children; fewer children are born to older parents. Conversely, the father's role has increased significantly. The father's heightened involvement is closely linked to a growing personal and family satisfaction when taking on this role. A good bond between father and children shows that everyone benefits at an overall health and social integration level. This applies to the children, as well as to the adult caretaker.

Nonetheless, at the start of this new century the situation is still not positive for men. Violence, abuse, drug addiction, and criminality continue to be viewed as mainly male behaviors. At the same time, many men are no longer providers, protectors or even procreators. Devoid of traditional functions and still considered emotionally limited, males nowadays seem out of place within society and family. The vicissitudes of a globalized world do not help either, as these demand certain "female" traits–flexibility, the capability of dealing with uncertainty–for which men are often not ready. In addition, a high unemployment rate is particularly damaging to males, when taking into account their traditional role.

There is not a single, "correct" description for the task of male parents nowadays. Nonetheless, we can attempt descriptions of bonds and practices that will enable us to attain a valid model for solving concrete problems, allowing a father to act more effectively as such. The aim of this description is to reconcile, to place this task in context.

The variety and network of relationships that make up a male parent has expanded significantly. Male parent sensitivity has grown to meet offspring needs, and this is more important than the deployment of strategies and resources to meet conflictive demands. With so many alternative formats at their disposal, male parents can now create trust units capable of supplying a richer and fuller sense to their lives.

POST-DIVORCE PARENTS

Our profession demands a matrix to sum up narratives in a unit. In addition to explaining the continuity of the processes, this unit should utilize the vocabulary of probability, not only to reach targets but also to reflect on the relative advantages arising from distinct concrete alternatives. To accomplish this task requires the understanding and explaining of the male parents role, redescribing it so that we can sympathize with him.

We have tried to construe descriptions so as to imagine a male parent in the post-divorce situation. As family therapists, this has aided us in increasing our sensitivity to his pain and humiliation. Thus, we are able to free ourselves from mere contemplation and have started to speak about contexts and perspectives, devising new metaphors and different accents. Thus, we were also able to move away from a moral vocabulary and to avoid highlighting any one feature of either parent. All this has fortunately facilitated an open debate so as to reach concrete agreements on ways of achieving parental purposes jointly. The ineffable and inevitable contingencies arising at meetings, in addition to the fact that we ourselves are also the product of the attitudes of others, significantly facilitated the redefinition of a father's role, which we are addressing here.

The emphasis on the post-divorce family situation–as with any historically conditioned situation–has modified our approach and made us curious about useful alternatives vis-à-vis the current role ideologies. Moreover, this recontextualization effort has meant defining interpersonal boundaries which lead us almost directly to moral responsibilities. For example, it has been very useful to describe family life in the aftermath of divorce: something suddenly different from what preceded it. It has also been useful to confirm that the new family solidarity is supported by reconciling the beliefs of both members of the parenting partnership, as regards the practical and concrete consequences of their actions. Finally, with its focus on the family, this is how the systemic approach shifts from the search for essences or individualities to that of effective joint rules of action.

We wish to stress that what really interests us is the condition of male parents as family members in the post-divorce situation, without resorting to categories which exceed the family framework itself, while recovering the history of achievements of the involved parts. Many people in the post-divorce aftermath often seek certainty, clarity, purity, rationality, the "truth." In other words they search for an order which, unintentionally, generates more skepticism. They fail to understand that the recontextualization of their relationship network will require accepting and adapting to the new family situation.

It is our belief that in order to reweave the typical habits of many male parents in relation to their children and their ex-wife, they must learn to extend their sensitivity and their parental know-how by putting aside the emancipatory, individualistic narratives in which they take refuge. Along these lines, there are in our culture different narratives offering male parents varied moral identities. These in turn pose different dilemmas but also various loyalty systems. In the case of parental coexistence, for example, the best narrative proves to be that which originates in the overlapping of the beliefs and wishes of both members. It is the one which allows an agreement: when both parties see themselves as valid interlocutors. (We are referring to an inclusive feeling, which is not indifferent to suffering, which reinforces a sense of shared moral identity and which will allow a better reorganization at a family level when there has been a divorce.)

Many male parents make significant progress in this field by visualizing coincidences with their ex-wife and they achieve it, not only by resorting to the law or arguing about ideologies, but by conforming new identities. This requires focusing on what is "coordinated" and "shared," making "belonging" a necessary element for empathizing and thus rebuilding the father's identity.

Of course, we are well aware that both divorce and post-divorce family arrangements are highly significant circumstances for the children. Emotional regulation strategies that offspring develop help them to evaluate, monitor, and modify their emotional reactions. Their ability to face things positively is closely linked to their strategies' flexibility, to their search for social and family support, and to the necessary redefinitions. Offspring of divorced parents learn to solve conflicts based on styles they have observed in their parents. When these styles appear aggressive or almost impossible to reconcile, the consequence will be an increase in behavioral problems (Cummings & Davis, 1994). We should also take into consideration the quality of the historical bond existing between mother-father and parents-children when evaluating the post-divorce emotional experience of the children.

Every family and social practice geared at favoring male parent responsibility post-divorce should help minimize conflicts at a parental level and therefore the ensuing consequences on the children (Leite & McKenry, 2000). This necessitates the continuation of shared parental authority with joint responsibility for the children's raising and education. As we have already mentioned–it also requires a clear outlining of the new roles and parental borders. The significance each parent gives to his or her identity shows the level of commitment. Parents tied to their pre-divorce experience and daily life, unable to bond among themselves and with their children in a different way and in the new context, have a high probability of failing in the family reorganization.

We are now admittedly in a context of unclear social expectations as to the post-divorce father's role. This ambiguity and lack of clarity generate an understandable dissatisfaction in the role's fulfillment. Marsiglio (1995) studied which social factors and attitudes, such as others' expectations, exert the greatest influence on separated parents. Marsiglio and associates in their research describe how this post-divorce complexity affects the father's identity, how rules regarding his "adequate" behavior change, and how their interpretation varies. Moreover, they clearly differentiate between the father as "visiting" (only one home–mother as primary parent) and as "local" (two homes–two parents simultaneously).

Though quite a number of fathers make an effort to continue having an active role in their children's lives, they often lack a clear road map on how to approach this transition. The large number of losses in different dimensions which a divorce brings about does not explain the greater or lesser loss of contact with the children; nor does the supposed "irresponsibility" explain the difficulties in initiating the rebonding. Many fathers desire to continue their committed and active presence despite being labeled "irresponsible." Nevertheless, they often fail to achieve it. In fact, there is still a high number of fathers who, for different reasons, do not see their children sufficiently. Research shows that this has significant consequences: Offspring who grow up without male parents may sometimes show lower academic performance, or have a higher probability of behavior problems, or else suffer from a shortage of all kinds of resources for problem solving.

What is now under discussion are the various parental post-divorce arrangements which may facilitate or hinder the father-children bond (uni-parental or shared custody). Which of the two best serves the interest of the children and teenagers involved? Our question leads us to a classic discussion on the rights and responsibilities of parents and children post-divorce and is consistent with various theories on child development and family interaction. A mother's uni-parental custody–almost the only option in Argentina–is supported by those who focus on the relevance of the primary parent and on the need for continuity and stability for the children in the post-divorce period. On the other hand, a bi-nuclear family, where both parents are active and influential participants in their children's development, sharing authority over the children after separation, points to a structure which seeks to prevent the mother from being overburdened and/or the father from being kept on the periphery. A prerequisite for this latter option is, of course, that there should be no chronic conflict at the parental level.

Given such complexity, the result is that adapting to divorce, on the part of parents and children, implies processes and stages difficult to describe if we only focus on certain variables. Additionally, the fathers' commitment and options toward his children will be determined by a multiplicity of factors, including cultural expectations and institutional practices in vogue (Doherty, 1998).

Clearly, a good parental and family subsystem reorganization is the foundation for the children's well-being after divorce. This presupposes adapting to the new circumstances, resolving the parental conflict, if there is one, and an adequate and sufficient rebonding among parents and children.

While almost all studies show that paternal presence positively influences children's well-being when there is low or no inter-parental conflict, there are serious difficulties when conflict is high and chronic. In the latter case, we agree with Hetherington, Cox, and Cox (1982) in that contact with the father significantly helps in reducing behavioral problems in children. A lack of interaction correlates with higher school drop-out rates, juvenile delinquency and suicide among adolescents. Thus, fathers' sustained commitment to their children is directly linked with the offspring's better handling of their impulses, a greater capacity for empathy and cognition and with fewer gender stereotypes (Radin, 1982; Radin & Sagi, 1982). Furthermore, although a father's rights and responsibilities may be legally codified, his parental intervention will depend solely and exclusively on his will to exercise his parental role and on the skills he is able to develop within this new situation, mainly an interaction that includes not only quantitative but also qualitative factors.

Another key element is the mediator's role played by mothers when facilitating a father's access to the children and transmitting his role values. In fact, when mothers do not portray a positive father image, the children's view becomes correlatively less positive, beyond the time and quality of the father-children interaction. Furthermore, if the ex-wife limits the children-father contact or conditions it inadequately, the result may influence the father's commitment to their children. Interestingly, there is evidence that fathers in this situation find it easier to continue their bond with their sons than with their daughters (Marsiglio, 1995). Also important are the attitudes the father held toward his children during the marriage, and how they operate after the separation. Regarding the father's possible new mate, the outcome of this relationship as well as his parental commitment will depend substantially on how much this new bond competes with the previous one (Furstenberg et al., 1983; Seltzer, 1991). The number, gender, and make up of the children or adolescents with whom the father now lives will affect his attitudes toward the children of his previous marriage. Additionally, the former spouses' level of autonomy will influence whether rebonding is eased or hindered. This delicate balance between old and new bonds, these different post-divorce autonomies and interpersonal boundaries, in which a certain proximity or distance can bring about better or worse rebonding, may cause many fathers, who find their parental duties painful or difficult, to end up opting to sever bonds. Whether temporary or definitive, this limited parental participation often expresses a loyalty conflict, which translates in children's difficulty in rebonding with their fathers (Hetherington, Cox, & Cox, 1978). Conversely, after a constructive divorce, and once bonds have been reorganized as a new family unit without exclusions, we usually see that fathers tend to acquire greater parental autonomy and child rearing experience on their own.

A dual residence for the children—what we have named two homes, two parents at the same time—though perhaps involving different periods with each, is related to a more satisfactory post-divorce adjustment, particularly for adolescents. Research points out that in this type of parental arrangement, children's bonds with both parents are stronger, and a higher commitment on the part of the father is achieved. This type of organization results in considerably higher levels of satisfaction for both parents and children (Folberg, 1991).

In intact families the mothers tend to evaluate the closeness of the fathers with their children in terms of the love, care, support and life norms they provide. Children do likewise; proximity is perceived as empathy and understanding. When divorce occurs this "parental responsibility" is assessed differently because mothers become more demanding in their evaluation of the father's bonding, within a context in which sons and daughters give differing information about the quality and nature of these bonds.

When after divorce the father has not gained custody, children actually tend to be less demanding than mothers in evaluating their father's closeness. Their commitment is different (Furstenberg, Morgan, & Allison, 1987). Fathers are an important, indispensable part of the offsprings' sense of stability and adequacy, in taking care of their vulnerabilities and also in the development of their gender identity. High parental commitment facilitates closeness and contributes to a sense of self-worth in the children. In turn, children view their fathers as more understanding and reliable when their conversation is more fluid. Thus paternal commitment entails a more positive evaluation of the paternal role itself. We have already mentioned that there is an ever-growing number of fathers who commit themselves to their children post-divorce (Gerson, 1993). The need and opportunity to widen the fathers' traditional repertoire is growing as well. Men show they can offer their offspring not only a material contribution but also emotional resources. They can transcend purely instrumental needs (Parsons & Bales, 1995) and thus significantly enhance the growth and development of the children (Hess & Camara, 1979; Wallerstein & Blaskeslee, 1989). This involves a stronger commitment in helping children to mature and also improving the overall health of all members of the reorganized family (Kimmel, 2000).

Nevertheless, many divorced parents still practice intermittent fathering, which becomes confusing and frustrating for every family member. They avoid discipline and are erratic in accepting their responsibilities: They neither confirm their bond with the children nor do they really establish it; some even abdicate fatherhood. Others, by becoming overly permissive or authoritarian, are either negligent or exclude themselves as fathers. The aforementioned are attitudes which increase the vulnerability of children affected and sensitized by a divorce.

PARENTING AS A CULTURAL CONCEPT

Social psychology studies, among other things, show how cultural attributes inherent in human femininity and masculinity are created, defined, and sustained in the course of social interaction. Also, they show how gender role ideology varies in use and significance according to each culture, and how these attributes explain or justify the behavior of men and women. Social psychology researches stereotyped beliefs which determine discriminatory conducts operating as positive or negative expectations. It teaches us, furthermore, how stereotype-based prophesies about gender roles tend to fail in situations or contexts where other social categories are more relevant.

Parenthood, as a cultural concept, varies according to time and place. As a code of conduct, it demands attitudes shared by others, and around this concept there are different models which are passed on from generation to generation, yet suffer changes in the course of time. Here, we are referring to the different ideologies on which a father's role is based and what is expected of fathers under these circumstances. The answer is not simple; perhaps it lies within a set of qualities and activities which differentiate fathers as such, qualities and activities which can at times be almost heroic, ideal goals which make many fathers flee from domesticity. Thus, fatherhood may become a problem when it is transformed into exasperated demands or, conversely, into *laissez faire*.

However, in order to offer fatherhood, one must have previously received it–and in sufficient fashion. Being a proper and full father implies displaying a male domestic role with the necessary commitment and reliability. It is a fundamental and substantial aspect of becoming a man, for those who perform it, and who directly bring to bear their intimate parental association capabilities. In other words, a father can, for instance, modulate the masculine development of his sons and the feminine development of his daughters. This generates emotional security for all family members involved, including himself (Pittman, 1993).

As a model male, the father may be present without resorting to exaggerated ways of being so. Keeping up his paternal commitment towards his offspring and his parental partner can express his maturity. We must therefore emphasize the importance of the narratives which forge parental commitment. To assume the responsibility implies a feasible agreement on the basic premises of child rearing. This language values the different contribution of each parent, each in his or her own manner, yet accepting and respecting the differences. Within those differences parents can increase mutual support in child rearing, beyond any specific conflict. This is possible if they are alternately in charge, in their own times and spaces, as post-divorce parents, clearly defining responsibilities and dividing up tasks. This will also contribute towards coordinating complementary tasks and defining domains and tolerance areas. Thus, when a father is in charge of his children, he is in a better position to develop an ample repertoire and with full responsibility.

For further information, see Belsky, Youngblade, & Rovine, 1991; Herscovici, 1986 a, b, c, 1991, 1994, 1995 a, b, c, 1999, 2001 a, b.

REFERENCES

Belsky, J., Youngblade, L., & Rovine, M. (1991). Patterns of marital change and parent child interaction. *Journal of Marriage and the Family, 53*, 487-498.

Cummings, Z. M., & Davies, P. (1994). *Children and marital conflict. The impact of family dispute and resolution.* New York: Guilford Press.

Doherty, W., Kouneski, E., & Erickson, M. (1998). Responsible fathering: An overview and conceptual framework. *Journal of Marriage and the Family, 60*, 277-292.

Folberg, J. (Ed.) (1991). *Joint custody and shared parenting.* New York: Guilford Press.

Furstenberg, F. F., Jr., Morgan, S. P., & Allison, P. D. (1987). Paternal participation and children wellbeing after marital dissolution. *American Sociological Review, 52,* 695-701.

Furstenberg, F. F., Jr., Nord, C. W., Peterson, J., & Zill, N. (1983). The life course of children of divorce. Marital disruption and parental contact. *American Sociological Review, 48,* 656-668.

Gerson, K. (1993). *No man's land. Men changing commitments to family and work.* New York: Basic Books.

Herscovici, P. (1986a). Terapia familiar. In M. L. Rovaletti (Comp.), *Matrimonio y familia en la Argentina actual (Marriage and family in Argentina nowadays).* Buenos Aires: Editorial Trieb. pp. 127-131.

Herscovici, P. (1986b). Padres e hijos de la separación (Parents and children of divorce). *Sistemas Familiares Año, 2 (3),* 23-29.

Herscovici, P. (1986c). Por el mejor interés y en defensa de los hijos de la separación (In their best interest and in defense of children of divorce). *Terapia Familiar, 15,* 75-82.

Herscovici, P. (1991). El divorcio y las nuevas organizaciones familiares (Divorce and new familial organizations). *Teoría y Técnica de la Psicoterapia Sistémica-Clínica del Cambio.* Buenos Aires: Nadir Editores, pp. 207-230.

Herscovici, P. (1994). Psicología familiar (Family psychology). In C. A. R. Lagomarsino, & M. U. Salerno, *Enciclopedia de drecho de familia.* Tomo III. Buenos Aires: Editorial Universidad.

Herscovici, P. (1995a). Panorama actual de la mediación familiar (A look at current family mediation). *Familias y Terapias Revista del Instituto de Terapia Familiar. Año, 3 (6),* 67-77.

Herscovici, P. (1995b). La mediación familiar interdisciplinaria (Interdisciplinary family mediation). *Revista de la Asociación de Magistrados y Funcionarios de la Justicia Nacional No14/15,* 193-204.

Herscovici, P. (1995c). Mediar y como mediar (Mediation and how to mediate). *Divorcio y Familia a fines del siglo XX Fundaih (5),* 64-66.

Herscovici, P. (1999). Justicia-familia (Justice-family). *Derecho de Familia Revista Interdisciplinaria (14),* 217-222.

Herscovici, P. (2001a). Divorcio (Divorce). In A. Rubinstein, S. Terrasa, E. Durante, E. Rubinstein, & E. Carrete (Eds.), *Medicina familiar y práctica ambulatoria.* Buenos Aires: Editorial Médica Panamericana.

Herscovici, P. (2001b). Qué podemos hacer por nosotros mismos (What we can do on our own). *Cuaderno de Doctrina No20 Temas de Mediación.* Colegio Público de Abogados de la Capital Federal.

Hess, R. D., & Camara, K. A. (1979). Post divorce family relationships as mediating factor in the consequences for children. *Journal of Social Issues, 35,* 79-97.

Hetherington, E. M., Cox, M., & Cox, R. (1978). The aftermath of divorce. In J. H. Stevens, & Matthews (Eds.), *Mother-child, father-child relationships* (pp. 149-176). Washington, DC: National Association for Education of Young Children.

Hetherington, E. M., Cox, M., & Cox, R. (1982). Effects of divorce in parents and children. In M. E. Lamb (Ed.), *Nontraditional families: Parenting and child development* (pp. 233-238). Hillsdale, NJ.

Hetherington, E. M., & Kelly, J. (2002). *For better or for worse: Divorce reconsidered.* New York: Norton.

Kaslow, F. W. (1981). Divorce and divorce therapy. In A. S. Gurman, & D. P. Kniskern (Eds.), *Handbook of family therapy* (pp. 662-696). New York: Brunner/Mazel.

Kaslow, F. W. (1986). La mediación en el divorcio y su impacto emocional en la pareja y sus hijos (Divorce mediation and its emotional impact on the couple and their children). In Divorcio y nuevas organizaciones familiares. *Terapia Familiar, 15*, 57-72.

Kaslow, F. W. (1987). Stages in the divorce process. In F. W. Kaslow, & L. L. Schwartz (Eds.), *The dynamics of divorce: A life perspective* (pp. 23-27). New York: Brunner/Mazel.

Kaslow, F. W. (1993). The divorce ceremony: A healing strategy. In T. Nelson, & T. Trepper (Eds.), *101 favorite family therapy interventions* (pp. 341-345). New York: The Haworth Press, Inc.

Kaslow, F. W. (1995). The dynamics of divorce therapy. In R. H. Mikersell, D. D. Lusterman, & S. H. McDaniel (Eds.), *Integrating family therapy: Handbook of family psychotherapy and systems theory* (pp. 271-283). Washington, DC: American Psychological Association.

Kimmel, M. S. (2000). *The gendered society.* New York: Oxford University Press.

Leite, R. W., & McKenry, P. C. (2000). Aspects of father status and post-divorce. Father involvement with children. *Journal of Family Issues, 23 (5),* 601-623.

Marsiglio, W. (Ed.) (1995). *Fatherhood: Contemporary theory, research and social policy.* Thousand Oaks, CA: Sage Publications.

Parsons, T., & Bales, R. F. (1955). *Family socialization and interaction process.* New York: Free Press.

Pittman, F. (1993). *Man enough.* New York: Perigee Books.

Seltzer J. A. (1991). Relationships between fathers and children who live apart. The father's role after separation. *Journal of Marriage and the Family, 53,* 79-101.

Wallerstein, J. S., & Blaskeeslee, S. (1989). *Second chances: Men, women and children a decade after divorce.* New York: Ticknor and Fields.

Death Does Not Do Us Part

Wencke J. Seltzer

SUMMARY. The author illustrates cotexting (use of the therapist's verbal additions to the client's verbalization of the story) in a co-constructed ritual as a way of breaking up a rigid, locked position that is maintaining a bereaved widow's unresolved bereavement situation and suicidal preoccupation. *[Article copies available for a fee from The Haworth Document Delivery Service: 1-800-HAWORTH. E-mail address: <docdelivery@haworthpress. com> Website: <http://www.HaworthPress.com> © 2004 by The Haworth Press, Inc. All rights reserved.]*

KEYWORDS. Bereavement and grief, cotexting, crisis intervention, ritual, therapy, silenced cultural issues, widowhood

Dear Florence,

Many great congratulations to you! You are an exceptional person and so is your man, Sol. The two of you have reflected togetherness, loyalty to one another and neverending support of your exceptionally exuberant relation for all

---

Wencke J. Seltzer was a member of IFTA from the time it was founded; she named and edited the *International Connection* (IFTA bulletin) for six years; and she was president of IFTA, 1997-1999.

Address correspondence to: Wencke J. Seltzer, Oscarsgate 80, 2356 Oslo, Norway (E-mail: wenck-s@online.no).

[Haworth co-indexing entry note]: "Death Does Not Do Us Part." Seltzer, Wencke J. Co-published simultaneously in *Journal of Family Psychotherapy* (The Haworth Press, Inc.) Vol. 15, No. 1/2, 2004, pp. 149-160; and: *Family Therapy Around the World: A Festschrift for Florence W. Kaslow* (ed: William C. Nichols) The Haworth Press, Inc., 2004, pp. 149-160. Single or multiple copies of this article are available for a fee from The Haworth Document Delivery Service [1-800-HAWORTH, 9:00 a.m. - 5:00 p.m. (EST). E-mail address: docdelivery@haworthpress.com].

the years I have known you, almost a couple of decades! It has always been a great pleasure to see the two of you together.

Florence, you "invented" The International Family Therapy Association (IFTA). It was a grandiose idea at the time, and some of us, whom you recruited as coworkers, were idealistic enough to join and we put all our efforts into it. Most of our endeavors went well, but there were also downfalls, hurt feelings and mistakes. At times we wondered if this fantastic world-travelling ship called IFTA would withstand the storms that came its way. Yet, it continued to sail, between continents of the world! Its first mission was to promote exchange of family therapy knowledge and skills across geographical, cultural, ethnic and political structures. IFTA congresses became highly valued as international family therapy events.

Strong friendships have been formed through IFTA, across all differential borders. In a world full of wars, violence and betrayal, IFTA's network of international, professional and personal friendships is extremely valuable. Thank you Florence, first of all for IFTA, and for your contributions to the field of family therapy. You, and all of us who took turns and served as crew on the IFTA vessel, are very happy and proud that this unique vessel is still going strong! That is exceptional!

Professor Wencke J. Seltzer, PhD
Oslo, Norway

HILMA'S STORY

In this piece of writing, I shall report on parts of a story told by a female client in dialogue with a team of therapists/researchers at a family clinic in a small community in rural Scandinavia. The story was originally voiced by 52-year-old Hilma, widow of Hilmar. I shall also report on how the multidisciplinary therapy/research team worked with Hilma through a period of severe crisis in her life.

CO-CONSTRUCTION AND COTEXTING OF THERAPEUTIC RITUAL

One particular therapy session is highlighted. In that session, a ritual was co-constructed and cotexted. Cotexting is a term that I have employed for several decades. It involves the therapist's verbal additions to the client's own verbalization of the story as therapeutic process evolves. The client voices her or his text, which is understood as the major and original text. The therapist may add to the client's original text by asking questions, commenting, and making other forms of verbal expressions. Cotexting is formed spontaneously in the therapy room, so that it fits the unique self-reported story of the client at hand. Cotexting influences the story, and may dislocate it and bring it out of rigid and/or locked positions, which often serve to maintain the client's problem. This story about Hilma, I assume, will illustrate this point.

RITUAL AS A SERIES OF COTEXTED SYMBOLIC ACTIONS

Rituals are most often composed of action saturated with symbolic meaning, frequently without shared talk. In religious ceremonies, a text may be read from the scripture, which is repetitious and fixed, as it has been for hundred of years. During the co-construction of therapeutic ritual, as in Hilma's case, cotexting is spontaneously formed to make it relevant for the client's particular situation. I have referred to the ceremony with Hilma as a ritual of individuation. The cotexting of the ritual reported on here emphasized a strengthening of Hilma's self-identity and individuation, separate from her dead husband's. In the ritual, Hilma was the central and celebrant actor.

HILMA AS A CULTURE BEARER

In the therapy room Hilma speaks as a culture bearer of a rural female and family life career. She also speaks about her extreme attachment to her husband, whose recent death reduced her into confusion concerning her own identity and left her, as she put it, as "only a half-body and half-person." This half-person status threatened her identity and future survival. The theme of the "half" woman without her man has been voiced, we believe, in the district where she lived and in similar areas all through Scandinavia for hundreds of years. This version of female identity in families may stand out as peculiar today, as different modern and postmodern family forms evolve. Yet, "dominant" discourse in terms of how the "ideal" family should be shows that many young people, as well as old, view the extended and traditional family as the ideal model by which to live. Today, her community and similar communities show a variety of family living, from prechristian, modern, and postmodern eras.

In her community's district, a well adjusted woman's status is still perceived as being achieved through bodily and psychological and economic merging with a man. Completeness as a woman is further achieved through the production of offspring. The man and the woman are viewed as "complementary" halves of one whole. In the work with Hilma in the clinic, I referred to Hilma and Hilmar's relation over 30 years as symbiotic, a relational position both had profited from, in a milieu where they felt expelled by their immediate social surroundings. In dialogues with myself, I termed this a case of culturally determined symbiosis. Hilmar's extended family, and others in the community as well, viewed Hilma as defective; she had failed to give birth to a child.

Yet, through mass media, and some contact with others, Hilma witnessed alternative voices and actions, often expressed by urban folks and younger generations who had settled in the community, or returned after periods of study and/or work in the cities. They exposed "new" ways of living, a variety of lifestyles, and accompanying functions, often referred to as postmodern. Thus, alternative values and living patterns were both distant and close to Hilma. Also, these opposites were possibly central components in her ambivalence as to the question of whether she could live on as a woman alone without her husband, or whether it was better for her to join her husband in his grave. Hilmar's death had left her feeling that she had lost her anchor in life and her sense of self-navigation.

At the time I write this story, I can gaze back into my own images of Hilma (four-five years after the sessions took place), see before me her bodily expression of pain and numbness, and hear her deep and desperate breathing amidst her forceful sobbing. At the same time I find myself wondering, as I did when the sessions took place, about her angelic, porcelain-like, smooth, childlike, and unstrained face, along with the sturdily framed body of a healthy country woman. There she was, with her strong body fully fit to continue life, yet she experienced extreme pain inside herself, and inside her medically declared healthy body. She was "left behind" at a station in rural Scandinavia, alone. Without her husband, she thought she would not be able to go on.

Aspects of Hilma's individual story could be recognized by females and families in many parts of the rural world. As women, we could recognize these themes in ourselves, in our mothers, and in our grandmothers. Thus, Hilma's story is also a collective one, and I thought an important one from which professional teachers, clinicians, and therapists may learn. In its more collective form, Hilma's story has taken us across individual, geographical, and cultural borders. It is collective and local, typically human–and, to some extent, gender specific.

THE CASE

Hilma was referred to the clinic by her physician, who felt that he could do very little about her complaints of headaches, painful muscles, and general numbness in the entire left side of her body. Following appropriate examinations and tests, the physician concluded that no organic explanations could be found for her numbness on one side of her body, her pain, and bodily discomfort. Hence, he referred her to the family clinic.

At the clinic, Hilma explained that she had lost her husband a few months prior to her consultation. She told a long story about an idyllic life with her husband Hilmar. They had met while they were both young, and worked together in a company for the first years of their marriage, in another part of the country. The industry which had first employed them then closed, and the couple moved to his family's home farm in the Mountainview county. As a son, born and bred on the farm, Hilmar was entitled to a piece of land on the farm grounds. The couple built a small house on the lot, which became their home for the remainder of their lives together.

Hilma was not "childborn" (a local term) in the county. It was common in the district to distinguish between those who were born and "belonged" there, and those who were more "transient" there. No doubt, those who were born and bred in the county were more highly esteemed than those who came from the outside. In the old days, the extended family settlements functioned like whole communities, where people slept, ate, worked, feasted, and socialized within the boundaries of the settlement, not unlike a total institution (Erving Goffman's term, Goffman, 1957). Such settlements were known to be protective of their social and geographic boundaries, and also inherently suspicious of those who entered the vicinity from the outside.

Since Hilma came from another part of the country, among those who were childborn there, she was clearly categorized as an outsider. Yet her function was to be a wife of one of the childborn sons in the family community. Commonly, such definitions of outsidedness of wives who moved to their husband's farms or home settlements were silenced after she had given birth to her first child. This physical presence of an offspring, which united the husband and wife in parenthood and "kinship," secured continuation of the family, and its future material position as well.

In Hilma and Hilmar's case, it became clear that they would never have a child. Hilma alone then was held responsible for the couple's barren life together. This was perceived as a flaw, which was attributed to her biology, based on no medical evidence. She became socially isolated. Her value in the community was hardly worth mentioning, except she did function as a good wife. She and Hilmar, in their isolation, became inseparable.

Hilma never elaborated on this theme in the therapy room. Yet, she mentioned this sad story in bits and pieces. It was not until far into the sessions that this theme of rejection was expressed. It was what I have called a silent story, silent within Hilma, and silent in the culture. Thus, Hilma seemed to feel it was "natural" that the locals excluded her. This behavior was so congruent with common attitudes in the culture that neither she, or anyone else for that matter, spoke against it or resisted it. However, she was very much aware that in the absence of the fact that she and Hilmar would never be fully accepted as worthy members of his family, the two had tightened the bonds between them into a protective and isolated "twosomeness." By becoming a closed unit they were insulated from the silent, yet painful exclusion from the outside. They did have their couple status, and that was impeccable. Hilma was a good housewife, and Hilmar was a loyal husband. Hilma explained to her therapist that Hilmar's family never showed any interest in them, and that the two of them were better off by themselves.

Hilma told wonderful stories about the loving relationship between herself and Hilmar. They took part in all activities together, and they had never slept apart during the almost 30 years that they had been married. Together, she and Hilmar visited a small place by a lake as often as possible. Here, they also became friends with other guests. In that place, Hilmar wrote a beautiful poem which he gave to his beloved wife on her birthday. The poem was about the beauty of life and all living creatures, and the beauty of his wife, "blooming in the springtime." Like flowers blooming in the spring, Hilmar wrote, human life should also be. Hilma kept the poem with her and recited it for her therapist.

Hilmar had become deadly ill. He was hospitalized, which forced a physical separation upon the two. Hilma stayed with Hilmar at the hospital most of the time for weeks. When she occasionally left the hospital building to have a bite to eat, or to draw some fresh air, he would get out of his bed and wander around looking for her. Since he was heavily drugged with pain-killing chemicals, he often needed help to find his way back to his bed. The night Hilmar died, Hilma drove home alone in the cold and dark winter night. When she arrived at their little house, nobody else was there. Hilda spent much time in complete isolation. She was scared at night, and thought she heard steps outside her house. She also received telephone calls from men who spoke to her in pornographic terms.

Hilma thought she felt Hilmar's presence by her side at night; she sensed his breathing, his odors, and even his physical body next to hers. Hilma began to hear voices located in her head. These voices were telling her to go to the grave and lay down by her husband. The voices were good and bad. Hilmar might be calling her into the grave with her, to free her from her unbearable grief, and protect her against the evil and estranged world in which she now found herself. She often woke up to her own screaming at night. She wondered if the voices came from someone who might be the devil, Satan himself, who wanted to fool her into taking her life and going to hell. She also had visions of slick, undefinable, and frightening creatures that came to her and invaded her body. She was desperate. In this period, she still went to the local grocery store a few times a week. Here, she talked with the lady at the cash stand. This social meeting became a point of orientation for her. She began to look forward to those meetings.

In that period, Hilma had developed a type of numbness (paralysis) on the entire left side of her body. This was the side of her body that had slept next to her husband's body every night for 30 years. Even though Hilma was paralyzed, she experienced pain in her left shoulder as well and had severe headaches. It was at this time she consulted the physician who declared her physically healthy and referred her on to the clinic.

In the sessions at the clinic, Hilma's therapist became the main point of orientation to Hilda. She came in regularly, and went through her traumatic story again and again. Her therapist listened patiently for a few months, and made certain Hilma was given the chance to grieve and recount the trauma that had come upon her. Hilda employed what the team of therapists and researchers had learned to call "a language of suicide."

Language of suicide is a term introduced by the cultural anthropologist Michael R. Seltzer, PhD. As a team member in the case reported here, he noticed that talk of suicide was rather common in the clinic's area. It would be expressed in terms such as "going to the mountain," "taking a walk to the river," and so on. In team discussions, we viewed this termed as culturally determined, implicitly meaning that the individual sees suicide as a possible solution to a problem but not in all cases indicating suicidal intention.

This language was commonly utilized as an indication of problem solving in the local area. Thus, it was a culturally based language, which indicated thoughts of suicide. Because of the common use of such language, it was difficult for the clinicians to distinguish serious suicidal threats from common expression of the wish to "get away." Examples of a language of suicide would be "Well, my aunt was wise–she climbed the cliffs up there and never came back," and so on. The language of suicide had a heroic and distanced feeling to it. This might have been a way to deemphasize emotional pain, for which there is little language in this community and similar Scandinavian rural areas.

Emotional pain is less accepted than physical pain as something to be spoken about. Consequently, a more respectable stance is to get out of the way, and take care of one's own problems, and not become a burden to others. In this context, taking one's own life is considered self-sufficient, and in the old culture viewed as a solution to unbearable pain. Reactions to such events in the community, although they cause people to grieve, also involve a flavor of heroism. The therapist encouraged Hilma to be more active socially, and her involvement in social activities increased some. Also, Hilma had a difficult time making ends meet financially. He also advised her regarding these problems.

One late afternoon Hilma called the therapist. During the night she had taken a large dosage of dangerous medication which Hilmar had accumulated during the terminal phase of his illness. She told her therapist she had had nightmares, and that she again had heard the voices calling her into Hilmar's grave. She took a handful of drugs, and hoped this would end her suffering. She became very ill, and began vomiting, which saved her life. The therapist made an agreement with her that from then on she would call the office every day. Hilma did. He also urged her to bring the medication which was left in her possession to be handed over to the office. Hilma did.

In the meantime, the therapist began to feel that he was stuck with the case. The team discussed the situation. Some of the thought that surfaced in the team discussion was that Hilma had begun to rely too much on the therapist, almost as if he were a father or a substitute husband. Some of us wondered if she had transferred some of her attachment behavior from Hilmar over to the therapist. If so, such a "transfer" would not be helpful for her in reorienting herself in her new single situation. The therapist had tried very hard to help her reroute her thinking into more positive terms. So, when Hilma, despite his efforts attempted to take her life, he felt bereaved as well. Hilma had become a demanding patient at this time. Also, the team wondered about the repetitive themes of loss and grief being voiced in the sessions by Hilma. Was it helpful, at this time, to play into the continuation of these themes?

The therapist invited me in as a guest therapist and the remainder of the team to view and to participate in the next sessions. In the team discussion I voiced my concern that perhaps Hilma was still psychologically united with Hilmar, in a kind of symbiosis, despite the fact that the other one in the two-sided union was dead. I thought of the symbolic meaning of the partial paralysis of the left side of her body following Hilmar's death. This side of her had died with Hilmar, and as such, belonged in the grave with him, the remainder of her continuing as a half alive person. I wondered how it might be possible to engage Hilma in such a way that she could begin to individuate from her dead husband (reduce the symbiosis) in body, feelings, thoughts, and actions. She was now a woman who had to make choices in life without Hilmar. In this spirit, the team mentioned the poem Hilmar had created for her, something that came from his inner self, telling her that life is sacred, and that all living creatures should cherish their lives. In their reflection, this was what the team thought Hilmar would have told her had he been with us at this time.

In order to bring in the deep unspoken voices of culture, it was emphasized by the team that it is not selfish to have friends and enjoy them. In the old culture, girls learn from the time they are small that one must learn to live for others and not be selfish. Further, a widow who never gave birth to a child must mourn for a long time, and her place in life may be viewed as meaningless. The team said it is natural to let go of the mourning and respect the wish of Hilmar for his beloved wife to live and let live.

The Ritual Session

The killer drugs as a symbol of continued attachment and faithfulness to Hilmar: The session began with Hilma bringing in the plastic bag filled with the dangerous drugs. I, as the guest therapist, thought about how to break into the repetitive and gradually destructive way Hilma had operated in since the death of her husband, which by this time had been nearly two years ago. Her self-destruction had become repetitive and stuck. Rational reasoning with her did not work. So, when learning that Hilma was bringing the plastic bag with Hilmar's killer drugs to the session, the idea struck me that this plastic object could be viewed as a transitional symbolic object (signifier) in a ritual of transition and individuation.

The following evolved: Hilma, her therapist, and I were gathered in the therapy room. The therapist explained to Hilma that in this session, as in the last one (we had met in one session before), Hilma and the guest therapist would do most of the talking, and he would be there as an observer. Behind the screen sat a team of therapists/research colleagues. In the past session, Hilma began the session by pointing to her painful shoulder, and the numb side of her body. She also expressed the feeling that she was not her old self any more. She was only partly a person, and she felt that she was called to the grave, either by Hilmar, or perhaps by the devil. Maybe Satan tried to fool her.

Hilma had placed the bag of deadly drugs in her lap. She was cuddling it, as if it were a dear and precious gift to her. Today, I said, we might concentrate on the life she still has, and that Hilmar no longer has. This, I said, made a great difference between the two, she was alive, and he was dead. I thought it was important to state the words alive and dead. At that time, those were key words.

I wondered if she would help me understand what meaning the drugs had to her. She then explained, as she covered her mouth with her hand, "I wanted to disappear" (language of suicide), and so her therapist had asked her to bring them in for him to take care of them. I said I wondered why he would want them. They were not his, and why should he accept a package full of drugs? She said they were dangerous drugs, and that they might take a person's life. I said I had heard from her therapist that she had used them for that purpose. She nodded. I wondered, by the way, were the drugs hers? No, she said, they belonged to her husband, he had left them behind. Again, I said I did not see how she could give away something that was really not hers? And why would the therapist be responsible for drugs delivered to him which belonged to someone who was dead? Was that the wish of the dead one? She repeated that the drugs were dangerous. I wondered if that meant that if the drugs were removed, she would be prevented from taking her life. As I understood the situation, the drugs had not forced themselves upon her, had she herself taken them out of their container and swallowed them? Her husband's drugs? She nodded, almost with a faint smile on her face. I felt she was being somewhat dissociative.

The absurdity of this discussion ended with my question of whether her delivery of the drugs to the clinic secured her life. No, she answered, "There are many ways a person can take her life, with or without drugs." I nodded, and added, "Yes, I see that. It is up to the person, isn't it?" She indicated her agreement. I felt we had made the point. I did not want to waste the time we had together by talking about the dangerous drugs. Since she knew how to dissociate, I felt it was important to associate the suicide attempt with her own actions, not that of the drugs. We did add, however, that Hilmar was not responsible for her suicide attempt either; he had not given his beloved wife drugs for her to end her life. She nodded and seemed to be relieved. She said the drugs should be given back to the physician since they were prescribed by a physician. We all agreed. We asked Hilma if she would explain to the physician why she wanted to deliver the drugs to him. The physician was one of our coworkers, who was observing behind the screen, and we called him into the therapy room.

THE COTEXTING OF A RITUAL OF INDIVIDUATION BEGINS

The physician entered the room holding up a cardboard box. We had worked together in many situations in the clinic, and the physician knew we had cleared the situation for enacting a leave taking ritual. The box, when the drugs were placed in it, had the potential of being viewed as a casket and as an object of transition. For a while the therapy room had the potential of becoming the site of a funeral.

The physician moved into the circle where Hilma, the therapist, and I sat, and I stood up to greet him. Hilma and the therapist stood up also. Now we were four people in a circle, around a cardboard box held in the middle by the physician. I introduced the physician to Hilma. She said: "The doctor is here, and so–therefore–you (the physician) should get these now." The physician opened the lid of the box and invited Hilma to put the bag with the drugs in it. Hilma moved toward the box and said: "Throw them away, destroy them!" She almost threw the bag in there, while staring at it. The doctor said he would take the responsibility for them, and she indicated that she was not worried about that. Then the physician shook hands with Hilma and was about to leave.

I said, "I wonder, before you leave, if I could add that from this moment on, there is no way Hilma can take her life with Hilmar's medicine." The physician nods and adds "no." Hilma says: "Yeah," breathing in as she is whispering her confirmation. I continued, "And, from this moment on," making a cutting hand motion between the box and Hilma, repeating, "it is the end of Hilma's thinking about killing herself with Hilmar's medicine." Hilma nods again, adding in a whispering voice "yes." The physician adds: "Yes, so I close this," and he turns the lid down on the box.

I place my hand on top of the closed box, and say, "So, when you leave with this case with Hilmar's medicine inside it, then Hilma is Hilma." The physician nods and continues: "So, I take with me Hilmar's casket, and the responsibility" (meaning implicitly, for the drugs). I continue: "Then Hilma must find her own means to continue her life, or end her life." Hilma adds "yes." I point to the box and continue: "So, now, do these (the medication) go back to the earth or–some other place?" The physician: "Yes, back to where they came from." Hilma is nodding, almost crying now. I say: "Shall we (turning to the physician), while you are still here (turning to Hilma and the therapist also), take farewell together, by placing our hands atop the carton (which all did)–that is really what this is about (implicitly meaning the symbolic and collective support extended to Hilma)?" All put their hands on Hilma's wrist and hold her like that for a moment. Then her therapist says: "Now Hilma has given away a possibility to die, and begins to live."

I place my arm around Hilma's shoulder and say to the physician as he is about to leave: "So, Hilma stays behind as the one who continues her life–who lives on." Hilma removes her glasses and begins to cry. I stroke her hair and say: "Hilma is now among the living, right?" Hilma is sobbing now, but manages to say "yes." I hold her around her shoulder for a while. Then each person returns to his/her own chair now, each holding his or her own pain. Everyone in the team also had misty eyes at this point. When the sobbing subsides, I say, turning to Hilma: "Once again you have taken farewell. Is that right?" She says yes, and continues to wipe tears. I take her hand and repeat: "So, one more time you took farewell and you remain here, and you are alive and you are Hilma."

A POST-RITUAL CONVERSATION

As a closing off of the ritual, I suggested that we (the group in the therapy room) change places with the team in the observation room, so that the team could share some of their thoughts with each other and us. In this post-ritual conversation, the team mainly talked about how they viewed Hilma's future. They brought in the poem that Hilmar had written to Hilma about the beauty of life, and talked about the friends Hilma had at the lake place where she and Hilmar had spent their free time. Also, the team mentioned several community activities which might be of interest to Hilma.

The therapist continued working with Hilma for some time. By then their conversations were much more directed toward Hilma's new life as a person on her own. She soon engaged in several community volunteer activities. During one of the last sessions at the clinic, she repotted, fertilized, and watered the almost wilted plants in the clinic. She said she could see that they needed nourishment and care. She would not let them die.

Again, it struck me that Hilma's story was like a speaking embodiment of a tale which could have been told by women in present and past times and places, and which could have crossed borders of ethnic and psychocultural milieus of many territories of the world. It was local and worldly at the same time.

REFERENCE

Goffman, E. (1957). Characteristics of total institutions. In *Symposium on Preventive and Social Psychiatry* (pp. 43-93). Sponsored by the Walter Reed Army Institute of Research, the Walter Reed Army Medical Center, and the National Research Council. Washington, DC: Government Printing Office. (Revised version of Goffman, E. [1956]. Interpersonal persuasion. In B. Schaffenr [Ed.], Group processes [pp. 117-193]. New York: Josiah Macy Foundation.)

Understanding and Treating the Family in Argentina

Cecile Rausch Herscovici

SUMMARY. Over a period of more than 300 years, Argentinean family customs and ways of life were shaped by the influence of colonial rule. At the turn of the twentieth century the family was modified by European immigration. Subsequently, economic and political turmoil have produced changes with major consequences. Currently, the contradictions between the traditional and the modern can be seen at various levels. Because the family structure remains more or less patriarchal in nature, the changing position of women accounts for many crises. In this predominantly Catholic country, in which divorce became legal only in 1986, open expression of affect is highly valued and intrusion into the private life of family members is commonplace as well as parental overprotection. Leaving home is problematic for youths, with regressions and developmental lags often not acknowledged. These characteristics and how they impinge on therapy will be described in a clinical vignette. *[Article copies available for a fee from The Haworth Document Delivery Service: 1-800-HAWORTH. E-mail address: <docdelivery@haworthpress.com> Website: <http://www.HaworthPress.com> © 2004 by The Haworth Press, Inc. All rights reserved.]*

Cecile Rausch Herscovici is Co-Director of TESIS Center of Systems Therapies, and Full Professor, School of Psychology and Masters in Family Sciences, Universidad del Salvador, Buenos Aires, Argentina.

Address correspondence to: Cecile Rausch Herscovici, J. Salguero 2745, Piso 1 Of. 13, (1425) Buenos Aires, Argentina (E-mail: cecilerh@ciudad.com.ar).

This is an updated version of the paper presented at the Symposia: State of the Art of International Family Psychology: A Millennium Update, American Psychological Association 108th Annual Convention, Washington, DC, August 2000.

[Haworth co-indexing entry note]: "Understanding and Treating the Family in Argentina." Herscovici, Cecile Rausch. Co-published simultaneously in *Journal of Family Psychotherapy* (The Haworth Press, Inc.) Vol. 15, No. 1/2, 2004, pp. 161-171; and: *Family Therapy Around the World: A Festschrift for Florence W. Kaslow* (ed: William C. Nichols) The Haworth Press, Inc., 2004, pp. 161-171. Single or multiple copies of this article are available for a fee from The Haworth Document Delivery Service [1-800-HAWORTH, 9:00 a.m. - 5:00 p.m. (EST). E-mail address: docdelivery@haworthpress.com].

http://www.haworthpress.com/web/JFP
Digital Object Identifier: 10.1300/J085v15n01_12

KEYWORDS. Family therapy, Argentina, clinical example, domestic violence

DEDICATION

I dedicate this article to Florence Kaslow, PhD, who, by tenaciously furthering the boundaries of the family therapy field, has made it more comprehensive and innovative. Dr. Kaslow has had the merit of publishing extensively, thus enhancing a scholarly access to state of the art knowledge. This has been carried out with a sharing spirit, one which has permeated her interaction with colleagues from every corner of the world. As an itinerant lecturer, Dr. Kaslow has been a model of keen sensitivity and respect for cultural idiosyncrasies; this article is a tribute to that aspect she has joyously nurtured.

A BEWILDERING NATION

Argentina is a bewildering country; in only a few decades it has managed to be displaced from the First to the Third World. In 1920, with an apparently stable democratic government, this thriving and prosperous nation had a highly educated population which made it more akin to Australia, Canada, and the United States than to any Latin American country (Shumway, 1993, 2002). Nevertheless, in spite of this promising scenario, during the following decades Argentina became torn apart by irresponsible governments, political chaos, economic instability, social dissolution, and a debt which has precipitated recent default with foreign creditors, to mention merely the least of the country's predicaments. Only a decade earlier, Argentina attained world notoriety on account of its infamous dirty war, during which state terrorism headed by three successive military juntas waged a systematic persecution of political opponents who were abducted, tortured and murdered in concentration camps. Explanations for such a dramatic decline of Argentina have been contradictory and often incomplete. An interesting idiosyncratic factor is what Ernesto Sabato has called "a society of opponents," referring to its failure in construing an ideological frame that allows for unity. Thus, often Argentines seem to be more intent on opposing their fellow citizen than in developing a viable nation.

The Argentine territory is vast and underpopulated, dotted with human and natural resources a well as beauty. It extends from the tropical forests of the Iguazú Falls to the Andean glaciers in Patagonia. During the decade extending from 1920-1930 Argentina was the fifth wealthiest country in the world. According to the national statistics bureau report (INDEC, 2003), currently, of the country's 36 million inhabitants, there are 20 million (57.8%) urban poor people, and one more million in the rural sector. Of these, over nine million (27.5%) are indigents, without sufficient income to cover the basic basket of food (US$200) for a family of four members. In less than a year, there are 6.9 million new poor in Argentina; currently 45.7% households are poor and 19.5% households are indigent. The increase in poverty is due to income (frozen wages); unemployment (17.8% of unemployed and 19.9% of sub-employed); inflation (41%); the increase in pauperization of the middle classes; and a dramatic unequal distribution of wealth. Half of the country's workers earn less than 40% of what they need to stay above the poverty line. The government's unemployment subsidies and other social support programs have no effect on poverty and indigence levels because they were developed as anti-conflict strategies and do not reach the neediest people, who live outside the patronage networks of politics.

CHANGES AT THE SOCIETAL AND FAMILIAL LEVEL

Argentinean family customs and ways of life were shaped by the influence of the colonial rule during a period of more than 300 years. At the turn of the nineteenth century, European immigration modified the family characteristics. As a result of alternating democratic and authoritarian regimes accompanied by many periods of political unrest, the country's development has been irregular. Currently, contradictions between the traditional and the modern idiosyncrasies can be seen at different levels.

In the 1990s, the greatest increase in unemployment affected those with highest education. Businesses reduced their personnel, and job opportunities decreased at a time when people increased their years of education. The once prosperous Argentine middle class was impoverished first by hyperinflation and then by hyper-unemployment. As social disparities were deepened, socio-economic insecurity became the trademark of the Argentine population with overqualified people often occupying the very scarce working positions. Many of these have chosen to migrate, with the hope of finding better working and living conditions. The jobless youths have duplicated and there are more than a million youngsters who do not study, work, or seek a job. As is to be expected, this group is frequently involved in health risk behavior (drug abuse, delinquency, violence, and so on). During the past two years, alcohol consumption among teenage females has increased by 150%, and begins at the age of 12 and 13 instead of the previous 16 and 17 years of age.

Women

Two million (20%) single, divorced, or widowed women are in charge of their offspring or other relatives. Single-parent families have had the highest increase (60-80% among the middle and upper classes), 77% of which are headed by mothers. Fourteen percent of all children under the age of 15 live in homes headed by mothers, and in most cases, the father is absent (Wainerman & Geldstein, 1996). Of the 700,000 newborn each year, 100,000 (14%) are born to mothers under the age of 19, and for 3,000 of them, the mothers are under 15. Some 80% of the "child mothers" (girls aged 9-13) have had babies with males who are at least 10 years older, and 25% of the remaining with men who are at least 20 years their senior, suggesting the possibility of abuse, rape, or incest (CEDES, 2002). As is to be expected, teenage pregnancy and maternity are more frequent among the underprivileged.

As in other countries, in Argentina most working women earn 24% less than men, and this is because they often work in less qualified positions. In the last three decades women have accessed all levels of formal education, and tend to be more consistent in completion of their studies. The number of university students has increased fivefold, and women account for a good part of this boost. Moreover, women have taken up careers traditionally considered masculine. This translates into later marriages, fewer children, and a higher participation in the work force. Accordingly, in this rapidly changing society, more democratic arrangements for living together are discussed and decided by the couple, and the traditionally patriarchal organization is slowly being transformed. Women's access to their own economic resources has brought along a greater personal autonomy. While traditional roles for couples are slowly changing, the traditional values of the family continue to exert a great influence on the couple and their offspring. These changes often parallel those occurring in psychotherapy, law, and the welfare system.

The Family

The changes at the familial level that have evolved during the past 40 years (INDEC, 1994) include: (a) the number of members per household has decreased from 4.5 to 3.2, indicating that couples are choosing to remain childless; (b) the number of children born out of wedlock (39%) has increased by 30%; (c) households headed by women have increased by 23%; (d) in Buenos Aires, the average age of marriage for women has risen from 25 to 28; (e) 30% of the marriages fail, and 30% of all marriages are remarriages; (f) 13% of the adult population lives alone (a 28% increase in the past 10 years), indicating the novel tendency of life arrangements different from the family; (g) nuclear homes have increased and extended ones have decreased, and the nuclear family is the most frequent sort of co-residence (Wainerman & Geldstein, 1996).

In a country in which divorce was made legal in 1986, 33% of those aged between 20-34 years do not expect their marriage to last until the death of their partner. Additionally, 30% of all men and women believe that legal marriage is not necessary. Thus, marriage is less frequent and takes place at a later age. Separation usually occurs around the fifth year of marriage and is more frequent in the higher class. Most divorces filed in the city of Buenos Aires come from middle-class couples (Grossman, 1985). In other words, in recent decades more people are without a partner, and this is due more to separation and divorce than to the choice of remaining single. However, the family does not tend to disappear; people continue to choose to live together, even though the union is not legally sanctioned, and these changes are more prevalent among the upper classes. The marriage institution is increasingly unstable, particularly in Buenos Aires, the very cosmopolitan and heavily populated capital city.

As women have gained more control over their sexuality, an increasing number of couples are choosing to live together before marriage. In the past this was the pattern of the lower class; presently it is prevalent among the middle class and to a lesser extent among the upper class (Wainerman & Geldstein, 1996). The number of all middle-class men who endorse a woman's right to remain childless in order to pursue her personal goals has almost doubled in the past 20 years (8-14%). In 1984, one-third of men agreed that ideally men and women should share housework and childrearing responsibilities; 10 years later this figure rose to 87%.

The current family structure inherited from the colonial past is mainly patriarchal, even though there are social class differences. The *machismo* attitude refers to men's need of constant reaffirmation that they occupy a position of authority in the family. The economic crisis of the past decade has contributed to familial strife derived not only from financial hardship, but also from changes in status between members of the marital couple. In this context, often unemployed men spend many more hours at home, and their wives are the breadwinners. This accounts for many crises concerning the changing position of women, with men trying to compensate for insecurities and sometimes attempting to fortify their dominant position by adopting an authoritarian stance at home (Falicov, 1983).

Domestic violence has been researched in Argentina only during the past 10-20 years, and therefore statistics should be taken with caution because they only inform on reported cases. It is overwhelmingly women (96%) who report physical abuse, and they are mostly cases of minor injuries among spouses or concubines. The most severe cases come from the lower class, while 73% of minor injury reports come from middle-class women. Interestingly enough, the victims of domestic violence are mostly women who work outside the home (62%), and half of them earn the same or more than their spouse. The conflict seems to pertain to a standard matrix; when the female spouse does not comply with expectations pertaining to gender roles, exchanges may escalate to violence. Usually when the man strikes, rather than a demonstration of force, it is an admission of impotence, a sense of losing power. The feminine attitude that the man often finds challenging is her demand of a more egalitarian distribution of power. His violence is legitimized as a way of correcting such "deviations." Men, regardless of age, social class, or level of education, express repentance after the incident (Mesterman, 1988).

THE THERAPY FIELD

Argentina is and probably will continue to be known for its psychoanalytic influence not only in the psychotherapy field but in most dimensions of human realm. Initially, Argentine family therapists strived to differentiate their therapy from the predominant psychoanalytic model. In this latter theory, the importance of meanings is emphasized, and isomorphism with reality or logic is not required. In Freudian theory, communication informs about an underlying order, and it is assumed that individuals can be freed from pathology by achieving insight of the meaning of symbols. Contrarily, following Bateson (1976), systemic family therapists stress the interpersonal nature of meanings and their acquisition through social learning, rather than their universal or idiosyncratic characteristic. At the beginning, Argentine family therapists often translated this new way of conceptualizing human problems and behavior (Sluzki, 1978) by becoming unduly responsible for the outcome of the therapeutic process. Importance was placed on making things happen quickly and on overemphasizing the present and the future, often rendering a spectacular version of therapy. Later on, having become more established, family therapy progressed to a stage of calmer consolidation. This postmodern stance allows for conversation as well as expert competence, one in which therapists have acquired discrete skills to deal capably with the variety of systems that characterize the individual and family life. This process has enhanced the introduction of the systems approach into the various public and private health and mental health services.

In sum, family therapy has been operating in Argentina for the past 25 years in different contexts, helping families and individuals solve their problems. As an institution, family therapy has begun to influence the practice and outcome of various interventions at the medical, psychological, legal and social level. However, the family therapy movement continues to suffer from a partly conceptual and partly institutional isolation compared to other therapy models (Herscovici & Herscovici, 1999). Its wealth, taking into account cost effectiveness as well as its multidimensional perspective and possibility of intervention, has so far failed to translate into mainstream practice, where the psychoanalytic deficit model continues to prevail.

However, currently many family therapists interacting with family lawyers and judges help couples conclude a relatively harmonious divorce and negotiate a fair settlement. Joint custody and different forms of shared parental involvement following a divorce and based on the decisions of both parents are beginning to replace "archaic" arrangements (Kaslow, 1981; Kaslow, 1995).

Within the family, open expression of affect is highly valued, and boundary diffusion is a routine finding. Intrusion into the private life of family members is commonplace; hierarchies are overemphasized in the lower class, and often subverted among the affluent. When a youth is the presenting problem, often regressions and developmental lags are not acknowledged. The leaving home transition, a frequent issue encountered in family assessment, is often delayed and problematic. Moreover, youth employment is rather new and public loans for studies or housing are practically nonexistent for this age group. The scarcity of opportunities further contributes to parental overprotection and protracted autonomy (Herscovici & Herscovici, 1999). Prior to marriage the young adult usually remains in the parental home and is supported by the parents, thus extending adolescence. Furthermore, many middle- and upper middle-class families of young adults live a higher standard of living than they can afford on their own, mainly through the financial help of their parents. In the past, Argentine society took pride in its rather easy upward mobility. Changes in recent years have made this a disappearing characteristic; however, parents sometimes overextend themselves to keep up with their youngsters' trendy demands. It is not unusual in our culture that they help their offspring purchase a home and get established when they get married or graduate, thus taking undue responsibility for their welfare far beyond adolescence. The trade off is the parental expectation that they remain close and loyal.

THE KOVACS FAMILY

This is a Hungarian, middle-class family that was introduced by Veronica's elder brother, a 33-year-old lawyer, who insisted on the urgency of the matter, since both he and his father had just discovered that this 29-year-old woman had been suffering from anorexia nervosa for more than 14 years.

Veronica's case is a paradigmatic example of how personal development can be arrested by a dysfunctional family organization which became exaggerated by unfortunate circumstances. Both parents were born in Buenos Aires;

they were a second generation of immigrants. The father, an accountant, and mother, a pharmacist, each worked independently and were able to attain a comfortable lifestyle for the family. They were hardworking, honest, intellectual, and disciplined people; passionately family-centered; and rather rigid in their ideology as well as organization. The mother, who was diagnosed with an inoperable brain tumor when Veronica turned 18, consistently deteriorated during the following 11 years before her death. Subsequent to the diagnosis of the mother's illness, the life of this family took a dramatic turn. The father resigned from his profession in order to assist his "beautiful and very elegant" wife at her pharmacy so that she could continue working. His whole life revolved around making his loving wife as comfortable as possible.

Veronica went on to study pharmacy and had a very poor social life because there was an implicit expectation that she should care for her mother in her spare time. Loneliness and isolation led her to construct a private world for herself. Veronica began writing letters to prison inmates and received their responses at a secret post office box. She would pick up the mail daily and sit at a café to answer the letters. Her choice was based on the thought that prison inmates were probably as lonely as herself, and she wanted to comfort them and give them hope of redemption. Veronica became increasingly drawn in with her new relationships and went to visit some of these men at prison, in spite of the vexing security controls she had to undergo. This activity remained her undisclosed life for various years; during that period Veronica dropped out of school and worked in the family's pharmacy, for which she received no pay.

One day, while writing letters in a café, she met and became involved with a young man who forced her to have sex and subsequently became a steady boyfriend who wanted to marry her. Veronica was suspicious he was marrying her in order to benefit from her family's better economic situation. In her words, in order to secure a marriage, this man plotted to make her pregnant with a pierced condom. All by herself, she arranged to have an abortion performed, and turned down the marriage option. The father knew about the abortion, yet never discussed the matter with his daughter. Instead he decided she was to leave the country for a couple of weeks because he had hired some racketeers to "handle" the failed groom. Veronica silently obeyed and returned to her secluded life. From then on, her father controlled every moment of her day, especially of the time she spent away from home. He even had her followed by detectives during several months. Veronica decided to go back to school, and once again she excelled. Her free time was spent at home taking care of her ill mother. In her loneliness, she started chatting on the Internet and became involved with a man she eventually fell in love with and once again became pregnant. After the abortion, the father discovered his daughter's plight by breaking into her computer and reading her e-mails. It was in response to that incident that Veronica came forth crying for help, confessing that she had an eating disorder since her adolescence, was intermittently anorexic, and had been purging for the past five years. She was distraught at her father's failure to realize what she had been going through. Veronica painfully expressed that "from [her] father and brother she had only experienced control but not care."

COMMENTARY ON THE CASE

The comments regarding this case will deal mainly with cultural idiosyncrasies that have been described earlier, and with special emphasis on the transitional gender issues. In a traditional Argentine family, a female is not expected to live on her own until she marries. Veronica was still living in the parental home and was not financially independent, even though she had worked in the mother's pharmacy during extended periods. This sort of non-differentiation is not infrequent in this culture, especially when one is working in a family enterprise. In a relational context in which adolescence is indefinitely extended, overinvolvement is to be expected. In this family, intrusion into the private life of family members was deemed an acceptable way of exerting the parental role, regardless of the daughter's age. Veronica's activity regarding the prison inmates is an amazing metaphor of an attempt to establish a boundary in which a private life could develop, yet one in which extreme external control guaranteed a safe distance from men. Additionally, as is often the case in prototypical anorexia nervosa personalities, Veronica pursued the inmates' "redemption" with the tenacity devoted to a superior cause.

This enmeshed family apparently had a transitional configuration at its outset (both professional, working parents, who seemed to share an egalitarian arrangement). However, as in a traditional family, the mother was in charge of rearing the daughter and the father was more involved with the son. Family life unfolded quite uneventfully until the mother became terminally ill. This crisis precipitated a family reorganization in which the father became totally devoted to his wife's care and Veronica was captured by the system. The once transitional family organization regressed to a traditional structure. As a female in a traditional culture, she was to aid in the mother's care while her brother went off to study law. The mother's contemporary stance of support of Veronica's gradual leaving home process was increasingly neutralized by the father, who felt overresponsible for his daughter and feared the external world. In his words, "I had to be father and mother at the same time." Veronica, isolated, unprepared, and in some ways unauthorized to enter and deal with a heterosexual world, became a victim; her body and soul took the blows.

This case required a broad range of therapeutic input, which will not be discussed here. Yet, the main family intervention is noteworthy because it was especially instrumental in reversing this malignant process. It was possible to recruit the father into a benevolent interaction with his daughter, by empathizing with him with the following construction: "The father, alone and desperate in his parental role, feeling guilty about his failure to care for and raise a daughter, expressed his impotence with violent control, distance, and abusive behavior. In his mind, this was a legitimate way of protecting his daughter. All this tragedy had developed because Veronica, captured by caring for her ailing mother, had remained unprepared to deal with the world. If I succeeded in recruiting his trust and help, we could both guide and support Veronica's entry into a safer world."

This case illustrates a pathetic story of failure to deal with a family crisis which stunted the daughter's emancipation process, resulting in Veronica's incompetence to deal with life. The identified patient's anorexia nervosa was an additional manifestation of this impairment. This is an example of how cultural idiosyncrasies impose an additional level of respect and caution regarding the differences within the client system. Beyond that, the systems perspective to family therapy continues to be the preferred theoretical frame for conceptualizing and intervening.

REFERENCES

Bateson, G. (1976). Some components of socialization for trance. In T. Schwartz (Ed.), *Socialization as cultural communication* (pp. 51-63). Berkeley, CA: University of California Press.

CEDES (2002). *Centro de Estudios de Estado y Sociedad.* (Center for Studies of State and Society). Buenos Aires: CEDES.

Falicov, C. J. (Ed.). (1983). *Cultural perspectives in family therapy.* Rockville, MD: Aspen.

Grossman, C. P. (1985). *El proceso de divorcio. Derecho y realidad.* (The divorce process. The law and reality). Buenos Aires: Editorial Abaco.

Herscovici, P., & Herscovici, C. R. (1999) Family therapy in Argentina. In U. P. Gielen & A. L. Communian (Eds.), *International approaches to the family and family therapy* (pp. 117-138). Padova: Unipress.

INDEC (1994). *Instituto Nacional de Estadísticas y Censos* (National Institute of Statistics and Census). Buenos Aires: INDEC.

INDEC (2003). *Instituto Nacional de Estadísticas y Censos* (National Institute of Statistics and Census). Buenos Aires: INDEC.

Kaslow, F. W. (1981). Divorce and divorce therapy. In A. S. Gurman & D. P. Kniskern (Eds.), *Handbook of family therapy* (pp. 662-696). New York: Brunner/Mazel.

Kaslow, F. W. (1995). The dynamics of divorce therapy. In R. H. Mikersell, D. D. Lusterman, & S. H. McDaniel (Eds.), *Integrating family therapy: Handbook of family psychotherapy and systems theory* (pp. 271-283). Washington, DC: American Psychological Association.

Mesterman, S. (1988). Los contextos de la pareja violenta. (The contexts of the violent couple). *Sistemas Familiares, 4 (1)*, 47-57.

Shumway, N. (1993, 2002). *La invencion de la Argentina. Historia de una idea.* (The invention of Argentina). Buenos Aires: Emece.

Sluzki, C. (1978). Marital theory from a systems theory perspective. In T. S. Paulino & B. S. McCrady (Eds.), *Marriage and marital therapy: Psychoanalytic, behavioral and systems theory perspectives* (pp. 366-394). New York: Brunner/Mazel.

Wainerman, C. H., & Geldstein, R. N. (1996). Viviendo en familia: Ayer y hoy. (Living in the family: Yesterday and today). In C. Wainerman (Ed.), *Vivir en familia (Family life)* (pp. 83-230). Buenos Aires: UNICEF/Losada.

The Family Chess Board
and Projective Genogramming:
Two Tools for Exploring Family Systems

Sandra E. S. Neil

SUMMARY. The Family Chess Board is a vehicle for creating differentiation, integration, and change in families. It was formulated by Sandra Neil and Robert Silverberg as a way of adapting Virginia Satir's notion of sculpting families to environments where movement of family members is impractical or undesirable. Family members are symbolically represented in complex three-dimensional "chessboard and pieces" interactions. Family rules are explicated. Family bonds and triangulations, boundaries, affectional and power roles, gender issues, and occupational issues are identified and transformed. The relationship to Florence Kaslow's Projective Genogramming is discussed. *[Article copies available for a fee from The Haworth Document Delivery Service: 1-800-HAWORTH. E-mail address: <docdelivery@haworthpress.com> Website: <http://www. HaworthPress.com> © 2004 by The Haworth Press, Inc. All rights reserved.]*

KEYWORDS. Family therapy, projective genogramming, Family Chess Board, family reconstruction, Virginia Satir

---

Sandra E. S. Neil is World Area Chair, International Council of Psychologists; Australian Representative, International Academy of Family Psychology; and Clinical Psychologist and Family Therapist, Satir Centre, Australia for the Family, Suite 2, 1051 A/B High Street, Melbourne, Armadale VIC 3143, Australia (E-mail: icp@netspace. net.au).

[Haworth co-indexing entry note]: "The Family Chess Board and Projective Genogramming: Two Tools for Exploring Family Systems." Neil, Sandra E. S. Co-published simultaneously in *Journal of Family Psychotherapy* (The Haworth Press, Inc.) Vol. 15, No. 1/2, 2004, pp. 173-186; and: *Family Therapy Around the World: A Festschrift for Florence W. Kaslow* (ed: William C. Nichols) The Haworth Press, Inc., 2004, pp. 173-186. Single or multiple copies of this article are available for a fee from The Haworth Document Delivery Service [1-800-HAWORTH, 9:00 a.m. - 5:00 p.m. (EST). E-mail address: docdelivery@haworthpress. com].

Digital Object Identifier: 10.1300/J085v15n01_13

FOREWORD

Florence Kaslow's work with families, and her many books and genogramming methods are a major contribution to family therapy and world practice. In Australia, at universities in Adelaide, Melbourne, and Sydney, her practical understanding of the dynamics of families, blended families, and transgenerational patterns are used in teaching methods. In private family practice, her work is an invaluable source of knowledge and insight, and to my knowledge, it is taught in Melbourne at the Alma Family Therapy Center and at the Satir Centre of Australia for the Family. Her contribution to practice and therapeutics has been useful for clinicians, students, teachers and others.

INTRODUCTION

In 2000, Florence Kaslow came to the Satir Centre of Australia in Melbourne to conduct a workshop on her technique, Projective Genogramming. We had known each other for years, as family psychologists with a strong humanistic appreciation of the possibility that people could learn, within their families, to be more fully human. In comparing notes, Florence Kaslow and I were surprised to discover that without knowing it, we had independently developed parallel methods to accomplish a similar thing. Projective Genogramming makes use of a genogram that is prepared without the usual specific instructions issued by a therapist when a genogram is prepared as part of an assessment. What results of course is a family map that brings forth the unconscious or repressed patterns, which can then be dealt with within the therapeutic process (Kaslow, 1995).

For years, we at the Satir Centre of Australia for the Family have used the Family Map in a comparable way, based on Virginia Satir's methods of elucidating family influences to facilitate movement of a family toward a more open system. By being alert to the ways in which the family reacts to stressors, a therapist can plan more effective interventions.

The Organic Growth Model of Virginal Satir (also called the Seed Model) emphasises the importance of process and feelings over cognition and content. There are several key theoretical concepts that are important in the Satir Model (Satir et al., 1991). Peace in the family starts with creating harmony within the self. Virginia Satir (1916-1988) was a major pioneer in family therapy. For nearly 50 years she helped people toward becoming more fully human. She believed in the healing of the human spirit through learning to make contact with others and ourselves in a meaningful way. She was a renowned author, lecturer, and teacher who trained many generations of therapists. Satir developed the therapeutic use of sculpturing, survival stances, metaphors, integration of parts, congruence in communication, and family reconstruction. She was warm and intuitive in her understanding of people. Her goal was to develop a conscious-ness toward peace inside and outside of ourselves, individual health, and social and personal responsibility. Her methods combined concepts of communication theory with humanistic notions of self-esteem, and a dynamic understanding of how increasing awareness of patterns learned in the family of origin can lead to change. The Satir approach is experiential involving families in exercises and activities during the sessions.

I have been personally involved with this process along with her, and have been working with and teaching methods based on the Satir Model throughout my career. I believe that the effectiveness is due to the combined use of tradi-tional individual psychoanalytically oriented therapy models and Satir's psycho-dynamically informed family therapy approach. In addition, her model stimu-lates an innate universal healthy growth process. It taps into the resilience of the person automatically, and it supports the implementation of familiar and com-fortable methods for a wide variety of therapists and clients. It is especially prac-tical for private practice where practitioners have the need to treat both individuals and families. Satir's approach is very adaptable and welcomes addi-tive methods that build on the basic pragmatic processes she pioneered. I strongly believe that Virginia Satir would have warmly welcomed the unique contributions of Florence Kaslow to the field of family psychology, as addi-tional ways of working with the idiom of emotions within the context of family therapy.

At the Satir Centre of Australia for the Family, we have long used the Satir tools of sculpting family patterns, along with family maps, to discover patterns of belief, rules, and values, as well as the wheel of influence and life chronology. These provide both assessment and therapeutic interventions. They are part of the larger family reconstruction process. But occasionally there are situations where the experiential movement of persons traditionally used in these methods proves impractical.

THE FAMILY CHESS BOARD

The Family Chess Board© method was devised by Sandra Neil and Robert Silverberg (1995) to adapt Virginia Satir's notion of sculpting families to a more limited environment, where movement of family members is impractical or un-desirable. This derivative family sculpture allows us to represent members of the family by chess pieces and to position the family members in two dimensions to indicate intimacy. In a second task, it allows us to indicate the optative, objec-tive, and the subjective positions between family members. All relations and posi-tions are recorded, including parents, siblings, step-siblings, and nonresidential members of the family. It is another vehicle for creating differentiation, integra-tion, and awareness for and of change in the family. It allows one or all members of the family to be symbolically represented in a less threatening, but equally rich and complex three-dimensional "chessboard and pieces" interaction. The language that a person uses is their own, and the chess pieces are labeled and named explicitly to fit with the perceptions of that person, and make the rules of the family explicit. Family bonds and triangulations, the boundaries of each family, the affectional and power roles, gender issues, and occupational issues are identified and often can be transformed using this brief, intensive, and process-oriented method.

Each person participating in The Family Chess Board needs a standard chessboard, chess pieces, and his or her own creative senses. No prior knowledge of chess is necessary, and, in fact, the game of chess is irrelevant to the process. The materials needed are a 64-square chessboard. Usually only chess pieces are used, although it is possible to use draughts, checkers, wooden beads, or other assorted items that are around in the room.

INSTRUCTIONS

Instructions are given to each member of the family. "In front of you (pointing to the chessboard and chess pieces), we have different figures which can stand for people in your family. One of them might be for your father, one your mother, and there are figures that could be for children, grandparents, and other people, animals, or things that you consider to be important in your family. We want you to put each of the pieces on the board to show how close or distant you feel to each one, and how close or distant they feel to one another. You can use the pieces in any way you wish to, using any of the spaces on the board. There is no right or wrong way to do this, just try to show how you see your family and what is important to you." Then the task begins, and each person records and explicates the most important pieces for him or her.

THERAPEUTIC QUESTIONS

Therapeutic questions that later arise include: "Tell me why you placed these people where you did; I want you to show me how you would like to change your family. Explain what it would look like if you did make changes. Would you like to tell me what you are thinking? Why did you move this person?" To us, these are reminiscent of the four-step questioning used in Florence Kaslow's *Projective Genogramming* (1995): "With whom did you begin?," "Why, whom did you omit or exclude?," "Whom would you like to eliminate?," and "Whom would you like to add?"

USES

The Family Chess Board has multiple uses. Remember that many of the symptoms in a family arise because of the interrelationship between the members. For example, if Peggy cries in the family, that might mean the dog runs away, and Dad yells at the dog, and Kathy hugs Paul, and Paul hides his head, and Mum yells at Dad, and Peggy cries again, and so on.

This method is suitable for use with individuals, couples, families, and organisations. It can be used alone with each member of a couple or family to discern their own family identifications, patterns of closeness and distance, affiliations, missing figures and objects, and desired future choices. The method can be used to look at turning points and times of change, which are inevitable, and is most important in understanding the development of the family's status quo. It has been pointed out by Minuchin and Fishman (1981), and other family therapists, that times of change are often the ones that are most important to be negotiated. Often, turning points are seen differently by different members of the family. We look to unblocking resistance to change. The Family Chess Board helps show each member reasons why the patterns of constructive or destructive behaviours occur.

The method lends itself to helping to eradicate the influence of the past on the future. As Satir said, "The past need not contaminate the present."

It is intended that in group and family therapy, the method focus on the inclusion/exclusion patterns between mother, father and child. For example, in the primary triad there may be an unwillingness by members to examine their assumptions about dependency, autonomy, and authority. The defences commonly used are projection, splitting, and withdrawal. Other patterns include an unwillingness to examine the assumptions about reciprocal influence, power, and control. Commonly, the defences involve projective identification and scapegoating.

The Family Chess Board is a method of following the development of adult children and generational equality and inequality. The method helps also in preparing grown children to feel equal with parents. It is a process in which family members can be of equal status and have an equal say in the functioning and processes of the family. It also promotes a means of communication wherein each member of the family can show their personal view regardless of age, language ability, and seniority. It is also a way of re-visiting, or "going home" at various developmental ages, without actually doing so.

Another way of using the method is to look at the needs of individuals in the family. After the determination of various fixations, times, and turning point times in the family history, one can look further to discover the unmet needs of each member. Critical decision points are highlighted and emphasised in the exploration using The Family Chess Board, and discussion of what happened and what might have happened occurs. For example, when a mother dies, the effects upon the surviving person are traced through their lifetime, and the effects of that wounding can be seen from the viewpoint of each of the siblings.

One can also use the method to look at the self of an individual. Althea Horner (1989) referred to one way of looking at motivation by conceptualising three parts: identity ("I am"); mastery ("I can"); and intentionality ("I will"). These can be observed and followed through at each of the individual's life turning points.

Further, the rules for the family can be explicated. Types of families are quickly diagnosed–enmeshed, distant, confluent, democratic. The rules of families proposed by Dr. Frederick Ford (1994) as "One for all and all for one," "Two of us against the world," "Until death do us part," and "For one to be happy, all to be happy" are often plainly illustrated by The Family Chess Board.

THE METHOD

The Family Chess Board has been adapted from clinical observations, improvisations, and therapeutic strategies. In order to accomplish the goals, a basic methodology has been found that seems to work. A therapist and family meet together. The therapist tells the family that they are about to use a technique which should be fun as well as serious, thereby introducing a useful therapeutic and diagnostic paradox.

MATERIALS

Any 64-square alternating-colour chessboard can be used, as well as any set of chess pieces. Chess sets that are culturally specific are useful in other cultures. For example, we found that using a water buffalo (as a Knight) from a Filipino chess set was useful in helping a European woman who had been seriously abused. She identified with the forced labour of the water buffalo. It might also be possible to use draught markers or checkers as representational objects, but we have found that chess pieces suit the purpose best.

GENERAL INSTRUCTIONS

As previously outlined in the Introduction, the family is instructed together. Generally, each family member produces his or her own version of The Family Chess Board. The person is told that sitting in front of them is a chessboard and chess pieces, which are designed to stand for people and objects in the family. One is meant to be father, one is meant to be mother, and there are figures for children, grandparents, and others who are important in the family. The person then selects chess pieces that represent important figures in their life, family, or self.

Other important figures, such as pets, special toys, friends, lovers, "ghosts from the past," or imaginary playmates and so on are similarly selected. Parts of the self, or "sub-selves" can be identified as well. Once this is done, the person is asked to put each of these "people" on the chessboard and is instructed to "show how close or distant you feel to each one, and how close or distant they feel to each other. You can use the pieces in any way you wish to, using any of the spaces on the board. There is no right or wrong way to do this, just try to show how you see your family and what is important to you."

The family member then generally selects and reselects the pieces to fit with his or her own internal image, and then places the pieces on the board. We have noticed that people represent emotional distance and closeness by distance and closeness between the pieces on the chessboard. While people portray distance differently on the chessboard, they usually are consistent throughout the exercise. Some people use the squares as units, others divide the squares. We have also noticed that people choose different pieces for different reasons. One would understand how a "King" could be "Dad," and a "Queen" could be "Mum," but often people select pieces for reasons that are quite idiosyncratic and do not adhere to stereotypic beliefs. For example, one business executive noted that whenever a black Queen appeared in her chessboards, that black Queen represented an overpowering figure in her life. At the first appearance, the black Queen was her dominant mother. At the next appearance, it was a female colleague who was competing for a position at the university. In a later board it was a male employer who was making her current job difficult, and in the final board the black Queen represented her future father-in-law, who did not accept her.

Once the layout is placed on the chessboard, the symbolic meanings can be elicited. It is useful to inquire why the person chose a particular piece. Colour, size and shape of the particular piece chosen take on symbolic idiosyncratic meanings.

The therapist might ask any question that makes the covert functioning of the family overt. For example, each family member could be asked, "Tell me why you placed these figures where you did on the board? Let's begin with the piece that represents you." The positions of all figures on the chessboard can be recorded on a standard form for inclusion in the clinical record.

The family member can then be directed, "This time I want you to show me how you would like your family to be, if things were as you would like them to be (ideally). If you would be able to make any changes that you want in your family, what would the family look like? Show me, putting the pieces on the board in the same way. You can move any of the pieces or leave them where they are." Once again, the positions of all the figures are recorded. The therapist then asks, "When you move the figures, you change them. Would you like to tell me what you were thinking or feeling? For example, why did you move this person (pointing to one of the figures)?"

The family sculpture, as symbolically represented by chess pieces, allows us to designate individual members of the family at a particular time in their life. The therapist will often ask family members to indicate the structure of the family as it is now, as it was at a particular turning point earlier in their life, and as they would like it to be in the future. The family members are often designated by specific pieces that remain constant throughout the exercise, although the pieces sometimes change if the symbolic representation of the person changes in the participant's experience. This often occurs with changes in time or developmental state. Intimacy is also depicted by the positioning of the pieces on the chessboard.

Typical family patterns on the chessboard will become obvious to the therapist, like reading a map. Often, simultaneously they will become obvious to the family observing it. At these points, some interpretation of the previously hidden patterns can be elicited from the family itself. Any missing pieces, such as a stepparent or an undesired relative, "the black sheep," can be pointed out to the family to see if the omission were intentional.

Using the combination mentioned above, the covert family rules for interaction can be made overt, tangible and visible. It allows families to see that rules, which once were comfortable coping mechanisms that have out lived their usefulness, now represent a well-worn pathway from which family members do not seem to be able to escape, even though things have changed.

A family can utilise the new insights to reposition pieces on the board to indicate desired changes in the family structure. Other family members, such as parents watching their children do this, will usually gain startling insights as to the real feelings of the children. Outmoded family patterns can be changed from old habits to new ways of seeing, doing and being.

THE CHESS DIRECTORY

The following are some of the major concepts, symbolic moves, and features that are observed during the course of a Family Chess Board session.

Distance

Virginia Satir (1967, 1975, 1987a; Satir & Baldwin, 1983) had a great deal to say about the importance of interpersonal space, boundaries and social distance, and closeness. She originated the concept of a "second skin" which extends about 45 centimeters out from the body of each person, and represents a distance within which two people can comfortably connect. Satir believed that in meeting another person, the most comfortable distance is approximately 90 centimeters, the distance of a handshake. If anger is present, the physical distance might be at the close range of a handshake of two people, but the felt emotional distance is generally far away at the farthest corner of a room. In depression, the emotional and physical distance is that one is in the shadow of the other person, too close for comfort. If intimacy is to occur, an invitation to move into the space of another must be present. Otherwise, it will be perceived as an invasion or abuse.

This concept of the second skin also relates to distance and closeness on The Family Chess Board. When the person is instructed to place pieces on the board wherever they wish, an important process to observe is how near and how far the pieces are placed. This gives information relative to the enmeshment, detachment, and social space that the person experiences. The chess pieces externalise and represent the internal phenomenal world of the family.

Family Patterns

Many of the family patterns become evident in The Family Chess Board. Patterns of enmeshment or disengagement, boundaries, alignments, and power can be externalised and transformed. The ability of family members to experience intimacy is also demonstrated in The Family Chess Board. The concept of "intimacy" we use has been defined by Satir as follows: ". . . It is simply the freedom to respect spaces between people: to go in when there is an invitation and not to invade when there isn't one. That is real intimacy . . ." (Satir, in Baldwin, 1987b). What also becomes evident is that as family patterns change over the course of therapy, the patterns on the chessboards also change accordingly. For example, an over-enmeshed family who fought constantly will produce a chessboard one year later that shows much more equality.

Patterns are also represented by one individual appearing in many "families" described over time. For example, one man, three times divorced, was able to explicate the patterns of his interactions with families and partners in a single two-hour session. The speed at which people externalise these patterns is remarkable. Some typical family patterns are presented at the end of this chapter.

Choice of Piece

The instructions to participants in The Family Chess Board are to choose pieces, assigning their own value and meaning to each of the pieces. Regardless of their meaning in the game of chess, this instruction reassures people who have never played chess, while those with a knowledge of the game of chess will often accept this paradoxical suggestion and use the symbolic meanings they are accustomed to. To some people, the size and structure of the piece is extremely important, and to others less important. Those who idealise their connections to others often use only Pawns to denote hoped-for equality of value. Often in families, the children will pick this up as an "ideal," and begin a discussion of the overidealisation in the family. The children have an opportunity to present their reality-based view. The choice of piece can represent both animate and inanimate objects. For example, quite spontaneously, business executives will build a "tower" of two chess pieces stacked one atop the other to represent "work." Sometimes people will look for and find other items in the room to use instead of just the chess pieces. Explanation of the meaning of their choice results in further insights.

Colour, Shape, and Size

Many of the participants specifically use the colour of the piece to represent some significant quality. Colour can connote closeness or distance (all those people who are close are all white or black), or gender, using black and white. Some simply ignore the second colour, using only pieces of a single colour. These choices always have symbolic significance to that person and are worth investigating. The other aspect of colour choice is sameness and difference. A person may say that those who are one colour are "similar to me," and those who are the other colour are "different to me."

Symbolic Meaning

This is one of the most interesting aspects of The Family Chess Board, since concrete and abstract thinking became evident on this dimension. Abstract thinking is connoted by the naming of the pieces. Some people think in highly symbolic ways, so that pieces can be chosen to represent abstract concepts such as their "meaning in life," "important books in my life," or "the parts of myself." These people are extremely abstract in their description of their board.

People who are more concrete in their thinking will have less understanding of these abstract connections between pieces and/or the possibility of utilising the pieces as anything other than representation of human figures. Using the chess pieces, little children are often very able to unfold the ways they symbolise their phenomenal and emotional worlds in far more direct ways than their parents. For example, a young child displayed her fears of death in a family chessboard session with her parents. She placed pieces representing four generations of ancestors she had detected in frequent visits to the cemetery with her aunt, who suffered from pathological mourning. The parents had not even realised the cemetery visits were occurring. Since this method is not language dependent, it can be used with very young children and in multicultural families.

Missing Pieces

This occurrence, the missing piece, is one of the most significant, and is critical to observe. Often people have difficulty in deciding which pieces to use on the board, which to leave unused, which should be counted in, and which should be counted out. For example, one man in a couples group had trouble in deciding whether to leave a piece, representing a good friend, on or off. After changing it six times, the therapist asked, "Well, is it on or is it off?" The man looked puzzled and said that he was not sure. Later it was found that this particular friend had, unbeknownst to him, just died in a car crash in another state. Jung termed this type of occurrence "synchronicity" (Jung, 1960, 1973).

Often, at a subsequent session, persons will say they have left an important piece off their chessboard. This type of "forgetting" can be an early indication of shame, humiliation, or an attempt to maintain dignity. Missing pieces may signify the lapse, or lack, of connection with significant others. For example, in a historically authoritarian-patriarchal family, if the father is no longer present in the family, the chessboard may be constructed with no piece to represent the father at all.

Rules from Childhood

There are many rules from childhood that continue to be followed in adult life long after their original usefulness has gone. Ford (1994) has written that these family rule systems can be classified based on the rules used. These rules are often explicated on The Family Chess Board, and the patterns observed often can be seen to match Ford's groupings, which are summarised here:

- *Two Against the World* is the system that is frequently exhibited by couples with disparate backgrounds, such as different skin colour, social, cultural, or ethnic origin, and/or markedly different ages. Children introduced into this system will not be excluded if they are essentially similar to the parents and are subservient to the rules. Children who are able to differentiate somewhat will become symptomatic or be treated as unwelcome guests rather than family members.
- *Children Come First* is defined as a family of children; although there are larger and smaller people, there are no leaders. The therapist can recognise this system when the number of children is greater than the number of adults and the family appears as a noisy cohesive unit in which much is happening but nothing is changing.

- *Share and Share Alike* is a pseudo-affective relationship in which an ambiguous type of sharing occurs. The system manifests itself in addiction, deceit, and/or deviance. The therapist can recognise this system instantly if it contains an addict or deviant. As the therapist is susceptible, recognition may occur much later if the manifestation is deceit. Families in this system talk about serious matters, are decorous and often appear successful. Paradoxically, there is an aura of superficiality and emotional poverty.
- Members of families caught in the *Every Man for Himself* system do not respect psychological space. Everything is deep, passionate, and packed with meaning, and the system may be recognised by the aura of menace. The consequent product is a variety of seemingly unrelated conditions, such as battered children, burglars, and petty thieves. It also spawns radicals, revolutionaries, and runaways. Children in this system may wish to grow up as quickly as possible and move away, but this is generally impossible. They either cannot leave or they leave and cannot stay away. The dependency relationships are unresolved.
- The family system called *Until Death Do Us Part* is a hostile dependent relationship in which there is an extreme closeness; the closeness is marked by sympathetic interaction that induces guilt rather than empathic interaction that communicates love. Although outwardly successful, the family inwardly experiences pessimism and doom. It must be suspected if there has been suicide or murder in proximate generations and when any family member has symptoms or disease that may lead to premature death.

These patterns are explicated on The Family Chess Board as people trace the developmental pattern of their relationships.

Group Processes

The applications of The Family Chess Board includes not only individuals, couples, and families, but other group settings as well. One example is a couples groups, which are multiple couples in conjoint couple therapy. Five couples meet in one room with the therapist(s), each couple privately arranging their chessboard and later discussing it with the other couples. The process during group therapy is illuminating to all, and often helps those members of the group who are more reticent or shy to feel their own presence within the group.

It is also is a method that can be used within family therapy, or with an individual, to follow the developmental life history and significant turning points. In organisations, the existing hierarchical structure is graphically demonstrated, with alliances, rivalries, and cohesions and conflicts becoming externalised.

Areas for improvement in the organisational system can be proposed, with distinctions between role and identity made clear.

Using the Moment (The Point in Time at Which a Change Occurs)

The moment of change during a chessboard session has to be recognised by the therapist, often to elucidate some unconscious or conscious difficulty. For example, if the pieces are used such that the King, a traditionally male piece, is used to represent the female, and the male is represented by the Queen, the therapist may intercede at that moment. Utilising other Satir methods such as drama, sculpting, a Parts Party, or the communication stances (placating, blaming, super reasonable, irrelevance, and congruence), the hidden can be made obvious at that moment in the therapy session.

The most important thing is to ask the person to unravel the meaning of their particular chessboard and to clarify their own personal symbolic understanding at that moment. The therapist needs to be extremely attentive, intervening, and interpreting rarely, permitting the person to work out personal meanings as much as possible at the moments at which change occurs.

Persistence of Old Patterns

The old patterns from childhood, learned from parents and other members of the family, often keep recurring at various points during The Family Chess Board session. The persistence of those patterns can be extremely elucidating. For example, a man who had been married several times showed the importance of romantic associations by constructing the male as a white Castle and the female as a white Queen. All other nonpassionate relationships, as he defined them, were constructed as two Bishops, male being the black Bishops and female being the white Bishops. He had no insight into recurrent patterns until he observed a repetitive pattern on serial chessboards representing four successive periods during his life. Each time a new female appeared in his life, who was later to become his new wife, he saw that there was a moment when the nonpassionate relationship turned into a passionate one by looking at the moment at which the white Queen reappeared, replacing a white Bishop.

Another example of the persistence of old patterns is a young adopted child who was able to say that his mother was often angry at his father, by using the chess pieces. The mother became outraged in the family session because the child had called attention to her role in maintaining the usual patterns and difficulties in the family. This in itself was a repeating occurrence and had to be transformed with the mother in the next family session.

Another example is the persistence of a "ghost." On her chessboard, a middle-aged woman depicted the sudden death of a boyfriend at age 16. The ghostly memory of the death continued to contaminate subsequent relationships and had never previously been adequately mourned or resolved.

CONCLUSION

It has been my experience that a humanistic, systems-oriented, experiential approach to families not only promotes the natural continued growth in a family, but also promotes resilience by allowing a family to update its own worldview, moving from the pessimistic toward the optimistic, the negative to the positive, from competition and fear toward cooperation and love. In comparing notes with Florence Kaslow concerning our two methods, it became apparent that therapists all over the world were still searching for methods of fostering congruence, promoting equality of personal value, and striving for better relationships in their families and the world.

REFERENCES

Ford, F. R., Doyle, M. M., & Skelton, J. (1994). *Morsense, theory and interpretation of mapping of rules* (MOR). c/o 13 Marchant Court, Kensington, CA.

Horner, A. (1989). *The wish for power and the fear of having it.* New York: Jason Aronson.

Jung, C. G. (1960 & 1973). *Synchronicity: A causal connecting principle.* Princeton, NJ: Princeton University Press.

Kaslow, F. W. (1995). *Projective genogramming.* Sarasota, FL: Professional Resource Press.

Minuchin, S., & Fishman, H. C. (1981). *Family therapy techniques.* Cambridge, MA: Harvard University Press.

Neil, S. E., & Silverberg, R. L. N. (1995). *The family chessboard: Sound moves for a sounder family.* Melbourne: Satir Centre of Australia.

Satir, V. (1967). *Conjoint family therapy: A guide to theory and technique.* Palo Alto: Science & Behavior Books.

Satir, V. (1975). When I meet a person. In R. S. Spitzer (Ed.), *Tidings of comfort and joy.* Palo Alto: Science & Behavior Books.

Satir, V. (1987a). Going behind the obvious: The psychotherapeutic journey. In J. K. Zeig (Ed.), *The evolution of psychotherapy* (pp. 58-72). New York: Brunner/Mazel.

Satir, V. (1987b). The therapist story. In M. Baldwin (Ed.), *The use of self in therapy* (pp. 17-27). Binghamton, NY: The Haworth Press, Inc.

Satir, V., & Baldwin, M. (1983). *Satir step-by-step: A guide to creating change in families.* Palo Alto: Science & Behavior Books.

Satir, V., Banmen, J., Gerber, J., & Gomori, M. (1991). *The Satir model: Family therapy and beyond.* Palo Alto, CA: Science & Behavior Books.

Childhood Background of Homelessness in a Chilean Urban Center

Arturo Roizblatt
Javier Cerda
Carolina Conejero
Marcela Flores
Christian Fau
Felipe González
Gustavo Quijada
Alberto Botto
Carolina Muñiz

SUMMARY. A random sample of homeless individuals (106 men and 106 women) residing in a shelter were interviewed using an interview schedule developed for this study. The main objectives were to study the sociodemographic characteristics and childhood history in an urban homeless population in a developing country (Santiago, Chile). The most salient finding is the high frequency of parent-child separation and placement with substitute parents during the early lives of the homeless

---

Arturo Roizblatt, Javier Cerda, Carolina Conejero, Marcela Flores, Christian Fau, Felipe González, Gustavo Quijada, Alberto Botto, and Carolina Muñiz are affiliated with the Department of Psychiatry, Faculty of Medicine, Campus Oriente, Universidad de Chile, Santiago, Chile.

Address correspondence to: Arturo Roizblatt, Malaga 950, Suite 52, Las Condes, Santiago, Chile (E-mail: ardasa@vtr.net).

[Haworth co-indexing entry note]: "Childhood Background of Homelessness in a Chilean Urban Center." Roizblatt, Arturo et al. Co-published simultaneously in *Journal of Family Psychotherapy* (The Haworth Press, Inc.) Vol. 15, No. 1/2, 2004, pp. 187-196; and: *Family Therapy Around the World: A Festschrift for Florence W. Kaslow* (ed: William C. Nichols) The Haworth Press, Inc., 2004, pp. 187-196. Single or multiple copies of this article are available for a fee from The Haworth Document Delivery Service [1-800-HAWORTH, 9:00 a.m. - 5:00 p.m. (EST). E-mail address: docdelivery@haworthpress.com].

we interviewed, 16% of men and 26.4% of women. A significant propor-
tion of the study participants reported incarceration before age 17,
13.2% of men and 9.4% of women. Seventeen point nine percent of men
and 20.8% of the women never knew their father; 7.5% of men and 5.7%
of the women never knew their mother. The childhood backgrounds of
the homeless in Santiago, Chile, are, in some aspects, similar to those described by researchers in the United States. *[Article copies available for a
fee from The Haworth Document Delivery Service: 1-800-HAWORTH. E-mail
address: <docdelivery@haworthpress.com> Website: <http://www.HaworthPress.
com> © 2004 by The Haworth Press, Inc. All rights reserved.]*

KEYWORDS. Homeless, childhood background, Chile, mental illness,
deinstitutionalization

FOREWORD

When I received an invitation to participate in Florence Kaslow's Festschrift, immediately I made an association with gratefulness. I met her first
through reading some of the papers she wrote, especially in relation to divorce
issues. I am referring to the late 1980s, when in Chile it was very difficult to
talk about this topic without being immediately labeled as a "prodivorcist." In
a trip to Florida, USA, I called her asking for an appointment because of my interest in sharing some thoughts on this topic. Then came my first surprise as I
started immediately receiving her generosity: The same morning that I contacted her, I shared with her an hour of therapy with a client, afterwards participated in a lunch with her staff at the Florida Couples and Family Institute, and
had the opportunity of talking about the reality of family therapy in Chile and
also the facts–that in Chile there was no divorce law, a situation which lasted
until 2004, when the Chilean parliament approved that law. In 1986 she accepted an invitation to do a workshop on divorce mediation in Santiago de
Chile, under the auspices of the Psychiatry Department of the Universidad de
Chile. This was a success, being the first workshop in the country with that
content. After that, Dr. Kaslow has visited Chile twice, winning a space in the
history of divorce issues in a country where this topic is so sensitive.

In every visit she left a feeling that in a very humble way she shared her experience and knowledge, being at the same time very respectful of the cultural
identity of the attendants to the workshops, not invading and always considering adequate timing, which is so important when receiving new knowledge
"imported" from a different culture, especially in topics so deeply linked to
values. Each time I meet Dr. Kaslow in any part of the world is an opportunity

to share with her a friendship that goes beyond a professional relationship. It is also relevant to mention that in this relation an important role is played by her husband, Sol, a loyal companion to whom she has been married for a lifetime.

Dr, Kaslow's accomplishments are numerous and in many domains: education, research, publications, and above all, in creating an international network of family therapists, which more than a group of professionals, can be defined as an "international family." Thanks to Florence Kaslow, I am very happy to belong to this family. Then, my second personal thought in relation to Dr. Kaslow is associating her name to the International Family Therapy Association, to which she has put so much energy, before, during and after her presidency. She surveyed the small organization and built a larger one, and I feel that her diplomatic and integrative efforts have helped a lot to keep the organization steady in difficult times.

A good picture that may summarize Florence Kaslow's work is the book, *Through Thick and Thin*, which she co-edited and is the result of gathering the research done in more than eight countries. This work shows very well her creativity, love, energy, sharing, transcultural gathering, and intellect that is put together in that product. This, I think, is what she has done permanently through her life, a gift to the human being in his or her relation through family connectedness.

Because of all the above-mentioned characteristics, it is an honor for me to send to this Festschrift this research, as it shows the relevant fact of linking family history and such a sad condition as being homeless, especially thinking of the importance that prevention may have in mental health and the role that the family may play in it.

–Arturo Roizblatt

INTRODUCTION

There are many published reports describing the social and psychiatric problems that the homeless population faces in the developed countries. (Sumerlin & Bundrick, 1997; Reilly, 1994; Breakey et al., 1989; Cohen & Thompson, 1992; DeMallie, North, & Smith, 1997; Holland, 1996; North, 1996; Abdul-Hamid, Wykes, & Stansfeld, 1993). In contrast, there is little information regarding the homeless population in developing countries. This report describes a pilot study of the homeless population in Santiago, the capital and the largest city in Chile, focusing on potential childhood antecedents of homelessness.

Health problems and chronic mental and neurologic disorders have been described in this population (Muñoz et al., 1998; Usatiene et al., 1994; Eddins, 1993). Contributing factors include exposure to adverse environments and to traumatic events, overcrowded institutions, substandard nutrition and hygiene, alcoholism, drug abuse, and mental health problems. American studies have suggested that homelessness among psychiatric patients may be due to a functional incapacity and to a poor implementation of the deinstitutionalization process. Specifically, drug abuse and psychiatric disorders are frequently associated with homelessness (Breakey et al., 1989). It has been suggested that the homeless population includes many that are disorganized, with poor problem-solving skills, and unable to maintain a stable residence (Lamb & Lamb, 1990). Compared to a non-homeless population, the homeless are 38 times more likely to have a diagnosis of schizophrenia, five times more likely to have a major depression diagnosis, and three times more likely to suffer from alcoholism (Robbins & Regier, 1991). Studies have shown high rates of self-reported depression and poor health in this group, related to social health problems, including teen pregnancy, child abuse and neglect, and HIV/AIDS and substance abuse epidemics (Burnette, 1999).

We studied the sociodemographic characteristics, childhood history and use of psychiatric services in a sample of homeless individuals in Santiago, Chile.

METHOD

Homeless participants for this study were drawn from a home run by a charitable organization known as "Hogar de Cristo" in Santiago, Chile. A random sample of 106 men and 106 women participated in the study. Demographic and historical information was collected by trained interviewers using an adaptation of the protocol used by Susser, Struening, and Conover (1987) in their study of childhood experiences of homeless men. Exclusion criteria included an active psychotic process and clinically significant cognitive impairment. Data are presented descriptively.

RESULTS

Demographic Information

As shown in Table 1, most men in the sample were 35 or older. In contrast, more than half of the women were under age 35. More than half of the women (58.4%) and 43.3% of the men in the sample were single at the time of the interview. Approximately 23% were married.

Almost two-thirds of the participants (62.7%) reported that their parents were married, and 9% were separated at the time the participants were interviewed (Table 2).

TABLE 1. Demographic Characteristics of Homeless Individuals in the Study Sample (n = 212)

	Men		Women	
Marital status	n	%	n	%
Single	48	45.3	62	58.4
Married	33	31.1	16	15.1
Living with a couple	1	0.9	3	2.8
Separated	15	14.2	17	16.0
Widowed	9	8.5	8	7.6
Age (years)	n	%	n	%
≤ 20	3	2.8	17	16.0
21-25	2	1.9	19	18.0
26-30	5	4.7	16	15.1
31-35	6	5.7	11	10.4
36-40	11	10.4	5	4.7
41-45	15	14.2	8	7.5
46-50	12	11.3	14	13.2
51-55	10	9.4	6	5.7
56-60	14	13.2	3	2.8
61+	28	26.4	7	6.6

TABLE 2. Marital Status of Parents of Homeless Individuals in Study Sample (n = 212)

	Men		Women		Total	
	n	%	n	%	n	%
Single	7	6.6	14	13.2	21	9.9
Married	79	74.5	54	50.9	133	62.7
Common law marriage	11	10.4	22	20.8	33	15.6
Separated	6	5.7	13	12.3	19	9.0
Widowed	3	2.8	3	2.8	6	2.8

Childhood History

It is noteworthy that 19.3% and 6.6% of the participants reported that they never knew their father and their mother, respectively. Approximately one-fifth (21.2%) of the sample lived away from both biological parents before age five, and women were more likely than men to have lived away from parents (26.4%) (Table 3). Approximately 20% of individuals in the sample had never met their father. Approximately 11% of individuals had been detained in a juvenile detention facility before age 17.

TABLE 3. Childhood History as Reported by Homeless Individuals in Study Sample (n = 212)

Ever met father	Number Men	%	Number Women	%	Total Number	Total %
Yes	87	82.1	84	79.2	171	80.7
No	19	17.9	22	20.8	41	19.3
Ever met mother						
Yes	98	92.5	100	94.3	198	93.4
No	8	7.5	6	5.7	14	6.6
Lived away from both biological parents before age 5						
Yes	17	16.0	28	26.4	45	21.2
No	89	84.0	78	73.6	167	78.8
Incarcerated before age 17						
Yes	14	13.2	10	9.4	24	11.3
No	92	86.8	96	90.6	188	88.7

As shown in Table 4, among those individuals who were not looked after by either biological parent before age five, grandparents were the most frequent caregivers. Aunts and uncles were the second most common caregivers during this period (age 0-5).

Psychiatric Care

Approximately one-third of the individuals (32.1%; see Table 5) reported at least one mental health contact with either a psychiatrist or a psychologist. Women were more likely to report admission to an inpatient psychiatric facility (13.2%) than men (6.6%).

DISCUSSION

Approximately half of the individuals in the sample (50.5%) were single at the time of the interview. This finding is consistent with previous reports. For example, Abdul and associates (1993) reported that 48% of homeless individuals in their sample were single. Approximately 15% of the participants in our study were separated, a higher rate than the national average (Rioseco, 1994). These findings suggest an association between homelessness and lack of significant attachments, as reflected by marriage, be it legal or common law. A similar association has been reported between mental illness and absence of

TABLE 4. Caregivers of Selected Homeless Individuals* When They Were 0 to 5 Years of Age (n = 62)

Caregiver/s	Number Men n = 29	%	Number Women n = 33	%	Total	%
Both grandparents	10	34.5	5	15.2	15	24.2
Neighbors	1	3.5	1	3.0	2	3.2
Grandmother only	3	10.3	13	39.4	16	25.8
Uncle/aunt	9	3.1	6	18.2	15	24.2
Others	6	20.7	8	24.2	14	22.6

*This table includes only those individuals who were not living with either biological parent from birth to age 5.

TABLE 5. Lifetime Psychiatric Services Reported by Homeless Individuals in Study Sample (n = 212)

	Men n	%	Women n	%	Total n	%
Any contact with a psychiatrist or psychologist						
Yes	32	30.2	36	33.96	68	32.1
No	74	69.8	70	66.04	144	67.9
Ever admitted to a psychiatric inpatient facility						
Yes	7	6.6	14	13.2	21	9.9
No	99	93.4	92	86.8	191	90.1

significant attachments (Usatiene et al., 1994), and another study showed that infants living in families with low financial resources or at psychosocial risk show a greater insecurity in their attachment relationships (Esterbrooks & Graham, 1999).

This study shows a striking age difference between the men and women interviewed. It is not known why the women were younger than the men. We speculate that men were able to fend for themselves for a longer period of time and therefore entered the shelter at a later age.

The main finding of this study is that homeless adults had a frequent history of separation from their biological parents, resulting in placement with substitute caregivers, e.g., relatives and foster parents. In the case of grandparents, a group identified as a rapidly growing population of "forgotten caregivers," studies show that they have very poor self-rated health and multiple chronic conditions (Burnette, 1999), and rearing children with special needs represents a significant secondary strain for this group.

A high prevalence of early parental death and of early parent-child separation has been previously reported in a homeless sample in the United States (Susser, Struening, & Conover, 1987; Feitel, 1992), and it is noteworthy that we observed the same pattern in this urban sample in Chile. There was a relatively high percentage of individuals in our sample who never met their parents (19.3% and 6.6% never met their father and mother, respectively). About a fifth (21.2%) lived away from both parents before age five. Thus, our research is consistent with the findings reported by Susser and associates (1987) in the United States. There is other evidence that individuals in our sample were at risk before they reached adulthood: as noted, 11.3% of individuals in our sample were sent to a juvenile detention facility before age 17.

By self-report, almost 10% of the individuals in our sample had been hospitalized in a psychiatric institution at least once in their lifetime. About one-third had had contact with a psychiatrist or psychologist. These figures are similar to those reported in epidemiological research studies in use by psychiatric services in Santiago, Chile (Vicente, 1992). Since these figures are based on self-report, they should be viewed cautiously.

This study has several noteworthy limitations. All information is based on self-report without independent confirmation or other independent evidence. Information about the past was obtained retrospectively and is therefore subject to all the pitfalls associated with the recall of distant events. The absence of a comparison group limits the interpretation of these findings. Nevertheless, this pilot study provided important information regarding a population that has received minimal attention from investigators: homeless urban dwellers in developing countries.

The main finding, the high frequency of a history of parent-child separation, is consistent with U.S. reports (Sumerlin & Bundrick, 1997; Lamb & Lamb, 1990; Susser, Struening, & Conover, 1987). Similarly, a childhood history of delinquency and/or running away from home was common in this sample as reported by other authors (Susser, Struening, & Conover, 1987; Feitel, 1992). The similarity of findings in societies as diverse as Chile and the United States suggests that certain childhood events, e.g., placement with substitute caregivers or institutionalization, might be common background of homelessness in a variety of societies and cultures. The mechanisms that link these childhood events to adult homelessness are not known and need to be investigated. Finally, we believe that the family plays an important role in preventing homelessness and related problems, and programs to enhance protective mechanisms in families at risk should be a main issue in public mental health programs.

CONCLUSION

As mentioned above, we believe that families play a significant role in reducing homelessness and associated problems. What we have found in this study of homeless persons in Santiago, Chile, implies that this study should be addressed from two angles, planning and practice, preventive and therapeutic. First, preventive work should involve working toward strengthening families that appear to be at risk. While not spectacular in terms of obvious contributions to mental health because it is hard to demonstrate the absence of something, preventive work can be judged on the basis of results with an at-risk population that is provided adequate support and subsequently produces lower rates of various kinds of pathology than would have been predicted. On the therapeutic side, our study appears to provide some support for the use of family interventions, including family therapy, with this population. The implications include some guidance regarding specific foci for interventions, such as attention not only to working to strengthen and reconstruct family structure and attachments where possible.

The finding that certain background characteristics of the Santiago homeless population match those found in homeless persons in other countries is reminiscent of the conclusion reached from a multinational study of long-term marriage that "Comparisons can be made between the countries, despite some sample difference, since the differences were found to be small and not very important" (Sharlin, Kaslow, & Hammerschmidt, 2000). What kinds of successful preventive and therapeutic programs and other family interventions have been found to be successful in other countries and can be successfully adapted in other societies? The answer to this question would be an invitation to follow Dr. Florence Kaslow's footsteps in working on the different aspects of families throughout the world and finding the way to help the world to become a better place to live.

REFERENCES

Abdul-Hamid, W., Wykes, T., & Stansfeld, S. (1993). The homeless mentally ill: Myths and realities. *International Journal of Social Psychiatry, 39(4)*, 237-254.

Breakey, W. R., Fisher, P. J., Kramer, M., Nestadt, G., Romanoski, A. J., Ross, A., Royall, R. M., & Stine, O. C. (1989). Health and mental health problems of homeless men and women in Baltimore. *Journal of the American Medical Association, 262(10)*, 1352-1357.

Burnette, D. (1999). Physical and emotional well-being of custodial grandparents in Latino families. *American Journal of Orthopsychiatry, 69(3)*, 305-318.

Cohen, C., & Thompson, K. (1992). Homeless mentally ill or mentally ill homeless. *American Journal of Psychiatry, 149*, 816-817.

DeMallie, D. A., North, C. S., & Smith, E. M. (1997). Psychiatric disorder among the homeless: A comparison between older and younger group. *The Gerontologist, 37(1)*, 61-66.

Easterbrooks, M., & Graham, C. (1999). Security of attachment and parenting: Homeless and low income housed mothers and infants. *American Journal of Orthopsychiatry, 69(3)*, 337-346.

Eddins, E. (1993). Characteristics, health status and service needs of sheltered homeless families. *ABNF Journal, 4(2)*, 40-44.

Feitel, B. (1992). Psychosocial background and behavioral and emotional disorder of homeless and runaway youth. *Hospital and Community Psychiatry, 43(2)*, 155-159.

Holland, A. C. (1996). The mental health of single homeless people in Northampton hostels. *Public Health, 110(5)*, 299-303.

Lamb, H. R., & Lamb, D. M. (1990). Factors contributing to homelessness among the chronically and severely mentally ill. *Hospital and Community Psychiatry, 41(3)*, 301-305.

Muñoz, M., Vazquez, C., Koegel, P., Sanz, J., & Burnam, M. A. (1998). Differential patterns of mental disorders among the homeless in Madrid (Spain) and Los Angeles (USA). *Social Psychiatry Psychiatric Epidemiology, 33(10)*, 514-520.

North, C. S. (1996). Are the mentally ill homeless a distinct homeless subgroup? *Annals of Clinical Psychiatry, 8(3)*, 117-128.

Reilly, F. (1994). An ecological approach to health risk: A case study of urban elderly homeless people. *Public Health Nursing, 11(5)*, 305-314.

Rioseco, P. (1994). Dimensión de las problemáticas de Salud Mental. *Review Psiquiatr.* (Santiago de Chile), *11(1)*, 4-8.

Robins, L. N., & Regier, D. A. (1991). *Psychiatric disorders in America: The epidemiologic catchment area study.* New York: Free Press.

Sharlin, S. A., Kaslow, F. W., & Hammerschmidt, H. (2000). *Together through thick and thin: A multinational picture of long-term marriages.* New York: The Haworth Press, Inc.

Sumerlin, J. R., & Bundrick, C. M. (1997). Research on homeless men and women: Existential-humanistic and clinical thinking. *Psychological Reports, 80*, 1303-1314.

Susser, E., Struening, E. L., & Conover, S. (1987). Childhood experiences of homeless men. *American Journal of Psychiatry, 144(12)*, 1599-1601.

Usatiene, R. P., Gelberg Smith, M. H., & Lesser, J. (1994). Health care for the homeless: A family medicine perspective. *Journal of American Family Physician, 49(1)*, 139-146.

Vicente, B. (1992). Trastornos psiquiátricos en diez comunas de Santiago. Prevalencia de 6 meses. *Review Psiquiatr.* (Santiago de Chile), *11(4)*, 192-200.

Study of "Sex-Less" (Sex-Avoidant) Young Couples

Israel W. Charny

Shlomit Asineli-Tal

SUMMARY. The phenomenon of reduced sexual activity in young couples is very common, with a high estimate being one out of three couples and a low estimate at one out of seven couples. Other than for couples who have become estranged and are angrily involved in a breakdown of their marriage, there is a prototypal situation where it is largely the wife who initiates the reduction or ends the regularity of sexual experience; the husband goes along with her; and the couple settle into a collusive marital and family lifestyle which involves a striking emphasis on the joys and meaningfulness of maintaining their shared home and raising their children while neglecting, minimizing, or com-

Israel W. Charny is Professor of Psychology and Family Therapy, Hebrew University of Jerusalem, POB 10311, 91102 Jerusalem, Israel (E-mail: encygeno@mail.com).

Shlomit Asineli-Tal is Director, Marriage and Family Therapy Clinic, Azor, Israel, Eliyahu Meron 28, Nes-Ziyona 74019, Israel.

The authors express appreciation to the graduate social work students who participated in Phase Two of the research reported: Oren Kochi, MSW; Naomi Melamed Goldstein, MSW; Orit Zafir, MSW; Roni Shalit, MSW; and Tal Shafir, MSW.

This paper was presented with the title, "Why do so many, even young couples, avoid having sexual relationships," at the XIIth World Family Therapy Conference of the International Family Therapy Association in Oslo, June 2000. An earlier paper, "Diagnosis and treatment of collusive house-parent marriages," was presented at the VIIIth World Family Therapy Conference of the International Family Therapy Association in Jerusalem in April 1997.

pensating for dysfunctions and gaps in their basic relationship and intimacy with one another. Sixty-nine percent of sex-avoidant couples demonstrated a marital profile that we characterized as "House-Parent Marriages," while only 23% of couples who maintain a more normal sexual frequency showed this pattern. *[Article copies available for a fee from The Haworth Document Delivery Service: 1-800-HAWORTH. E-mail address: <docdelivery@haworthpress.com> Website: <http://www.HaworthPress.com> © 2004 by The Haworth Press, Inc. All rights reserved.]*

KEYWORDS. Sex-avoidance, limited marital sexuality, young couples, marital collusions, "House-Parent Marriages"

"SEX FOR KASLOW"

Is it crude, rude, or, worst of all in our society, "politically incorrect" for me to reveal that the present paper for the Festschrift in honor of Florence Kaslow has been listed in my computer as "Sex for Kaslow"?

Between two long-time friends it feels like good fun.

Over the many years that I have known Florrie, there were times that I wrote or spoke formally of her very outstanding professional work and leadership. She has been a sound thinker and a voice for a commonsense integrity in respect of many aspects of human experience and behavior such as values in family life, the management of crises of divorce, or fighting the lure of cults; and she has been an innovative and tireless leader of wonderful professional initiatives and organizations, such as the Coalition on Relational Diagnosis, and founding and giving leadership for many years to the International Family Therapy Association.

So enough professional compliments, however well deserved. It's time to play, and I submit the attached article on young couples who stop "doing sex" to this Festschrift as my gift and tribute to Florrie, hence "Sex for Kaslow."

– With warmest wishes,
Israel W. Charny

INTRODUCTION TO THE PROBLEM OF SEX-AVOIDANT MARRIAGES

This is a study of young couples who engage in reduced sexual activity–which in the present work is defined as no more than two reported events of sexual intercourse a month. The phenomena of seriously reduced sexual activity is surprisingly, and to many of us distressingly, quite widespread.[1] The phenomenon has also been underrecognized and understudied in both the clinical and research literatures for many years.[2] Although in practice one frequently sees such couples in counseling and psychotherapy practices, it nonetheless has been a phenomenon that is not frequently discussed among therapists and about which most clinicians have read relatively little. Nonetheless, when one brings up the subject conversationally, there is generally immediate recognition that it is quite commonplace in just about everyone's practice.

PREVIOUS LITERATURE ON LIMITED MARITAL SEXUALITY

A comprehensive review of the more sociological rather than clinical literature shows that the phenomenon has been reported many number of times in statistical studies. The statistical studies of this phenomenon generally are parts of rigorous demographic inventories of overall marital functioning where there has been no focus on the specific phenomenon of the reduced sexuality and certainly no efforts at study or interpretation of the phenomenon. However, these data are in their own right significantly substantiating of the clinical observations. (The reader is referred to Barrett et al., 1999; Call, Sprecher, & Schwartz, 1995; Doddridge, Schumm, & Berger, 1987; Frank, Anderson, & Rubinstein, 1978; Greenblatt, 1983; Jasso, 1985; Rao & Demaris, 1995.) All the statistical data we have seen are in agreement that following an initially high sexual frequency at the beginning of marriage, there is a progressive and surprisingly early and intense decline in the frequency of intercourse. Greenblatt (1983) sums up the phenomenon as follows:

> Marital sex does not appear to be very important to many people. Despite the highly sex-oriented media and social environment, the frequency of intercourse in these couples [referring to the research being presented by the author], all in the early years of marriage, is not very high. Furthermore, first-year rates are not maintained by most persons, particularly in the face of increased work and parenthood pressures. (p. 298)

As noted, the literature for the most part has remained at the static level of description. What is also known scientifically about the decline following the initial excitement of marriage is that the decline deepens statistically with age and the duration of the marriage, and is also statistically correlated with the number of children. A series of secondary observations also come up in the literature about a peaking of the phenomenon of reduced sexuality following birth of a child (Barrett et al., 1999). Thus, in one sample of 98 postnatal women, 44% reported a definite loss of sexual desire. Of these same 98 women, 58% reported symptoms of dyspareunia, so that the experience of pain is probably the single most defined cause for the loss of sexual desire. Other studies suggest that women with low sexual desire to begin with are the ones who are most susceptible to a need to reduce their sexual functioning subsequently in their marriages (Trudell, Landry, & Larose, 1997).

There have been periodic and largely anecdotal references in the clinical literature to the surprisingly high frequency of reduced sexual functioning even in many young couples. Thus, Talmadge and Talmadge (1986) noted: "Over the last several years low sexual desire has been more frequently reported by both men and women. Our clinical experience supports this" (p. 3). Looking at sexuality on the level of the couple relationships, a number of studies observe that the incidence of sexual functioning is correlated with the experience of being in love with one's mate. Pioneering sex therapist and psychotherapist, Helen Kaplan (1974, 1979), was among the first to bring to the fore the issue of reduced sexual desire and to identify it as a common clinical issue. As is also well known, Helen Kaplan's descriptions of her own efforts at treatment of this condition, like the reports of many other researchers (see Beck, 1995; Bennun, Rust, & Golombok, 1985; Dekker & Everaerd, 1983; Hawton, Catalann, & Fagg, 1991; Lief, 1977; LoPiccolo, 1980; Schover, 1986; Snyder & Berg, 1983), reported relatively poor results in treatment of low sexual desire. Kaplan was especially unusual for her focus on the truths of the real quality of the marital relationship. She even insisted that sex therapy–in its prescription and monitoring of a series of sexual behavior tasks as originated in the innovative works of Masters and Johnson (1970), and then somewhat modified by herself (1974)–not be undertaken so long as there were evidences of what she identified as "sexual sabotage" in the marital relationship. Whereas Masters and Johnson had accepted as an operational criterion for participation in their treatment program any explicit readiness of a couple to undergo sexual behavior tasks together, Kaplan insisted that a discerning eye was needed to see if the couple really were or were not welcoming one another as sexual partners, and she insisted that the initiation of active treatment through sexual behavior tasks was actually contraindicated if serious rejection or negation of a partner was evident.

Nonetheless, even in respect of Helen Kaplan's work, it has been suggested that her focus was much more on the psychodynamics of a given mate who was withdrawing from sexuality than on the relationship process itself. In general, the single most definitive criticism of efforts at therapy of low sexual desire has been that insufficient attention is given to the couple's basic relationship process. Talmadge and Talmadge (1986) say, "Sex therapy techniques have a poor record of success in treating low sexual desire largely because of insufficient attention to the emotional relationship of the persons involved and to psychodynamics" (p. 5). The authors provide an alternative picture of the basic context in which reduced sexual functioning appears as a symptom:

> Sexuality is a physical expression of primary emotional bonds. At no other time in the life of the couple do they confront themselves and each other in a more vulnerable way than when they are engaged in sexual pleasuring. This primitive vulnerability is the core of the difficulties so many couples experience in their sexual and marital relating. (p. 6)

The Talmadges emphasize as a *sine qua non* of sexuality a capacity for intensity of feeling, the absence of which creates "an experience of numbness," and they suggest that couples who exclude negative feelings from their relationship end up creating a "smooth relationship at the expense of their intensity and passion" (p. 10). They see intimacy as a capacity and willingness to share hurt feelings, and a capacity to be dependent, and that sexuality also requires a readiness to contain dysphoric, negative and conflictual emotions, including a measure of hostility, as natural processes of meaningful intimacy.

DESCRIPTION OF THE SEQUENCE OF THIS STUDY AND A SUMMARY OF BASIC FINDINGS

The main purpose of our research is to contribute to the analysis of the dynamics of sex-avoidance, and not so much to information about the statistical incidence of reduced sexual behavior. The present report presents new results not previously reported from two earlier phases of an unfolding sequence of studies of marital interaction in general and the validation of a psychometric instrument for mapping or describing and assessing clinically the dynamics of a marriage, the Existential/Dialectical Marital Questionnaire (EDMQ) (Asineli, 1992; Charny & Asineli, 1996; Asineli & Charny, 1997), as well as the results of an entirely new study.

Table 1 summarizes the full sequence of the three phases of the research.

The original basic study, to which we refer as Phase One, included 60 couples who were in marital therapy compared with 61 "normal" couples or couples who had not sought marital therapy (see Table 2).

This basic study was then followed by additional research in Phase Two which was specifically intended to recruit conflict-avoidant couples and sex-avoidant couples in order to examine each of these two groups of couples who are defined by a decided pattern of avoidance of a normal function, in the one case conflicts, in the second case sexual relations. In this second phase of the studies, 10 conflict-avoidant couples were identified and 14 sex-avoidant couples were identified (see Table 3). The research of the sex-avoidant couples in Phase Two was assigned as a year-long group project to graduate students in a seminar on marital therapy in the Marriage and Family Therapy Program at the School of Social Work at Tel Aviv University which was conducted by the senior author. This phase of the study conducted by the graduate students included 12 cases provided by the students and two additional cases from the senior author's clinical practice. It provided a first opportunity for an in-depth look at the dynamics of sex-avoidant couples who were well known to their therapists, and hence an opportunity to solicit not only a reconstruction of the facts of the decline in sexual functioning as reported to the clinician, but also psychodynamic and relational interpretations by the clinicians of the meanings of the reduction or cessation of sexual activity.

Phase Three of the study was a multipronged evaluation of three different subgroups of couples, from all of which a combined sample of sex-avoidant couples was constructed while tracking the specific sources of each of the subgroups that make up the larger sample. The three subgroups were: (1) a group of 15 kibbutz couples, (2) a group of 13 therapist-spouse couples, which means that at least one of the spouses was a practicing therapist, and (3) a group of 28 couples undergoing marital therapy who were brought into the study by their therapists who were then students in the post-graduate Program for Advanced Studies in Integrative Psychotherapy at the Hebrew University of Jerusalem in a seminar on marital therapy conducted by the senior author. In the first of the subgroups, six couples out of 15 or approximately 40% were sex- avoidant; in the second subgroup of 13 therapists and their spouses, there were no sex-avoidant couples reported; in the third sample, 10 couples out of 28 or 36% were sex-avoidant. The overall total was a sample of 16 couples out of 56 or 29% who were sex-avoidant (see Table 4).

As stated, Phase Two of the study involved 14 sex-avoidant couples specifically chosen by their therapists from their caseloads as couples evidencing sex-avoidance, and Phase Three of the study yielded a total of 16 sex-avoidant couples, so that together Phases Two and Three produced a total of 30 sex-avoidant couples out of a total population of 80 couples.

Overall, If we add these 80 couples to the 121 couples who were the subjects of Phase One of the study who underwent evaluation on the EDMQ and thereby were also subject to evaluation of some aspects of their sexual functioning, the number of subjects in the unfolding sequence of studies of marital sexuality reported here reaches a total N of 201 couples. In Phases Two and Three, moreover, 30 sex-avoidant couples were identified for more in-depth study.

TABLE 1. A Study of Sex-*Avoidant* Young Couples

POPULATIONS STUDIED	PURPOSE OF STUDY AND MAJOR RESULTS
Phase One (previously published): Asineli, 1992; Charny & Asineli, 1996; Asineli & Charny, 1997	*Validation of marital questionnaire (EDMQ) in course of which comparisons were made of scores of patient couples and normal couples on "Attraction and Sexuality."*
60 COUPLES IN MARITAL THERAPY 61 "NORMAL" COUPLES (WHO DID NOT SEEK MARITAL THERAPY)	*Patients had many more complaints and much less idealization of one another, and normals had much fewer complaints and much greater idealization.*
Total N = 121	
Phase Two (previously published): Charny & Asineli, 1996; Asineli & Charny, 1997 10 CONFLICT-AVOIDANT COUPLES 14 SEX-*AVOIDANT* COUPLES	*Although sex-avoidant gave many more complaints on "Attraction and Sexuality," they also gave a remarkable number of satisfactory and even idealizing ratings. This funny pattern also carried over to other areas of marriages espe - cially in respect of "Family Management" and "Parenting."*
Total N = 24	
New Findings of Phase Two: **THERAPIST ANALYSIS OF 14 CASES OF THE SEX-AVOIDANT COUPLES:**	*PRECIPITANTS OF DROP IN SEXUAL FUNCTIONING: 4 AFTER BIRTH, 4 AFTER BANKRUPTCY OR OTHER ECONOMIC CONFLICT. WHO MADE THE DECISION NOT TO HAVE SEX? IN 8 CASES THE WIFE, 3 CASES THE HUSBAND, 3 CASES BOTH. PROTOTYPAL DYNAMIC PATTERN: 10 HUSBANDS WERE GENERALLY PASSIVE TO DOMINANT WIVES.*
Phase Three: CURRENT STUDY 15 Kibbutz Couples of which 6 SEX-*AVOIDANT* and 9 SEX-*FUNCTIONING* 13 Therapist-Spouse Couples of which 13 SEX-*FUNCTIONING* 28 Couples in Marital Therapy (Hebrew University Students) of which 10 SEX-*AVOIDANT* and 18 SEX-*FUNCTIONING*	*16 OR 29% (OR 1 OUT OF 4) OF 56 COUPLES QUALIFIED AS SEX-AVOIDANT.* *20 OR 36% (APPROACHING 2 OUT OF 5) COUPLES WERE IDENTIFIED AS "HOUSE-PARENT MARRIAGES."* *69% OF THE SEX-AVOIDANT MARRIED COUPLES AND ONLY 23% OF THE SEX-FUNCTIONING COUPLES SHOWED A "HOUSE-PARENT MARRIAGE" PATTERN.*
Total N = 56 of which 16 SEX-*AVOIDANT* and 40 SEX-*FUNCTIONING*	*"HOUSE-PARENT MARRIAGES" OF THE SEX-AVOIDANT TENDED TOWARDS DENIALS OF RELATIONSHIP DYSFUNCTIONS, WHILE THE SEX-FUNCTIONING TENDED TOWARDS IDEALIZATION OF ONE ANOTHER.*
Total N of all Phases = 201 of which *30 SEX-AVOIDANT*	

TABLE 2. Distribution of Scores (Percentages) of Four Different Groups of Couples on the Existential/Dialectical Psychometric Questionnaire of Marital Interaction on Each of Five Major Areas of Marital Functioning and Five Marital Relationship Values

	COUPLES IN THERAPY (N = 60)*				NORMAL COUPLES (N = 61)*				CONFLICT-AVOIDANT (N = 10)				SEXUALITY-AVOIDANT (N = 14)			
	+	√	+√	−	+	√	+√	−	+	√	+√	−	+	√	+√	−
AREAS OF MARITAL FUNCTIONING:																
FAMILY MANAGEMENT	10	2.5	72.5	27.5	24	67	91	9	66	32	98	2	46	26	72	29
COMPANIONSHIP	5	60	65	35	27	69	96	4	62	4	96	4	38	27	65	35
RELATIONSHIP & COMMUNICATION	4	60	64	36	33	59	92	8	62	26	88	12	36	26	62	38
ATTRACTION & SEXUALITY	7	60	67	33	32	60	92	8	60	36	96	4	31	28	59	41
PARENTING	12	65	77	23	33	63	96	4	64	35	99	1	53	24	77	23

	+	√	+√	−	+	√	+√	−	+	√	+√	−	+	√	+√	−
MARITAL RELATIONSHIP VALUES:																
COMPETENCE	9	54	63	37	31	63	94	6	68	30	98	2	42	20	62	38
COMMITMENT	11	65	76	24	33	61	94	6	67	30	97	3	48	27	75	25
RESPECT	5	63	68	32	37	59	96	4	71	29	100	0	41	27	68	32
CONTROL	7	62	69	31	11	75	86	14	37	44	81	19	34	30	64	36
CLOSENESS	7	62	69	31	38	60	98	2	71	29	100	0	39	25	64	36

*Note: The percentages in each area of functioning or value is based on N = 300 combined scores (Husband/wife's rating of self combined with spouse's rating).

−   Reports of Dysfunctional Couple Functioning
√   Reports of Effective Couple Functioning
+   Reports of Idealized Couple Functioning
+ √ Combined Reports of Effective and Idealized Couple Functioning

Phase One of the Study:
Validation of the Existential/Dialectical Marital Questionnaire (EDMQ)

As noted, the first phase of the research has been reported extensively in earlier publications. The overall finding with regard to all aspects of marital functioning was that couples in therapy had a significantly higher number of complaints about dysfunctions averaging in the province of 30%, while normal couples who were not in therapy had much lower statements of complaints about dysfunctions, in all cases below 10%. In addition, normal couples were seen as having much greater idealization of one another in re-

TABLE 3. Distribution of Scores (Percentages) of Four Different Groups of Couples on the Existential/Dialectical Psychometric Questionnaire of Marital Interaction [EDMQ]

SUBJECTS	N	REPORTS OF COUPLE FUNCTIONING			
		+ Idealized	Effective	+√ Effective & Idealized	— Dysfunctional
COUPLES IN THERAPY	60	8%	61%	69%	31%
'NORMAL' COUPLES (NO HISTORY OF THERAPY)	61	30%	64%	94%	6%
CONFLICT-AVOIDANT COUPLES	10	63%	32%	95%	5%
SEX-*AVOIDANT* COUPLES	**14**	**41%**	**26%**	**67%**	**33%**

TABLE 4. Distribution of Couples Having Two or Fewer Events of Sexual Intercourse per Month (N = 56)

	SEX-*AVOIDANT*	SEX-*FUNCTIONING*	N
KIBBUTZ	6 = 40%	9 = 60%	15
THERAPISTS	0 = 0%	13 = 100%	13
(Jerusalem) COUPLES IN MARITAL THERAPY	10 = 36%	18 = 64%	28
TOTALS	**16 = 29%**	**40 = 71%**	**56**

spect of their various marital functions, approximately in the range of 30% of reported statements, while couples in therapy had much lower idealization scores, ranging from four to 12%. In other words, the couples in therapy and the normal couples showed mirror images of one another in that about 1/3 of the statements by couples in therapy were descriptions of dysfunctions, and about 1/3 of the statements by normal couples were idealizing perceptions of their marriages. These results are summarized in Table 2.

Two of the published reports of the above study (Charny & Asineli, 1996; Asineli & Charny, 1997) also included a preliminary statement of the overall statistical findings of the then just-completed data of Phase Two of the study. Beyond showing that the questionnaire differentiated between these groups meaningfully, we were struck with the fact that the sex-avoidant couples did report higher levels of dysfunctions in respect of sexuality at a level corresponding the approximately 1/3 complaints that were previously seen to be characteristic of couples in therapy with respect to all areas of marital interaction. *Simultaneously* the sex-avoidant couples continued *nonetheless* to give a surprising number of satisfied and even idealized ratings, together equaling 67% of their reports, with regard to their sexual functions. In other words, even though these sex-avoidant couples do very little sex, they say their sexuality is good to great!

We found a similar pattern of idealization generalizing across all areas of marital functioning when we looked at the pattern of conflict-avoidant couples. Conflict-avoidant couples report extremely few scores of dysfunctionality– with a slight suggestive exception in the area of Relationship where the scores of dysfunctionality are still more comparable to normal couples rather than couples in therapy. The scores of adequate or idealized functioning of conflict-avoidant couples reach percentages in the high 90s. In other words, we were struck by the fact that even as the sex-avoidant couples acknowledge and report the facts of their sexual dysfunctions, they also utilize a pattern of denial of experiencing any problem in respect of their sexual functions that reminded us of the ways in which conflict-avoidant couples avoid experiencing disturbances and dissatisfactions in all areas of their marriage.

Table 2 above also shows a comparison of 10 conflict-avoidant couples and 14 sex-avoidant couples. In their idealization of one another, almost all the idealizing ratings of the conflict-avoidant couples were above 60%–with the exception of scores in the area of Control, where indeed one outstanding price of conflict-avoidance is a spouse yielding their sense of mastery and leadership in the relationship in order to appease the other. Similarly, conflict-avoidant couples did report some complaints of dysfunctions, especially in respect of lack of Control and to a lesser extent in the area of Relationship and Communication. But overall, and certainly in marital functions other than Control, conflict-avoidant couples prove to be, as one would expect, consciously 'happy campers' idealizing their trouble-free marital universe and their mates.

What is most relevant for our present report is the corresponding data for the 14 sexuality-avoidant couples. The comparative perspective here is no less interesting in showing that in respect of their idealization of one another, these couples as a group moved far from what was seen in normal couples in the direction of the conflict-avoidant couples. The percentage of idealizing scores ranges from 31 to 48, or below the 60% figure seen in the conflict-avoidant couples, but higher than the 24 to 38% ratings that were seen among normal couples (with the exception here too in the area of Control where normal couples also reported less idealization of their sense of control in the relationship). Although all of the sexuality-avoidant couples indeed did report a much higher percentage of dysfunctions in the area of Attraction and Sexuality (41% complaints of dysfunctionality), they also reported a surprising and actually illogical number not only of adequate functions in respect of their sexuality (28%) but a considerable number of idealizing responses (31%), which together yield a composite score of reports of effective plus idealizing statements equaling 59%.

This finding that couples who are not functioning well in their sexuality, who had specifically been selected by their therapists for the study based on their reduced sexual functioning, and who admitted in the EDMQ to sexual dysfunctions at the same time nonetheless described themselves in good and even glowing terms in respect of their sexuality led us to think about what was to emerge as a new proposal of a model of a collusive relationship which we call "House-Parent Marriages," about which we will report more fully shortly.

Table 3 provides a condensed summary of the comparisons of the four groups studied in Phase One of the study, the group of couples in therapy and the group of normal couples both of which were studied extensively in this first phase of the study, and then the two groups of the conflict-avoidant and sexuality-avoidant couples. In each case, the scores provided are those for idealized functioning, effective scores, combination scores of effective and idealizing scores, and scores of dysfunctional functioning. As previously reported, idealized functioning is especially characteristic of conflict-avoidant couples, but also suggestively higher in sex-avoidant couples than is seen in normals. Dysfunctional scores run equally high in couples in therapy and sex-avoidant couples.

Phase Two of the Study:
10 Conflict-Avoidant Couples and 14 Sex-Avoidant Couples

As noted, the 14 sex-avoidant couples in the second phase of this study were couples in therapy for whom we have depth analysis by their respective therapists in addition to the results of the couples' performances on the EDMQ. For each case the therapists completed a detailed systematic questionnaire which gave an interpretation of the dynamics of the cases, including evaluations of each of the spouses and of the couple system. These analyses are reported here for the first time and give us a more in-depth look at sex-avoidant couples as seen by marital therapists who know them well.

In virtually all cases, both spouses were under the age of 40–the few exceptions were a number of husbands who had just recently passed that age. In each case, the couple had been identified by the therapist as underfunctioning in their sexuality in that both husband wife reported two or less events of sexual intercourse a month.

All of the couples in this study had reported a drop in their sexual functioning one to two years before the time of their seeking couple therapy. The therapists who knew these cases provided us with a picture of how the virtual cessation of sexual activity came about. Two immediate precipitants for the stopping of sexual activity that were reported fit other information that has long been available in that four out of 14 cases were after the birth of a child, and another four out of 14 cases followed a breakdown in the economic functioning of the husband and couple unit–bankruptcy or other major economic conflict. Two cases reported a drop in sexuality as a result of sexual dysfunction: In one case, the decrease in desire was not associated with any known cause but seemed to follow simply the fact of being married; In two cases no precipitating event was described; only in one case was the drop in sexuality connected with a process of major conflict leading to divorce. Of course, the above findings are not based on sufficiently large statistical samples to be acceptable as scientifically significant, but they are consistent with earlier reports in the literature, and they are also consistent with basic clinical theory, namely that major life transitions are a context for the emergence of many difficulties. The birth of a child is certainly a major shift in meaning for many women towards a much greater emphasis on motherhood rather than on romantic and sexual aspects of couplehood, and the development of major economic difficulty would of course be a huge blow to the self-esteem of working men and the self-esteem of the couple unit as well.

Most importantly, this study provided a rare opportunity for tapping the understanding of the therapists as to the psychodynamics of the decrease in sexual functioning. A major finding was that in the majority of cases, the husbands were generally passive in their orientation to their dominant wives, and the predominant role in initiating the period of the symptomatic drop in sexual functioning fell to the wives. In eight out of 14 cases, the decision not to have sex was explicitly made by the wife and the husbands reacted to the decision passively; in three cases the decision was made by both the wife and husband; and only in three cases was the drop in sexual functioning attributed to the husband. Overall, in 10 out of the 14 couple systems, the men were described as passive, and their passivity was coupled with a dominant woman. In the four remaining couples the couples as interactive units were described as disengaged from one another. Although this is not the same as a picture of male passivity in relation to female dominance, a pattern of disengagement in itself can also be thought of as including a form of passivity in the male, so that it is again true that in all cases the males do not show the energy, activity or leadership to seek to overcome the distance and gap that has developed between them and their wives. It may be correct, therefore, to conclude that, for all 14 couples who showed reduced sexual functioning, whatever the original reasons for its development, a major contribution to maintaining and transforming the problem into a chronic pattern of dysfunction was a basic passivity in the style of the husband. The emergence of dysfunctional sexuality was not taken as a trigger for active emotional work and correction by the husband–nor by their spouses, of course–but led to a rigidification of the pattern.

At the same time, in almost all cases the therapists also emphasized a difference between the husbands and wives which has been widely reported in the literature of sexuality, namely that males relate to sexuality far more as a need to have sexual release and to achieve sexual pleasure, while females contextualize the sexual contact much more as an aspect of keeping the marriage going and as part of the couple's intimacy. The women, therefore, are much more sensitive to the presence or absence of romance in the relationship as enabling them to engage in sexual activity.

When asked for their interpretations of the central dynamic in the couples' loss of sexual experiencing, the therapists reported in six out of 14 cases that fear of intimacy was the key dynamic; in seven out of 14 cases, there was a failure or decline of respect for the spouse in the heart and the mind of at least one spouse toward the other; and only in one out of 14 cases was an actual sexual dysfunction seen as the cause of the drop in sexual functioning.

Phase Three:
Correlation of Sex Avoidance with "House-Parent Marriages"

Phase Three of the study was based on an examination of three subgroups of couples to identify among them sex-avoidant couples. As noted, 15 kibbutz couples, 13 therapist-spouse couples,[3] and 28 couples in marital therapy were the subjects in this phase of the study, with the total of 56 couples yielding 16 sex-avoidant couples.

By now our ongoing studies of marital process using the EDMQ had also led us to a conceptualization of a specific collusive pattern (see Charny, 1987) among many couples who turn toward valuing the two traditional sociological functions of marriage of maintaining a home and bringing up children at the expense of the quality of their relationship as a couple–their Companionship with one another, Relationship and Communication, as well as Attraction and Sexuality. This kind of pattern was now designated by us (Charny & Asineli-Tal, 1997) as a collusive pattern of "House-Parent Marriages." We saw this pattern as providing an escape and compensation from an undeveloped or unsatisfactory couple relationship, especially with regard to dimensions of intimacy, via an escape into overvaluing the structure of the marriage in providing a marital and family home and a context for bringing up one's children. In this collusive marital pattern, the couples define their marriages for themselves as satisfactory, or even better than satisfactory, while denying the importance or consequences of the discrepancy between their management of family organization and parenting on the one hand and their much lower level of functioning in aspects of their marriage which pertain to their relationship with one another.

Earlier dissertation studies of marital interaction supervised by the senior author had shown that collusive patterns reduce capabilities for managing stress. Machlin (Machlin & Charny, 1991a, 1991b) had studied six cases in which a husband had suffered a stroke at a relatively young age when the husband was still employed and while the couple were still involved in active parenting of children. Kirschner (1988) studied couples who presented for marital therapy in a crisis that erupted at the time of the "empty nest" or the last child leaving home. Erel (1990) studied the interaction of couples in which at least one spouse was the child of a Holocaust survivor. All three studies arrived independently at the conclusion previously reported, that greater vulnerability to stress and poorer marital functioning are associated with a pattern of marital interaction which involves ostensibly good functioning in the areas of Family Management and Parenting, but at the same time a degree of dysfunction in one or more areas of Companionship, Relationship, Communication, and Attraction and Sexuality. The emphasis and often pride in family management and parenting may enable couples to live in collusive self-deception for years at a time, but they are more susceptible to decompensation and breakdown in the event of crises.

Based on these earlier findings in respect of our knowledge that couples who do not function at a normal level in their sexuality nonetheless engage considerably in idealization of their relationship, we were on the lookout for how the sex-avoidant couples qualified their sexuality specifically and their relationship in general. In analyzing EDMQ results, the statistical definition we use for House-Parent Marriages is based on either one of two formulae:

a. the couple earns scores idealizing House and Parent functions (Family Management and Parenting) to an extent that is twice as much as either their idealization scores, or scores of competent functioning, or a combination of the two in the areas of Relationship functions (Companionship, Relationship and Communication, Attraction and Sexuality);

b. the couple earns scores of disturbed or dysfunctional functioning in the areas of Relationship functions to an extent that is twice as much as their scores of disturbance or dysfunctionality in House and Parent functions.

Table 4 shows that, as noted, in Phase Three of the present study 16 of the 56 couples, or 29%, were found to be sex-avoidant. Table 5 shows that out of the 56 couples, 20 couples, or 36%, demonstrated a House-Parent Marriage pattern. (The samples of each of the subgroups here are too small to warrant conclusions, but one cannot help but note suggestively that the kibbutz couples, a society which has long been described as suffering from an undue degree of emphasis on family-wide functioning with a corresponding loss in vitality in marital experiencing, show the highest percentage of House-Parent Marriages.) Table 6 tells us that there is a significant difference between the sex-avoidant couples and the sex-functioning couples in respect of the frequency of the House-Parent Marriage pattern: 69% of the sex-avoidant couples showed the House-Parent Marriage pattern, while only 23% of the sex-functioning couples showed the same pattern.

TABLE 5. Distribution of Couples Showing Collusive House-Parent Marriages (N = 56)

	HOUSE-PARENT MARRIAGE	*NOT* HOUSE-PARENT MARRIAGE	N
KIBBUTZ	8 = 53%	7 = 47%	15
THERAPISTS	5 = 38%	8 = 62%	13
(Jerusalem) COUPLES IN MARITAL THERAPY	7 = 25%	21 = 75%	28
TOTALS	20 = 36%	36 = 64%	56

TABLE 6. Relationship Between Reduced Sexual Activity (Sex-*Avoidant* Marriages) and House-Parent Marriages (HPM)

	Sex-*AVOIDANT*	Sex-*FUNCTIONING*	N
KIBBUTZ	6 = 40%	9 = 60%	15
of which HPM	6 = 100%	2 = 22%	
THERAPISTS	0 = 0%	13 = 100%	13
of which HPM	—	5 = 38%	
(Jerusalem) COUPLES IN MARITAL THERAPY	10 = 36%	18 = 64%	28
of which HPM	5 = 50%	2 = 11%	
TOTALS	16 = 29%	40 = 71%	56
of which HPM	11 = 69%	9 = 23%	

Although only suggestive in terms of the extent of data available, a difference also emerged in the dynamics of the construction of the House-Parent Marriage pattern. The sex-avoidant couples showed a House-Parent Marriage pattern based more on denial of relationship dysfunctions which existed, while the sex-functioning couples showed a House-Parent Marriage pattern that was more in the direction of idealization of these classic functions of marriage, and less on the basis of denial of dysfunctions that were present in their relationship. Table 7 highlights these findings about the inner dynamic structure of the construction of House-Parent Marriages. Of 11 out of 16 (69%) sex-avoidant couples who showed a House-Parent Marriage pattern, eight of the 11 (73%) did so on the basis of denial of their relationship dysfunction, and only three of the 11 did so on the basis of idealizing the relationship. Of the nine out of 40 (23%) sex-functioning couples who showed a House-Parent Marriage pattern, five of the nine (56%) did so on the basis of idealizing the relationship, and four of the nine (44%) did so on the basis of denial of the relationship dysfunction. The suggestive conclusion of greater denial of relationship dysfunction

TABLE 7. Dynamic Structure of Collusive House-Parent Marriages Compared in Sex-*Avoidant* and Sex-*Functioning* Marriages

	Sex-*AVOIDANT*	Sex-*FUNCTIONING*
KIBBUTZ (6 out of 15 Sex-*AVOIDANT*) HOUSE-PARENT MARRIAGES	6	2
• Idealization of relationship	0	1 of 2
• Denial of relationship dysfunction	6 of 6	1 of 2
THERAPISTS (0 out of 13 Sex-*AVOIDANT*) HOUSE-PARENT MARRIAGES	–	5
• Idealization of relationship	–	4 of 5
• Denial of relationship dysfunction	–	1 of 5
(Jerusalem) COUPLES IN MARITAL THERAPY (10 out of 28 Sex-*AVOIDANT*) HOUSE-PARENT MARRIAGES	5	2
• Idealization of relationship	3 of 5	0 of 2
• Denial of relationship dysfunction	2 of 5	2 of 2
TOTALS (16 out of 56 Sex-*AVOIDANT*) **HOUSE-PARENT MARRIAGES**	**11 (69%)**	**9 (23%)**
• **Idealization of relationship**	**3 of 11 = 27%**	**5 of 9 = 56%**
• **Denial of relationship dysfunction**	**8 of 11 = 73%**	**4 of 9 = 44%**

in sex-avoidant couples and more idealization of the relationship in sex-functioning couples seems to be deserving of further study.

IMPLICATIONS FOR TREATMENT

Marital educators and marriage therapists need to be aware to counsel still-young couples that there is a likelihood of a considerable reduction of their sexual activity following the early phase of their marriage, especially following a birth of a child and/or following some kind of major economic loss with its realistic meanings and stresses as well as its attack on the self-confidence and esteem of the male and the couple; hopefully, anticipatory attention to these issues might provide some protection against a severe decline in sexuality.

The basic pattern that seems to obtain when sexual functioning drops seriously is that the wife is generally the mate who stops wanting and being available to engage in sexual intercourse, and this option is characteristically exercised by a woman who has a dominant role in the marriage with her husband playing a passive role, so that now the husband shows the same passivity in response to his wife's cessation of sexual functioning. In other words, according to these findings, the basic pattern which clinicians are advised to address preventively or to treat in cases where there already is reduced sexual activity is one of a husband who reacts passively to the frustration and insult imposed on him by a characteristically dominant wife, including when she now calls a relative to absolute halt to their sexual activity. At the same time, the fact that most women tend to view sexuality from a point of view of their overall emotional relationship with their partner is encouraging that treatment work that helps men to be more related and loving may contribute meaningfully to some degree of unlocking the closed doors. From a systemic point of view, or looking at the couple as a whole, the findings point to couples who have not created a pattern of equality between them, and a sense of processing or dealing actively with emotional disappointments, frustrations and problems as they arise in the marriage.

Charny (1992b) has described sexuality as a kind of high speed film on which all basic dynamics are registered immediately and with fine-grain intensity. Many clinical observations of marriage have suggested that only couples who engage in a respectful ability to process emotions, and especially the dysphoric or disrespectful, critical, angry, and hostile emotions (Charny, 1992a), have a possibility of arriving at a relationship in which there is trust and a faith in being able to handle difficulties. When applied to a cessation of sexual functioning, the pattern of being unable to process difficulty only reinforces the drop in the highly sensitive and emotionally charged functions of sexuality.

The sad facts are that any number of couples report enormous relief, and then also actual pleasure, at the cessation of sexual activity. They emphasize that they now achieve an absence of upset and a calm restfulness that they did not have before. What they are saying does not necessarily speak for the joy at the cessation of sexuality as such, although that too is true for some, but for the overall collusive bargain that is achieved by foregoing sexuality in order to achieve peace. These are couples who are afraid of sexuality along with and as a part of fearing many other aspects of emotional processing intimacy, and especially ambivalences and conflicts, and the intensity of emotional closeness. As Talmadge and Talmadge have concluded:

> The idealizing requires exclusion of negative feelings from the relationship; the end result of which is an exclusion of all affect. Gradually they turn down the intensity of the feeling between them so that there is an experience of numbness. They create a smooth relationship at the expense of their intensity and passion. (1986, p. 10)

Many couples, however, are able to maintain the smooth facade at the expense of intimacy for their entire lives together. This bound up energy may also result in physical, emotional, or psychosomatic symptoms in the partners or in their children. (1986, pp. 10-11)

Given that sexuality is a very special opportunity for intimacy on the level of primary feelings of dependency, vulnerability, needs for another person, and the ability to process negative feelings, unless couples are able to handle the processing of emotions they are going to be more susceptible to a cessation of sexual activity, and also are going to be less able to respond appropriately to the symptom of cessation of sexual activity, and any pattern of under-functioning sexually is likely to become structurally entrenched.

Perhaps the most poetic, and, in our judgment, entirely accurate, statement about what is optimal marital sexuality that has appeared in our professional literature to date is by David Schnarch (1997). In a wonderful chapter entitled, "Fucking, Doing and Being Done: It Isn't What You Do, It's the Way You Do It," Schnarch writes:

> Fucking involves *doing* and *being done*–as in doing your partner and be-
> ing done by him or her. It doesn't make sense to think of fucking as syn-
> onymous with intercourse because many who've done the latter have
> never experienced the former. Some people "make love" specifically to
> avoid it. (p. 263)
>   Do you know what it feels like when somebody's *doing* you–not
> just bringing you to orgasm or having intercourse–but really doing you?
> Do you know what it feels like to *do* somebody else? (p. 264) . . . Being
> done involves surrender, union, and the power of receiving (p. 266) . . .
> Fucking is the subjective experience of doing each other and being done
> simultaneously. Sound simple? It's not. In fact, it is difficult for people
> to really *fuck* their spouse (in the most wholesome, erotic sense of the
> word). Many people, male or female, have a hard time cracking loose
> their eroticism with the person they married. (p. 267)

Schnarch's emphasis is on the ultimate relational intimacy, on the essence of the one lover meeting, tasting and simultaneously being tasted by the other lover in an exchange of giving and receiving by the two people. He estimates that perhaps 10 to 20% of couples experience this level of intimacy. The present senior author (Charny, 1992a) has otherwise estimated that approximately 10% of marriages achieve what has been described as a level of a co-creative relationship, and although obviously the overall quality of marriage should never be reduced only to its sexual component, the similarity in percentages is probably not by chance, basically because what is in common is a degree of significant emotional intimacy between the two spouses.

CONCLUSIONS

The present study reports an unfolding trail of research which leads to the following picture: There is convergent evidence that the phenomenon of reduced sexual activity in young couples is very common, with a high estimate being one out of three couples and a low estimate at one out of seven couples. Other than for couples who have become estranged and are angrily involved in a breakdown of their marriage, there is a prototypal situation where it is largely the wife who initiates the reduction or ends the regularity of sexual experience; the husband goes along with her and is unknowing and unable to challenge her or repossess her; and the couple settle into a collusive marital and family lifestyle which involves a striking emphasis on the joys and meaning fulness of maintaining their shared home and raising their children while neglecting, minimizing, or compensating for dysfunctions and gaps in their primary relationship with one another. A strong statistical finding in the present study showed that some 69% of sex-avoidant couples demonstrated a marital profile that we characterized as "House-Parent Marriages," while only 23% of couples who maintain a more normal sexual frequency show this pattern. In addition, there are suggestive data that the "House-Parent Marriages" of couples who for the most part have ceased to have a sexual relationship with one another are based on compensatory idealization and accommodation to the absence of sexuality on the basis of denials of any relationship dysfunctions in their lives. When the same pattern of undue emphasis on home and parenting is found in couples who are maintaining a more natural sexuality, it tends to be more on the basis of idealization of their house and parenting functions over the marital relationship, and less on compensation for and denials of dysphoric and dysfunctional emotional relationship experiences. The present study also suggests to marital therapists that attention to greater caring and loving of wives by their husbands is one key to correcting reduced sexuality, and that therapeutic work on greater equality between spouses–including correction of patterns of female domination and male passivity, and enhancement of intimacy processes including the ability to handle conflict–are among the best ways to protect the continuation of couples' sexuality.

NOTES

1. I have seen and heard over the years estimates ranging from one out of seven young couples to one out of four. A newspaper report of a just-published book by well-known psychologist Carol Gilligan (2002) which I have not yet seen reports her as writing of an even higher incidence: "One out of three married couple suffer a decline in desire if not a complete loss of desire." Quoted from Kazin, Edna (2003). Books and magazine articles all warning of a decline of sexual desire of married couples, and especially among married women. *Ha'aretz*, February 5. (Hebrew)

2. Perhaps the silence is just now lifting. Along with the above-mentioned book by Gilligan, there has been another recent book by Michelle Wiener Davis (2003).

3. Professional readers may be relieved that our colleague therapists did not embarrass us since none of the therapist-spouse couples reported being sex-avoidant–assuming that we can trust their replies, of course.

REFERENCES

Asineli, S. (1992). *Development of a psychometric instrument for evaluating couple interaction based on an existential/dialectical model: A bridge between theory, research and practice.* Unpublished master's thesis, Tel Aviv University, Bob Shapell School of Social Work, Israel. (Hebrew)

Asineli, S., & Charny, I. W. (1997). Development of a questionnaire for couples to assess marital functioning and interaction based on an existential/dialectical model. *Bamishpacha (Journal of the Israel Association for Marital and Family Therapy), 39,* 7-26. (Hebrew)

Barrett, G., Pendry, E., Peacock, J., Victor, C., Thakar, R., & Manyonda, I. (1999). Women's sexuality after childbirth: A pilot study. *Archives of Sexual Behavior, 28*(2), 179-191.

Beck, J. G. (1995). Hypoactive sexual desire disorder: An overview. *Journal of Consulting and Clinical Psychology, 63,* 919-927.

Bennun, I., Rust, J., & Golombok, S. (1985). The effects of marital therapy on sexual satisfaction. *Scandinavian Journal of Behaviour Therapy, 14*(2), 65-72.

Call, V., Sprecher, S., & Schwartz, P. (1995). The incidence and frequency of marital sex in a national sample. *Journal of Marriage and the Family, 57,* 639-652.

Charny, I, W. (1987). "Marital Trap Analysis" - Incompetence, complementarity and success traps: Identifying potential future dysfunctions based on a couple's current collusive agreements. *Contemporary Family Therapy, 9,* 163-180. *See also*: Foley, Vincent D. Going beyond symptoms: A comment on Charny, 181-184. Kaslow, Florence W. Marital trap analysis reanalyzed: A comment on Charny, 185-187.

Charny, I. W. (1992a). *Existential/dialectical marital therapy: Breaking the secret code of marriage.* New York: Brunner/Mazel.

Charny, I. W. (1992b). Marital sexuality: Joyful and loving sexuality versus "good marriages" with no sex and "bad marriages" with good sex. In *Existential/dialectical marital therapy* (pp. 199-219). New York: Brunner/Mazel.

Charny, I. W., & Asineli, S. (1996). A validity study of existential/dialectical marital questionnaire [EDMQ]: A psychometric questionnaire for assessing marital interaction. *Contemporary Family Therapy, 18,* 41-59.

Davis, M. W. (2003). *The sex-starved marriage: A couple's guide to boosting the marriage libido.* New York: Simon & Schuster.

Dekker, J., & Everaerd, W. (1983). A long-term follow-up study of couples treated for sexual dysfunctions. *Journal of Sex and Marital Therapy, 9*(2), 99-113.

Doddridge, R., Schumm, W. R., & Bergen, M. B. (1987). Factors related to decline in preferred frequency of sexual intercourse among young couples. *Psychological Reports, 60,* 391-395.

Erel, D. (1990). *Marital interaction of children of Holocaust survivors: The inter-generational transmission of post-traumatic impacts on marital functioning* [An exploratory study of five couples in marital therapy]. Unpublished master's dissertation, Tel Aviv University, Bob Shapell School of Social Work, Israel. (Hebrew)

Frank, E., Anderson, C., & Rubinstein D. (1978). Frequency of sexual dysfunction in "normal" couples. *New England Journal of Medicine, 299*, 111-115.

Gilligan, C. (2002). The birth of pleasure. *A new map of love.* New York: Knopf.

Greenblatt, C. S. (1983). The salience of sexuality in the early years of marriage. *Journal of Marriage and the Family, 45*, 289-299.

Hawton, K., Catalan, J., & Fagg, J. (1991). Low sexual desire: Sex therapy results and prognostic factors. *Behaviour Research and Therapy, 29*(3), 217-224.

Jasso, G. (1985). Marital coital frequency and the passage of time: Estimating the separate effects of spouses' ages and marital duration, birth and marriage cohorts, and period influences. *American Sociological Review, 50*(2), 224-241.

Kaplan, H. S. (1974). *The new sex therapy: Active treatment of sexual dysfunctions.* New York: Brunner/Mazel.

Kaplan, H. S. (1979). *Disorders of sexual desire.* New York: Brunner/Mazel.

Kirschner, P. (1988). *Changes in marital functioning and interaction following treatment of couples in mid-life crisis.* Unpublished master's thesis, Tel Aviv University, Bob Shapell School of Social Work. (Hebrew)

Lief, H. I. (1977). Inhibited sexual desire. *Medical Aspects Human Sexuality II*, 94-95.

LoPiccolo, J. (1980). Low sexual desire. In Leiblum, S. R., & Pervin, L. A. (Eds.), *Principles and practice of sex therapy* (p. 25). New York: Guilford Press.

Machlin, R., & Charny, I. W. (1991a). Changes in marital functioning and interaction of couples following a stroke. *Chevra vRvachach (Society and Welfare), 11*, 395-406. (Hebrew)

Machlin, R., & Charny, I. W. (1991b). Changes in the quality of the marital relationship after a stroke. *Bamishpacha (Journal of the Israel Association for Marital and Family Therapy), 34*, 18-27. (Hebrew)

Masters, W. H., & Johnson, V. C. (1970). *Human sexual inadequacy.* Boston: Little Brown.

Rao, K. V., & Demaris, A. (1995). Coital frequency among married and cohabiting couples in the United States. *Journal of Biosocial Science, 27*(2), 135-150.

Schnarch, D. (1997). Fucking, doing and being done: It isn't what you do, it's the way you do it. In *Passionate marriage: Love, sex and intimacy in emotionally committed relationships* (pp. 261-287). New York: Henry Holt & Co.

Schover, L. R. (1986). Sexual dysfunction: When a partner complains of low sexual desire. *Medical Aspects of Human Sexuality, 20*(3), 108-116.

Snyder, D. K., & Berg, P. (1983). Predicting couples' responses to brief directive sex therapy. *Journal of Sex and Marital Therapy, 9*(2), 114-120.

Talmadge, L. D., & Talmadge, W. (1986). Relational sexuality: An understanding of low sexual desire. *Journal of Sexual and Marital Therapy, 12*(1), 3-21.

Trudel, G., Landry, L., & Larose, Y. (1997). Low sexual desire: The role of anxiety, depression and marital adjustment. *Sexual and Marital Therapy, 12*(1), 95-99.

How Do Young Adult Children Deal with Parental Divorce? A Generational Prospect

Eugenia Scabini
Vittorio Cigoli

SUMMARY. Research during the last decades has paid great attention to the long-term developmental outcomes of parental divorce for young adult children in several domains of their life. Recently some studies have started to consider the qualitative aspects associated with the resolution process of this traumatic experience. This contribution is based on data drawn from in-depth interviews conducted with 30 Italian young adult children (20-26 years of age) who experienced parental divorce. The purpose is to provide a comprehension of how young adults deal with the past experience, as well as to examine the quality of the intergenerational exchange and to explore the young adults' future representations related to the topics of filial responsibility and personal family projects.

Eugenia Scabini is Professor of Social Psychology of the Family; Dean, Faculty of Psychology; and Head, Center for Family Studies and Research, Catholic University of the "Sacro Cuore" of Milan.

Vittorio Cigoli is Professor of Clinical Psychology of the Family, Faculty of Psychology, and Director, Postgraduate School of Psychology "A. Gemelli," Catholic University of the "Sacro Cuore" of Milan.

The authors thank Cristina Giuliani, PhD, researcher at the Center for Family Studies and Research, for pointing out the object of the research, developing interviews, and administering the "Double Moon Test."

[Haworth co-indexing entry note]: "How Do Young Adult Children Deal with Parental Divorce? A Generational Prospect." Scabini, Eugenia, and Vittorio Cigoli. Co-published simultaneously in *Journal of Family Psychotherapy* (The Haworth Press, Inc.) Vol. 15, No. 1/2, 2004, pp. 219-233; and: *Family Therapy Around the World: A Festschrift for Florence W. Kaslow* (ed: William C. Nichols) The Haworth Press, Inc., 2004, pp. 219-233. Single or multiple copies of this article are available for a fee from The Haworth Document Delivery Service [1-800-HAWORTH, 9:00 a.m. - 5:00 p.m. (EST). E-mail address: docdelivery@haworthpress.com].

219

Gender differences are also examined, comparing data of male and female interviewees. *[Article copies available for a fee from The Haworth Document Delivery Service: 1-800-HAWORTH. E-mail address: <docdelivery@ haworthpress.com> Website: <http://www.HaworthPress.com> © 2004 by The Haworth Press, Inc. All rights reserved.]*

KEYWORDS. Divorce, generational effects of divorce, gender differences

INTRODUCTION

The theme of divorce and its personal and generational effects is central in the clinical research of Florence Kaslow. Its value is that of having used an admirable diaclectical approach and overcoming the barriers between the various theoretical directions. It has remained possible to continue work on the characterised phases and stages of the pain of divorce to which correspond emotions-feelings and actions-behaviour, both specific and recognisable (Kaslow, 1980, 1981, 2000a; Kaslow & Schwartz, 1987). Phases and stages outline a kind of "virtual line" for getting over the pain that characterised the failure of a couple's ties, pain that begins even before the separation through the feelings of delusion, alienation, and emotional withdrawal from the relationship with the other. On the other hand the "virtual line" that leads toward the psychological divorce that we define as the transition of divorce (Cigoli, 1998; Scabini & Cigoli, 2000) is bound to encounter multiple obstacles along the path toward restructuring identity and reopening of trust-hope in the relationship with the other.

For the clinical psychologists who occupy themselves with couples, families, and divorce, the research of Florence Kaslow constitutes a true and proper milestone. In meeting single people and couples who live through the painful experience of divorce, they can in fact tend to take into account the phases that the person crosses and the obstacles they encounter.

As for the phase of conflict during divorce, which may turn into a perpetual family discord, we have in our research highlighted two obstacles we consider crucial: First, the firm hope for reunification with the former partner and that he or she may do something to change the nature of the relationship, and, second, the compulsory schism with the other. In order to save oneself as a valid source of tie one has to delete the other's presence (Cigoli, Galimberti, & Mombelli, 1988; Cigoli, 1998).

The interpersonal and generational outcomes of the two forms, i.e., ties/ anti-ties, are the following: The first case requires the maintenance of the ties with the other partner-parent in all ways, including also at a long distance from the divorce, in particular making use of the children; the second case requires getting rid of the other, canceling even the existence of the relationship and separating the children from the ex-partner. From this point of view, the parental alienation research (Gardner, 1989) is nothing but the behavioural deed with its techniques of "brainwashing" and seduction of the children of a mental process in order to face the pain of divorce.

The other merit of Florence Kaslow is that of paying attention to the influence of divorce on the generational dynamics (Kaslow, 1996, 2000b). In general, the scientific literature that deals with the "long-term effects" of divorce makes reference to the social adaptation and the quality of the emotional ties of the children in late adolescence, of the age of young adulthood and that of adults (Wallerstein & Lewis, 1998). The generational position is, however, a different prospect, i.e., another paradigm, since the core of research and the clinical intervention lies in the exchange among the generations. Such exchange consists not only of emotional and cognitive aspects, as in the case of beliefs and the "visions of life," but also ethical aspects.

According to Florence Kaslow, the promotion of legal action against the parents, the claim for damages, both in terms of the inheritance of goods and in terms of abuse undergone, are considered signs of unhealed wounds and ways of silencing the generational pain of divorce. The violation of the family loyalty and the iniquity of the actions within the relationships between parents and children, if not faced, spread the negative effects into future generations.

From our part, inside of a line of research clearly marked in family-generational terms, we have constructed, applied, and submitted to empirical checking both an intergenerational model of psychological consultancy directed at the judges of the court and the divorced families sent for counselling and a model of family and intergenerational mediation directed at parents and children. In both cases, particular attention is paid to the origins of family pain and the possible ways to repair guilt, injustice, and disloyalty to rekindle the hope and the trust in the relationship with the other (Cigoli, Gulotta, & Santi, 1983; Cigoli, 1997, 1998; Scabini & Cigoli, 2000).

DIVORCE AND GENERATIONAL EFFECTS

Late adolescence and young adulthood are characterised, with regard to the transitions into adult life and the undertaking of responsibility, as a crucial time for observation and evaluation of the dynamics within the relationships connected to the parental divorce. The recent literature dedicated to the "children of divorce" is in accord with the discovered importance of the long-term effects related to marital breakdown. Quite a few critical effects are said to be manifest during these phases affecting many different areas of the life of a young adult: adaptation and personal well-being, successful completion of school and setting out into professional life, and the quality of family relationships and feelings which, together with the behaviour of adolescents and young people as regards marriage, have in particular drawn the attention of researchers.

Moreover, according to some authors, it is in the age of the young adult that gender-bound specific effects of divorce are found. So, for example, the males display behavioural problems with more frequency and have difficulty in finishing their studies (dropout), while the females would more frequently experience unsatisfactory relationships with their mothers and have major preoccupations connected with the formation and maintenance over time of loving relationships (Amato, 1988, 1996; Zill, Morrison, & Coiro, 1993; Booth, Brinkeroff, & White, 1984; Amato & Keith, 1991; Gabardi & Rosen, 1991, 1992; Hetherington, Law, & O'Connor, 1993; Aquilino, 1994; Amato, Rezac, & Booth, 1995; Johnson, Wilkinson, & McNeil, 1995; Nichols et al., 2000; King, 2001).

It was with the outset of pioneering research by Wallerstein and Blakeslee (1989) that the problematic outcomes in the field of interpersonal relationships have been documented, particularly for female children. As is already well known, authors have spoken about the presence of a "delayed effect" (sleeper effect) of divorce that remains dormant during the preceding years and is related to the emergence of dangerous feelings in the area of intimate relationships. Such dangers examine the construction of bonding feelings, the fear of betrayal and being abandoned, and the distrust of the male partner.

Subsequent research has shown evidence that the female children of divorcees have sexual experiences earlier than the female children of married parents. Moreover, this research refers to the greater number of experiences regarding love and feelings (Gabardi & Rosen, 1991; Durana-Aydintung, 1997). Their style of attachment results in them being predominantly of anxious type and living with a higher level of difficulty in heterosexual relationships (Aro & Palosaari, 1992; McCabe, 1997). Finally, the risk of divorce often appears higher for women that have experienced the divorce of their parents in respect to their male counterparts.

However, not all researchers are in agreement over the presence of negative consequences of parental divorce in the age of the young adult. In fact, a few of these young adults show evidence of some positive effects, such as the example of the development of a greater independence, a richer social competence, and the capacity to comprehend and stay emotionally close with the mother.

As always, the results of the research, being referred to the different theoretical paradigms and using different methodology (and not just the techniques of analysis of the specific data), request a deeper reading of the studied phenomenon. This, in any case, is a turning point in the research from a study centred exclusively around the adaptation or lack of it in the face of divorce; the researchers have in fact always directed more of their attention to the aspects of emotional cognitive coping and to the relationships of the people involved in the situation of divorce. So, for example, other research has focused on the feelings of injustice that cross the family relationships following the marital breakdown, while still others have agreed to consider if and why the parents and their adult children search for reciprocal clarification (Arditti & Prouty, 1999; Shulman et al., 2001; Jurkovich, Thirkiend, & Morrell, 2001; Cigoli, Giuliani, & Iafrate, 2002). We would like here to underline how the time is occupied in the research of themes concerning the justice-injustice and the loyal-disloyal relationships (Boszormenyi-Nagy & Krasner, 1986; Jurkovich, Thirkiend, & Morrell, 2001). This means to take into account the ethical side of the family relationships and not only the emotional-cognitive aspects.

OBJECTIVES AND METHODOLOGY

The present contribution of research focuses on the young adult phase of children from divorced families in the context of Italian culture. Its objective is to analyse the modality through which children of that age seek to elaborate on the experience of parental divorce.

The theoretical context of the research is the relational-symbolic paradigm (Scabini & Cigoli, 1991; Cigoli, 1992, 1997; Scabini & Cigoli, 2000). This puts at the centre of study of family relations the connections (of couples, siblings, with the original family, between parents and children) that form ties between the members and the generations and their symbolic foundation. "Symbolic" is here intended in its original meaning of "syn ballein," that is to say, kept together, or connect (in our case of family relations). Apart from the cultural differences present in the family system, the symbolic foundation appears to centre itself on the themes of trust and of the hope in relationships with another (where the opposites are distrust and desperation), as well as the themes of justice-equality in the exchange (in which injustice and iniquity are the opposites). Emotional principles and ethical principles result in this way to be closely interrelated.

In particular, the paradigm assumes that the symbolic foundation, made by the quality of the exchange, whether between the family members or between the generations, emerges in the critical transitions, that is to say, in the fundamental passages in respect of the family (marriage, birth, adolescence, death) and in other critical passages (illness, divorce). In this sense, the divorce is not considered at all "a phase of the cycle of life," but rather a critical passage and at times impracticable for interpersonal or intergenerational exchange. In short, the transition of divorce puts to the test the symbolic foundation of the family relationship. In the specific transition of divorce, that is to say, the possibility to constructively elaborate or else the impossibility of doing, it is seen with the eyes and listened to through the feelings and the beliefs of the young adult.

In particular, the questions that this research intends to respond to are the following:

1. Is the young adult condition an opportunity to deal again with the pain of divorce? And if so, how?
2. Keeping in mind the cultural context, what can we say about gender differences in respect to the mental treatment of the parental divorce?
3. Once it is recognised that the pain of divorce can undermine the trust of the children in stable relationships during adult life, is it possible to find the presence of antidotes (resilience factor) in respect to the jeopardy?

It is clear that from a certain point of view, divorce cannot be considered a pathology, neither does it even out the idea of their normality being very widespread in the culture of the western world (and only in this). The research of answers to questions can address the clinical-social interventions in favour of the young and their families.

The qualitative characteristic research involved 30 Italian young adults (15 male, 15 female) aged between 20 and 26 years old (average = 23.7) who came from separated families. These sample subjects had experienced the separation of their parents during childhood and adolescence. Their average age at the time of separation was 9 years old, and the time passed since the parents' separation averaged 14 years. The sample young adults, whether university students or working, turned out to have been given to the mother, with exception of one case which involved joint care between the parents. (In Italy, more than 90% of children are given to their mothers, with different forms of the father's presence.) The major part of them, as in the typical Italian cultural context, still live in their family unit consisting of the mother and possible brothers and sisters. None of these young adults have a stable 'live-in' relationship, neither have they built their own family unit.

The qualitative research scope focuses on the emotional-cognitive-ethical modalities through which male and female children deal again with their parents' divorce during young adulthood.

The participants in this research were given a clinical interview, specially prepared, and the projected-graphic test, the "Double Moon" (Greco, 1999). The themes of the dialogues offered in these clinical interviews made reference to the family experiences, past and current, of the subjects, focussing in particular on the dynamics of the generational exchange (giving, receiving and repaying among the generations).

After a phase of warming-up, the first proposition for the subjects was the theme of generational inheritance (the resource-origin and the source of pain).

There is then a proposal to them, through the representation of the couple's and family's future, the theme of the revision of family relations in a generational sense (expectancy, responsibility, feeling of jeopardy). The interviews were analysed through the software Atlas.ti in its most recent version, proceeding according to the methodology typical of "grounded theory" (Denzin & Lincoln, 2000; McLeod, 2000; Strauss & Corbin, 1990).

After a phase of relaxation, the young adults eventually do the graphic test, the "Double Moon." It is a projected-graphic test that focuses on the theme of boundaries and the feelings of belonging within the family, always including, however, reference to the "missing element." The criteria for interpretation of the test focus in particular on: the presence of poles in conflict; their double representations (that is to say, for each pole); avoidance of conflict; and the modality of the responses of the projected-graphic of the participants at the request to insert the missing element (in our case it is almost always the father and his original family).

According to a long and profitable experience of clinical research, it seems very important to compare the "saying" and "telling" of the interview, with the "doing" of the projected-graphic test. It is in fact from this comparison that the hypotheses of sense can be given value to or not.

In the following section the results of the articulated research according to the produced themes are presented. Following this will be the search to give answers to the questions.

GENERATIONAL INHERITANCE

The Resource-Origin

All of the young people interviewed recognised having received something good from their family. It is important to point out the constant presence of the following sequence: the communication given to the interviewer, in narrative and dialogue form, starting regularly from the positive inheritance, while the reflections on the painful aspects are postponed to a second moment and, in some cases, even omitted. One might say that from a generational point of view, it is fundamental to be refuelled by a beneficial source.

In the characterisation of the beneficial generational source, the young adults make reference to two different means of approach. In the first case it is the mother who is recognised as the only good source, while the father is not nominated and is also excluded from the graphical representation. This source qualifies as the stability/continuity from the presence and from the care. To be demonstrated, it is this temporality, not often sacrificial, that it is put in opposition with the paternal disengagement and even abandonment.

The resource-origin is presented with typical personality characteristics: the tenacity and the bravery to deal with life, the capacity to not become overwhelmed by adversity, and the trust in the possibility of change and relational growth. It is always from the mother that the young people, whether male or female, recognise the transmission of ethical and spiritual values: honesty and a sense of duty, the sense of family and faith.

Equally, the narration and the graphic action bring to light completely opposite polarities (the mother, the father) that may suggest an underlying presence of a schism between the parents. Rather than talking of "fading fathers," the young people seem to evoke the "phantom of the only parent" (Cigoli, 1998), the belief that, within the family relationships, one parent is enough to build a family and have offspring. In fact, the recognition of a beneficial source that involves the father is absent. In case there is the need to nominate something positive attributed to the father, it is marginalized to the passion for sport or the fact of being honest at work.

In the second case, instead, the beneficial resource-origin is indicated in the parental couple ("my parents"). The origin is qualified as the sharing presence within some fundamental values of the divorced parental couple, and even the capacity to transmit them to the children through concrete choices of life. The demonstrated values comprise of honesty, altruism and generosity; a sense of duty and of responsibility; correctness and loyalty within personal relationships; and the respect of family traditions. What is important from the generational point of view is that the young adult children preserve in this way the unity of the couple in spite of divorce and beyond.

We could think that the couple has managed to safeguard the parental joint exercise, moreover the custody of the child to one of the two parents, but also that the children search within themselves for such safeguards.

The Sources of Pain

The sources of pain for all the people interviewed consists of the drama-event of the divorce of their parents, with everything it provoked in the couple's relationships, and, above all, their children. In particular it is the lack of a couple as a stable point of reference to be perceived as the source of pain within the self of all people interviewed. The characteristics of this pain, however, come from a differentiation in the relationships of every parent and in relation to the general difference. We could speak of the proposal of specific form of pain for males and females in the young adult years.

However, considering the father, the source of pain consists principally in a relationship with his children characterised by distance or even detachment (spatial dimension) and discontinuity and even the break-up of the relationship (temporal dimension). These aspects constitute the leitmotif of the children's accounts about the relationship with the father who does not have custody be they male or female.

The pain generated from a connection lived as something fragile and discontinuous shows different characteristics for males and females. In fact, for the sons, this includes the marginality and the lack of the father, the absence of the parent who establishes the rules, who guides and hands down useful rules for life. For the daughters, the lack and marginality of the father is above all the absence of a partner close to their mother. This produces the loneliness of the mother and the identification with her suffering. So the husband-partner of the mother is missing, which is also perceived as a boundary in respect of the maternal presence which risks being excessive and invasive.

The source of pain attributed to the mother coincides in fact with the excess of her presence and closeness, a theme that distinguishes above all, if not exclusively, the relationship between her and her female children. It refers to both the spatial dimension of the interpersonal boundaries (interference and involvement) and the temporal dimension (sacrifices of the mother and her spirit of abnegation for the children). In particular, the projected-graphic Double Moon Test has provided important indications of the relationship with the father and the mother. In the first case, drawings highlight the difficult or absolute lack of access of the father through his omission or his marginal/external arrangement in respect to the family space. Conversely–in the case of the mother–drawings emphasize a risky relational intimacy which turns out to be too tight.

From the Involvement of Pain to the Search for Understanding

So what are the experiences connected to this excessive presence and closeness and what are the possible ways of facing them? If we consider the female children, the presence of a mix of feelings made of fear regarding the sensitivity of the mother in the face of psychological injuries, of guilt for the feelings of inadequacy with regards to the feeling of duty to comfort and protect the mother, of confusion between their own suffering and the maternal suffering, of anger for the emotional blackmail undergone and for the heavy debt due to the burden regarding the sacrificial behaviour of the mother. This results in the female children finding themselves wrapped up in an involved relationship without being able to see a way out.

The males, on the other hand, remove themselves from the situation through avoidance and emotional distance. In cases of involvement, the dominating feeling is anger: anger at having to face the mother's feelings of loneliness, anger for dividing the world into good and bad, and anger for being attacked if the male child is similar to his father.

They are, however, much more sensitive to the experienced loss, to the disappointment connected with the "disappearance" and to the scarce interest of the father towards them. In this case anger easily takes the form of resentment for having felt lonely, having had to get by in the world, and, quite often, this creates a very dangerous mix with the feeling of impotence felt in the face of the relational situation.

Furthermore, it must be said that for the males it is more difficult to understand the theme of the generational exchange (giving-receiving). While the females immediately pick up on the aspects of debt towards their parents and responsibility towards them, the males are disoriented and bewildered by words like "obligation," "duty towards," "responsibility," and easily claim their right to receive. It is like saying that mentally they focus with more difficulty on the logic of generational exchange.

There are, however, situations of young adults, whether males or females, marked by other experiences. There are present, for example, feelings of esteem towards their parents, of understanding their limits and their needs, but also of the risk of the ties. Even in the presence of notable emotional closeness, the mother-daughter relationship is coloured in calmer and more delicate shades; the father-son relationship, even in the presence of a weak closeness of the father, is coloured in shades of understanding compared with the difficulty and pains of his experiences.

In short, the overcoming of this generational barrier (Williamson, 1981, 1991) or its involvement are characterised by a comparison with the parent of the same sex. Antidotes for the pain need to be found to overcome the generational barrier: They consist of feeling esteem for the other, identifying with the reasons of the other and their pain, as well as understanding the complexity of life and the risks within the ties involved. Naturally, this research, focusing only on young adults' representations and experiences, does not allow us to draw any correlation between the divorced parents' relational patterns and their children's representations. In any case, it seems particularly important considering the antidotes' typology.

GIVING, RECEIVING AND EXCHANGING:
THE GENERATIONAL PROSPECT

The theme of generational inheritance, central to the presented qualitative research, looks at the past-present of young adults by finding the resource-origin and the source of pain and it opens into their future-present through the idea of a future couple and family. To this purpose it must be said that all the interviews are marked by two keywords: mistake (of the parents) and redemption (one's own). The mistake of parents can be a true personal fault, but also as an unfortunate incident or a mixture of both. In any case, for the females, the redemption comes through the need to have children, possibly early. (This "need" is in contradiction with respect to the Italian cultural context where the lowest birth rate in the world is found and where the young adult women are, like the males, much more focused in self-realisation). The need emerges also in the projected-graphic test.

This is contrasted with the fear of not being able to guarantee to the children what they themselves were not able to experience: the family unit and the presence of both parents. From here comes the first thought, that of looking for the "right man," capable of giving the guarantee of not being abandoned. The redemption, therefore, is in the relation to the mother and her fault of having chosen the wrong partner, while the fear concerns the danger of once more exposing the child to the loss of the family unit.

The males also anticipate a family future and bringing up children. However, they do not deal with a true personal need, and the fear focuses on the possibility of repeating the mistake of the father. So, together with the desire to safeguard the father-mother-child relationship (also related to the problems of the couple and to the original families) and to have the relationship alive and profound with the child, we find continuing doubts concerning their own ability to commit and to assume responsibility towards future generations. The redemption concerns again the taking on of generational responsibility (which for the father was very difficult and at times impossible), and offering the children a security they had little chance to experience during their own childhood.

So, whereas young adult women seem to be guided by the need of having a family and are at the same time "obsessed" with the idea of searching for a suitable partner who will keep the family united, the young adult males figure out a future family, but are "obsessed" with the idea that they could repeat their father's mistake, i.e., of not being capable to offer security to his own family, especially to his children.

CONCLUSIONS

In the present research we have dealt with young Italian adult children who experienced the pain of their parents' divorce. It aims, along with Florence Kaslow's idea (2000a, 2000b), at considering the possible generational effects as well as the relation between resource and relational jeopardy as experienced by young adults. As is typical with qualitative research based on epistemological premises and the use of peculiar techniques (Strauss & Corbin, 1990; Denzin & Lincoln, 2000; McLeod, 2000), we started by asking some questions.

The first examines the way young adults reflect on their personal experience, where they find the origin-resource, and which ones are the sources of pain and what jeopardises them. From the research emerge two beneficial sources: one, more widespread, can be attributed to the mother and, specifically, to the stability and continuity of her presence and care. The other, more rarely, is attributed to values the parental couple used to share and have handed on to their children. (The mother is seen as a beneficial source in almost all the subjects [male and female], while parental couple sharing is seen as a beneficial source significantly more in females. This is not surprising considering their particular attention at the relation [see: attention to the father as the mother's partner].) It is therefore interesting to point out that the two sources coincide with the belief of clinical psychologists that this is the appropriate way to tackle the pain of divorce. Some underline the importance of ongoing care and of finding the parent who is capable of ensuring it (Goldstein, Freud, & Solnit, 1973). Others, however, highlight the importance of shared values and custom of the parental couple (Cigoli, Gulotta, & Santi, 1983, 1997).

The source of pain is unanimously found by both males and females in the missing of a parental couple acting as a stable point of reference. Father and mother occupy the position of "missing" and "excessive presence" respectively and attain specific attributions from male and female young adults. So, for males, the parent who sets up the rules and gives the guidelines is missing, whereas for the females it is their mother's partner. Given the excessive maternal presence and high female sensitivity as regards the relationship with another person, the daughters are easily involved sentimentally, making it difficult to overcome the generational boundary (Williamson 1981, 1991).

Males, however, do admit an excessive maternal presence, but keep feelings of obligation and duty towards their mother at a far distance and focus much more on the missing (absence, marginal role, precariousness) of their father.

At this point it can be observed that young adults relate to their same genders (males to males; females to females), bringing to light the crucial role which in the human mind is performed by the identification with the similar gender. The second question is related to trust/distrust in respect to family and couple ties where again we can find a gender difference. When projecting their present into the future, the females surely see themselves with children and are already searching for a partner who is capable of ensuring their children the security of a united family. As far as the males are concerned, they do wish a future as a couple and family, but feel more doubtful about it, since they are afraid of themselves, i.e., repeating their father's error and guilt.

So we understand that for the males the aspect of identification with the same gender is crucial, whereas for the females there is a "relational shift" aiming at what is different, specifically at the partner their mother did not have or was not able to tie to herself for good.

The last question relates to the antidotes for mental and relational jeopardy. To this may be said that young adults, who have succeeded in saving their parents by, for instance, acknowledging their common values, or in saving their life by accepting their parents' personal limits and by understanding that the bond is open to the unpredictable and may generate pain that cannot be treated easily, have more strings to their bow to cope with the pain of divorce. But as was stated before, this is a minority. Most young adults in fact are still implied either in the schismatic process dominated by the thought of eliminating the other, or in the process of involvement where anger, guilt and impotence form a mix of feelings which is difficult to cope with.

We believe that the knowledge offered by the present research may be useful for clinical psychologists who deal with the pain of divorce. In fact by making a start from the capability of identification with the other's (in our case the young adult's) sufferings as well as searching for their available resources, we will be able to orient the work of support and cure.

REFERENCES

Amato, P.R. (1988). Parental divorce and attitudes toward marriage and family life. *Journal of Marriage and the Family, 5*, 453-461.

Amato, P.R. (1996). Explaining the intergenerational transmission of divorce. *Journal of Marriage and the Family, 58*, 628-640.

Amato, P.R., & Keith, B. (1991). Parental divorce and adult well-being: A meta-analysis. *Journal of Marriage and the Family, 53*, 43-58.

Amato, P.R., Rezac, S.J., & Booth, A. (1995). Helping between parents and young adult offspring: The role of parental marital quality, divorce and remarriage. *Journal of Marriage and the Family, 57*, 363-374.

Aquilino W.S. (1994). Impact of childhood family disruption on young adults' relationships with parents. *Journal of Marriage and the Family, 56*, 295-313.

Arditti, J.A., & Prouty, A.M. (1999). Change, disengagement and renewal: Relationship dynamics between young adults and their fathers after divorce. *Journal of Marital and Family Therapy, 25*, 61-81.

Aro, H.M., & Palosaari, U.K. (1992). Parental divorce, adolescence, and transition to young adulthood: A follow-up study. *American Journal of Orthopsychiatry, 62*, 421-429.

Booth, A., Brinkerhoff, D.B., & White, L.K. (1984). The impact of parental divorce on courtship. *Journal of Marriage and the Family, 46*, 85-94.

Boszormenyi-Nagy, I., & Krasner, B.R. (1986). *Between give and take: A clinical guide to conextual therapy*. New York: Brunner/Mazel.

Cigoli, V. (1997). *Intrecci familiari. Realtà interiore e scenario relazionale*. Milano: Raffaello Cortina.

Cigoli, V. (1998). *Psicologia della separazione e del divorzio*. Bologna: Il Mulino.

Cigoli, V., Galimberti, C., & Mombelli, M. (1988). *Il legame disperante. Il divorzio come dramma di genitori e figli*. Milano: Raffaello Cortina Editore.

Cigoli, V., Giuliani, C., & Iafrate, R. (2002). Il dolore del divorzio: adolescenti e giovani adulti tra riavvicinamento e distacco alla storia familiare. *Psicologia clinica dello sviluppo, 3*, 423-439.

Cigoli, V., Gulotta, G., & Santi, G. (1983). *Separazione, divorzio, affidamento dei figli*. Milano: Giuffrè (Nuova Edizione, 1997).

Denzin, N.K., & Lincoln, Y.S. (Eds.) (2000). *Handbook of qualitative research (2nd ed.)*. Thousand Oaks, CA: Sage Publications.

Duran-Aydintung, C. (1997). Adult children of divorce revisited: When they speak up. *Journal of Divorce and Remarriage, 27*, 71-83.

Gabardi, L., & Rosen, L.A. (1992). Intimate relationships: College students from divorced and intact families. *Journal of Divorce and Remarriage, 18*, 25-56.

Gardner, R. (1989). *Parental alienation syndrome*. New York: Cresskill.

Goldstein, J., Freud, A., & Solnit, A. (1973). *Beyond the best interest of the child*. New York: Free Press.

Greco, O. (1999). *La doppia luna. Test dei confini e delle appartenenze familiari*. Milano: Vita e Pensiero.

Hetherington, E.M., Law, T.C., & O'Connor, T.G. (1993). Divorce: Challenges, changes, and new chances. In F. Walsh (Ed.), *Normal family processes* (pp. 208-234). New York: The Guilford Press.

Johnson, P., Wilkinson, W.K., & McNeil, K. (1995). The impact of parental divorce on the attainment of the developmental task of young adulthood. *Contemporary Family Therapy, 17*, 249-264.

Jurkovic, G.J., Thirkield, A., & Morrell, R. (2001). Parentification of adult children of divorce: A multidimensional analysis. *Journal of Youth and Adolescence, 30, 2*, 245-257.

Kaslow, F.W. (1980). Stages of divorce: A psychological perspective. *Villanova Law Review, 25*.

Kaslow, F.W. (1981). Divorce and divorce therapy. In A.S. Gurman & D.P. Kniskern (Eds.), *Handbook of family therapy* (pp. 662-696). New York: Brunner/Mazel.

Kaslow, F.W. (Ed.) (1996). *Handbook of relational diagnosis and dysfunctional family patterns*. New York: John Wiley and Sons.

Kaslow, F.W. (2000a). Families experiencing divorce. In W. Nichols, M.A. Pace-Nichols, D. Becvar, & A.Y. Napier (Eds.), *Handbook of family development and intervention* (pp. 341-368). New York: John Wiley and Sons.

Kaslow, F.W. (2000b). Children who sue parents: A legal route for family destruction? In F.W. Kaslow (Ed.), *Handbook of couple and families forensics: A sourcebook for mental health and legal professionals.* New York: John Wiley and Sons.

Kaslow, F.W., & Schwart, V. (1987). *The dynamic of divorce: A life cycle perspective.* New York: Brunner/Mazel.

King, V. (2002). Parental divorce and interpersonal trust in adult offspring. *Journal of Marriage and the Family, 64*, 642-656.

McCabe, K.M. (1997). Sex differences in the long-term effects of divorce on children: Depression and heterosexual relationship difficulties in the young adult years. *Journal of Divorce and Remarriage, 27*, 123-135.

McLeod, J. (2000). *Qualitative research in counselling and psychotherapy.* London: Sage.

Nichols, W.C., Pace Nichols, M.A., Becvar, D., & Napier, A. (Eds.) (2000). *Handbook of family development and intervention.* New York: John Wiley and Sons.

Scabini, E., & Cigoli, V. (1991). L'identità organizzativa della famiglia. In E. Scabini, & P.P. Donati (a cura di), *Identità adulte e relazioni familiari.* Studi Interdisciplinari sulla famiglia, 10. Milano: Vita e Pensiero.

Scabini, E., & Cigoli, V. (1997). Young adult families. An evolutionary slowdown or a breakdown in the generational transition? In A.J. Cherlin, E. Scabini, & G. Rossi (a cura di), Delayed home leaving in Europe and the United States. *Journal of Family Issues, 18, 6*, 608-626.

Scabini, E., & Cigoli, V. (1998). The role of theory in the study of family psychopathology. In L. L'Abate (a cura di). *Family psychopathology. The relational roots of dysfunctional behavior.* New York: Guilford Press.

Scabini, E., & Cigoli, V. (2000). *Il famigliare. Legami, simboli e transizioni.* Milano: Raffaello Cortina Editore.

Shulman, S., Scharf, M., Lumer, D., & Maurer, O. (2001). Parental divorce and young adult children's romantic relationships: Resolution of the divorce experience. *American Journal of Orthopsychiatry, 71*, 473-478.

Strauss, A.L., & Corbin, J. (1990). *Basics of qualitative research: Grounded theory, procedures and techniques.* Newbury Park, CA: Sage Publications.

Wallerstein, J.S., & Blakeslee, S. (1989). *Second chances: Men, women and children a decade after divorce.* New York: Ticknor and Fields.

Wallerstein, J.S., & Lewis, J. (1998). The long-term impact of divorce on children: A first report from a 25-year study. *Family and Conciliation Courts Review, 36*, 368-383.

Williamson, D.S. (1982). La conquista dell'autorità personale nel superamento del confine gerarchico intergenerazionale. *Terapia Familiare, 11*, 77-93 (ed. or. 1981).

Williamson, D.S. (1991). *The intimacy paradox.* New York: Guilford Press.

Zill, N., Morrison, D.R., & Coiro, M.J. (1993). Long-term effects of parental divorce on parent-child relationship, adjustment and achievement in young adulthood. *Journal of Family Psychology, 7*, 91-103.

Family Togetherness:
The Impact of Florrie Kaslow's
Contributions on Her Family of Procreation

Nadine J. Kaslow
Solis Kaslow
Howard I. Kaslow

SUMMARY. Members of Florence Kaslow's family of procreation share their insights into the myriad ways in which her professional contributions in family psychology and international psychology have had an impact on their family life. Particular attention is paid to the family life of psychotherapists, healthy family functioning, healthy long-term marriages, sex therapy, military psychology, family business consulting and the use of projective genograms, and international family psychology. *[Article copies available for a fee from The Haworth Document Delivery Service: 1-800-HAWORTH. E-mail address: <docdelivery@haworthpress.com> Website: <http://www.HaworthPress.com> © 2004 by The Haworth Press, Inc. All rights reserved.]*

Nadine J. Kaslow is Professor and Chief Psychologist, Emory University School of Medicine, Department of Psychiatry and Behavioral Sciences, Grady Health System, 80 Jesse Hill Jr. Drive, Atlanta, GA 30303 (E-mail: nkaslow@emory.edu).

Solis Kaslow is a financial consultant, and Howard I. Kaslow is Vice-President-Investments and a financial consultant, Smith Barney, Golden Bear Plaza, Suite 200, 11780 U.S. Highway 1, North Palm Beach, FL 33408.

[Haworth co-indexing entry note]: "Family Togetherness: The Impact of Florrie Kaslow's Contributions on Her Family of Procreation." Kaslow, Nadine J., Solis Kaslow, and Howard I. Kaslow. Co-published simultaneously in *Journal of Family Psychotherapy* (The Haworth Press, Inc.) Vol. 15, No. 1/2, 2004, pp. 235-250; and: *Family Therapy Around the World: A Festschrift for Florence W. Kaslow* (ed: William C. Nichols) The Haworth Press, Inc., 2004, pp. 235-250. Single or multiple copies of this article are available for a fee from The Haworth Document Delivery Service [1-800-HAWORTH, 9:00 a.m. - 5:00 p.m. (EST). E-mail address: docdelivery@haworthpress.com].

http://www.haworthpress.com/web/JFP
© 2004 by The Haworth Press, Inc. All rights reserved.
Digital Object Identifier: 10.1300/J085v15n01_17

KEYWORDS. Healthy marital and family functioning, military family psychology, family business consulting

As Florence (Florrie) Kaslow, PhD's, family of procreation, we are delighted to have the opportunity to contribute to this collection honoring Florrie's contributions to the fields of family psychology and family therapy.

Let us begin by introducing ourselves. Solis (Sol), a financial consultant, and Florrie have been married for close to 50 years. Sol has enjoyed participating with Florrie in her international travels. Together, Florrie and Sol have two children, Nadine and Howard. Nadine is a clinical psychologist with a special emphasis in family psychology/family therapy. Like her mother, Nadine has been actively involved in organizational activities within psychology. Just as Florrie was committed to an academic career at the University of Pennsylvania, Hahnemann Medical College, Florida School of Professional Psychology, Duke University Medical Center, and Florida Institute of Technology (Kaslow, 2000a), Nadine was on the faculty at the Yale University School of Medicine and currently is Professor and Chief Psychologist at Emory University School of Medicine based at Grady Health System. Nadine and Florrie share a passion for dance, particularly ballet. Howard, like his father, is a financial consultant. Howard and Sol have worked together for 20 years. Some have asserted that occupation is a sex-linked gene in our family. Howard is married to Denise and they have three children, Rachel, Ethan, and Naomi. Their three children will also share some of their insights on how their grandmamma, Florrie, has touched their lives.

We have decided to organize this article around some of Florrie's key contributions to the field and how these contributions are reflected in our family interactions and dynamics and each of our own personal development. Specifically, we will focus on the family life of psychotherapists, healthy family functioning, healthy long-term marriages, sex therapy, military psychology, family business consulting and the use of projective genograms, and international family psychology. Her writings in many other fields, including relational diagnosis (Kaslow, 1993a, 1993b, 1996), teaching/supervising and mentoring (Kaslow, 1986b), forensic psychology (Kaslow, 2000c), divorce including divorce mediation and divorce ceremonies (Kaslow & Schwartz, 1987; Schwartz & Kaslow, 1997), families and cults (Kaslow & Sussman, 1982), learning disabilities (Kaslow & Cooper, 1984), and dialogues among families of Holocaust survivors and perpetrators (F. W. Kaslow, 1995; Kaslow, 1997a, 1998), are not directly relevant to the life and functioning of our family, and thus they will not be covered in this article.

THE FAMILY LIFE OF PSYCHOTHERAPISTS

In her dedication to one of her numerous edited books, *The Family Life of Psychotherapists: Clinical Implications* (Kaslow, 1987), Florrie wrote, "To my family of procreation, Solis, Nadine, and Howard, who have intuitively known my desire to live fully in two worlds–the personal and the professional–keeping them somewhat apart yet definitely interwoven." It is her contention that although there must be some boundaries between our personal and professional lives, the two are inextricably intertwined and should be mutually enhancing and compatible (Kaslow, 1990). We firmly believe that while Florrie always has been passionate about living in both worlds, she has consistently communicated that her family life has come first. The day she received her doctorate, Nadine asked, "Should I call you Mommy Doctor or Doctor Mommy?" Florrie responded, "I will always be your mommy first." As a wife, mother, teacher, supervisor, lecturer, and psychotherapist, Florrie has aptly conveyed the ways in which there is a reciprocal impact of one's personal and professional worlds. She has validated how people, particularly women, often must struggle and juggle the multiple complexities and often overt and covert roles of wife, mother, and professional simultaneously in their lives. Florrie also has emphasized the influential impact of the reactions of partners and children on the lives of professional women.

All of us in the family have been served well by the recommendations that she has presented professionally for people to achieve a balance between their personal and professional lives. These include therapy for the therapist (Kaslow, 1984; Kaslow & Friedman, 1984), networking, self-care and replenishment, disengaging from one's professional role, and paying attention to the warning signs of stress and burnout.

One of the ways in which our family replenishes itself is through engaging in activities with Howard and Denise's children. They are fortunate to live near their grandparents and to see them often. Rachel, her 10-year-old granddaughter, says the following about Florrie, "she is caring, likes to have fun, travels a lot, and she always brings us back presents from her trips." Rachel loves to go to the ballet with her grandmother and enjoys it immensely when they do large puzzles together. Her 7-year-old grandson, Ethan, describes grandma as "kind, nice, and beautiful." He likes when she and Sol take the entire family on annual trips. The youngest grandchild, Naomi, age 5, says with an impish grin, "Grandma likes watches, and necklaces, and earrings." Naomi likes to play with her, especially when they do puzzles together and play with stuffed animals.

PROFILE OF THE HEALTHY FAMILY

Florrie has been a major contributor to family system's thinking regarding the healthy family (Kaslow, 1981). In this section, we review the key concepts that she articulated as components of a profile of the healthy family and share our views regarding these dynamics within our family.

Systems Orientation

First, she notes that healthy families reflect a systems orientation, such that the family has a sense of itself as a unit in which all members perceive themselves as having very special relationships with each other. The family enjoys spending time together in various activities but also welcomes others into their life. There is no question that we have a strong bond as a family unit of four, that each dyad within our family has special connections, and that we each have very strong friendship networks and connections with our extended family and with Howard's family of creation. As noted later in this paper, our family loved to travel together, both in the United States (U.S.) and abroad. We enjoyed attending cultural and sporting events together, and still do so. Howard's family is now included in such events. Some examples of our special connections as dyads follow. Nadine and Florrie enjoy their mutual psychology activities together through the American Psychological Association, co-authoring articles and chapters (Kaslow, Kaslow, & Farber, 1999; Kaslow & Kaslow, 1981), and taking trips together to see the ballet and shows in New York. Howard and Nadine have a very strong sibling bond, and talk with each other multiple times per week. They share a passion for baseball and love going to games together. Since they have very different skills and talents, they often help one another in areas in which they each excel.

Boundary Issues

A second characteristic of a healthy family concerns boundary issues. Although "family togetherness" was our theme song, and there has always been a great deal of cross-generational sharing within our family, there was never a question that the parents were the parents, the children were the children, and the grandparents had a unique role. As Howard and Nadine were growing up, Florrie and Sol shared in a very egalitarian manner all of the caregiving responsibilities, leaving Nadine and Howard free to be involved in school and their myriad extracurricular activities (e.g., piano, ballet, violin, drums, theater, marching band, Hebrew School). Howard and Nadine always enjoyed playing together and, during high school, were involved together in theater activities and thus had overlapping friendship circles. Sol's parents died when

Nadine was young and before Howard was born, so they were not active in our family life. However, Florrie's parents, who both emigrated to the United States from cities on the Russian-Ukraine border when they were preschoolers early in the 20th century, were very involved in our family life. They each emigrated from Russia to escape anti-Semitic pogroms and military conscription. We spent all of the Jewish holidays with them, and they always communicated to us how fortunate we were to reside in a country where there was political freedom and liberty. We visited with them frequently, and they helped out taking care of Howard and Nadine when Florrie and Sol began traveling abroad. They were also on-call for Nadine and Howard when both Florrie and Sol had to work and one of the children became sick. There is no doubt that just as Florrie had a special relationship with her grandparents, Nadine and Howard had a special tie with Florrie's parents that was treasured by all.

Contextual Issues

Contextual issues reflect the third dimension of healthy family functioning. A high value has always been placed in the family on clear and direct communication. Even in times of disagreement, an emphasis has been placed on open lines of dialogue. When someone in the family has issues, these are discussed openly and efforts are made to resolve the difficulties. These discussions of differences allow for each person in the family to develop his or her own and very different identity, while simultaneously feeling very close to others in the family.

Power Issues

Power issues are the fourth gestalt in the healthy family profile. Florrie and Sol have always had an unusually egalitarian relationship that was mutually supportive. Way before the feminist movement and role sharing became popular, Sol was helping out making breakfasts and lunches. When Florrie was "dissertating," Sol took the children out each Sunday on outings to provide Florrie time to work. Florrie and Sol served as co-PTA Presidents when the children were in elementary school, a fact that attested to the value they placed on participating in their children's education and their comfort in working together. Florrie was committed to Nadine and Howard not being latchkey children, and thus arranged her schedule to be home and available to the children after school and for extracurricular activities, dinner, and homework time. She then worked after the children went to bed. In elementary school, Nadine once said, "When I went to bed, Mommy was typing and when I woke up, Mommy was typing. Does she type all night?" It was hard for Nadine and Howard to split Florrie and Sol, as they made decisions together and supported the decisions made by the other. As Nadine and Howard matured, they had an increasing voice in decision making. However, there was always an emphasis placed on shared family decision making when appropriate. For example, together as a family we made decisions about summer vacations, movies to see, and so on.

Autonomy and Initiative

The fifth dimension of the healthy family profile is the encouragement of autonomy and initiative. Florrie and Sol were committed to providing Howard and Nadine with the nurturance, guidance, and limits they needed, while supporting their emancipation and independence. This was partially accomplished by Florrie and Sol modeling both closeness and separateness in their relationship with one another.

Affective Issues

With regard to affective issues, there always has been support for the expression of a wide range of emotions in the family. People comfort one another in the family when someone is particularly distressed and share in people's happiness and successes. Of course, each of us has been through difficult times in our own lives, and we have each felt very supported, in terms of both emotional and instrumental support, during these trying times. We love playing together as a family, as well as playing with Howard's family. For example, as a three-generation family, we enjoy going to Disney World together.

Negotiation

As a family, we negotiate by hearing each person's perspective, prioritizing what matters most and to whom, and then making a decision that everyone can live with. Sometimes, negotiating is actually fun in the family, even if it can be tense during the process. Topics that we have had to negotiate about over the years have included money, adolescent limits, parental expectations regarding grades and Hebrew School attendance, and degrees of autonomy versus connection. Annually when Howard and Nadine were growing up, we negotiated about such topics as should we build a pool or go on a trip, or where we would go on our summer trips. With regard to negotiations around task performances, each person had clearly identified tasks and yet we were able to trade tasks with others in the family.

Transcendental Values

The final component of a healthy family profile refers to transcendental values. Everyone in the family shares high ethical standards in one's personal and professional life, an appreciation of the importance of community involvement and participation, an awareness of the importance of education at all stages of the life-span, the attainment of one's personal best, and a reverence for social justice. Thus, it is no wonder that everyone in the family is very active, busy, conscientious, successful, and involved in the community. Our family's values are similar to those Florrie described as capturing the essence of both her family of origin and Sol's family of origin, "thrift, diligence, perseverance, self-reliance, and family loyalty" (F. Kaslow, 1995). Just as Florrie's father emphasized to her and her sister the intellectual, academic, and politically attuned aspects of life and her mother fostered the emotional, creative, and fun-loving components of living (Kaslow, 1990), our family values a blending of the two.

LONG-TERM "GOOD" MARRIAGES:
THE SEEMINGLY ESSENTIAL INGREDIENTS

For two decades, Florrie and her colleagues have portrayed healthy couples and in recent years have conducted research on long-term "good" marriages (Kaslow, 1982a; Kaslow & Hammerschmidt, 1992; Kaslow, Hansson, & Lundblad, 1994; Kaslow & Robison, 1996; Roizblatt et al., 1999; Sharlin, Kaslow, & Hammerschmidt, 2000). They have identified eight essential ingredients for long-term satisfying marriages. In this section, Sol shares his perspective on how these ingredients appear in his marriage to Florrie.

Problem-Solving and Coping Skills

With regard to good problem-solving and coping skills, Sol notes that when problems arise in his relationship with Florrie, they are able to each strongly present their case and then work out a mutually satisfactory resolution. "We never let a problem fester, but always try to resolve it within a reasonable amount of time." He also indicates that when they are confronted with problems external to their marriage, he often defers to her because of her natural intuition regarding dealing with people. However, he reports that they certainly together identify what the problem is, discuss various solutions, and then figure out a plan that mostly satisfies each of them.

Trust

In terms of trust in each other that includes fidelity, integrity and feeling "safe," Sol underscores the fact that they have made a firm commitment to having a monogamous relationship and have explicit trust in and respect for each other. He remarks that this commitment allows each of them to tolerate and accept the other's close relationships with people outside the marriage. "We feel safe enough to share our vulnerabilities with one another and to receive the support we need. We have always respected each other's chosen professions and activities."

Permanent Commitment to the Marriage

According to Sol, there is no doubt that he and Florrie have a permanent commitment to the marriage. Even in stressful times, "we have never viewed divorce as an option." He comments that part of what has made a permanent commitment to the marriage possible is that they have open, honest, and good communication. Another factor that supports their investment in the future of the relationship is the fact that they enjoy spending time together and having fun together, while simultaneously appreciating some spaces in togetherness for separate activities. There are enumerable ways in which they have fun together. Florrie and Sol enjoy physical activities with one another, such as tennis, dancing, long walks, aerobics, and workouts in the fitness center. They also relish their involvement in cultural activities, and are avid theater-, ballet-, concert-, and museum-goers. Other shared activities include going on long drives together and taking in the scenery, entertaining, and traveling in our country and abroad.

Shared Value System

In addition to their shared interests and activities, they have a shared value system. Sol indicates that they were very compatible in their views on raising the children and their relationships with their respective family's of origin, and have always had relatively comparable views on politics, spending money and associated financial responsibilities, and where and how to live. "We have similar priorities in life as to what we wanted to accomplish." He points out that their relationship has always been marked by consideration, mutual appreciation, and reciprocity. "Long before it was in vogue, we had a very egalitarian relationship in terms of roles and responsibilities. Whether it was simple things like dividing household chores or more complex sharing such as childcare duties in a dual-career marriage, we have always been considerate in our negotiations and have had an easy give and take. When Florrie was in graduate school and needed time on the weekends and late nights for her studying and her dissertation, I assumed considerable weekend responsibilities for the children so that she could concentrate on her assignments." Florrie portrays Sol's cooperation during this time as a "steady force" and notes that he was her "greatest cheerleader when [she] felt overwhelmed" (Kaslow, 1990). Similarly, when Sol had times when he was dealing with significant management responsibilities at work, he found Florrie to serve as an excellent sounding board.

Physical Attraction

Finally, Sol comments that their physical attraction for each other has been present from the outset and over the years, and says "I believe that we have found each other's inner beauty" to be appealing, desirable, and comforting. As a result, there is no doubt that their love for one another is deep and abiding and has grown stronger through the years.

SEX THERAPY

Not only has Florrie written about sex therapy (Kaslow, 1988), but she has also trained and supervised many sex therapists. She is a Certified Sex Therapist through the American Association of Sex Educators, Counselors, and Therapists, as well as a diplomate in Clinical Sexology. Of course, it would not be appropriate to discuss her sex life with Sol in this article. Suffice it to say, she and Sol practice what she preaches. And according to Sol, "we have enjoyed a very healthy sex life so we have been able to avoid the need for a sex therapist." Florrie and Sol took a stance of being open with the children growing up in terms of educating them about sex and conveying a positive attitude regarding sexuality.

MILITARY PSYCHOLOGY

Probably the first person in our family to be interested in the psychology of the military was Sol, who was on a PT boat in World War II and participated in the Normandy invasion. Through his experience in the navy as an older adolescent and young adult during wartime, Sol found that his PT crew was like family. Since his boat was small, holding only 14 men, he learned about adjusting in close quarters to people from different geographical locations in the country, which had different values and styles of interacting. Sol has shared his wartime experiences with our family in multiple ways. In addition to visiting members of his PT crew on our journeys around the country, Nadine joined Sol at a reunion of his crew held near a PT base off of Rhode Island. Florrie and Sol had the opportunity to travel together to Normandy, where Florrie witnessed the intense and powerful emotions aroused in Sol as he returned to this battle site. Sol has shared films of PT boats during the war with his grandchildren, and his grandson Ethan was delighted when for his birthday, Sol gave him one of the medals he had received commemorating D-Day. Recently, Sol, Florrie, and Nadine visited the D-Day Museum in New Orleans, and this visit led to fascinating discussions about the effects of war on the family.

It is likely that the powerful role that the military played in Sol's formative young adult years influenced Florrie's decision to begin to consult with the military and to focus on military families during peace and war (Kaslow, 1986a, 1993c; Kaslow & Ridenour, 1984). She has lectured at many military installations and for many years has consulted for the U.S. Navy and the U.S. Army, as well as for the Israeli military (Kaslow, 1990). She first became involved with military psychology while on the faculty at Hahnemann Medical College, when the psychiatry residents from the local Naval Hospital trained with her in family therapy (Kaslow, 1990). Florrie has written articulately about common problems focused by the military family in war and peace including frequent separations, relocations, reunions, and all too often, physical danger. Her work also has highlighted the rigors of daily life in a highly regimented society in which the needs and natural tendencies of the family must always be tempered by the exigencies of the larger family of which it is a part.

FAMILY BUSINESS CONSULTING
AND THE USE OF PROJECTIVE GENOGRAMS

Long before our family learned about the concept of family business consulting, we were using effective strategies to run a family business to guide our efforts to be a successful dual-career family. Florrie went to graduate school when Nadine and Howard were in elementary school, and began her academic career upon her graduation when Nadine was in sixth grade and Howard was in third grade. Thus, in accord with principles of family business, we had a weekly family meeting in which roles and responsibilities were discussed for the upcoming week. Everyone had age-appropriate tasks that they were expected to do. We handled these negotiations relatively well and in an egalitarian fashion. There is no doubt that Sol and Howard have built upon these early experiences as they work together in the same office on a daily basis and have done so for the past twenty years.

In her book on projective genograms (F. Kaslow, 1995), Florrie articulates the ways in which her and Sol's experiences in their own family's of origin led to their involvement in family business consulting. After Florrie's parents grew up, met, and married and had two daughters, they went into the grocery business–together–with the living quarters attached to the store for much of Florrie's childhood. Similarly, Sol's parents, who also emigrated to the United States from Russia when they were very young, also went into a "Mom and Pop" dry-cleaning business that was adjacent to their home. Both Florrie and her sister, Cecily, and Sol and his sister, Mildred (Millie), helped out in their parents' businesses.

Given Florrie's expertise in family dynamics, and Sol and Howard's skills in financial management, the three of them have teamed together to consult to family businesses. One of only a few two-generation families involved in family business consultation, Sol or Howard join Florrie in this work when some of the issues under consideration involve financial planning, investments, capital expansion and other money matters, and intergenerational strife within the context of the business or professional practice. Florrie and Sol co-authored a chapter on the family that works together: special problems in family business (Kaslow & Kaslow, 1992) and presented together at the Family Firm Institute Annual Conference. In their work, they emphasize the evolution and stages of family businesses; the steps of the consultation process; issues frequently encountered by a consultation team comprising a family, a systems-oriented psychologist, and an investment broker-financial planner; and the unique perspective of the family business consultant (Kaslow & Kaslow, 1992).

INTERNATIONAL FAMILY PSYCHOLOGY

Long before Florrie became a leading international family psychologist, we were practicing international family psychology within our home. As our nuclear family was growing up, we hosted a graduate student and sometimes his or her family each year through the International House at the University of Pennsylvania (Kaslow, 1990, 2000a). This entailed orienting them to Philadelphia, life in America, and life in our family. We often had them over for dinner and holidays or went sightseeing with them. We learned a great deal from them as well about their home cultures, including traditions, food, dress, and rituals. We hosted students from such diverse cultures as India, Japan, Korea, Mexico, and the Philippines, and remain in contact with some of these individuals. This stimulating exposure likely accounts for the fact that everyone in our family enjoys a varied and diverse friendship circle. In addition, this activity also laid the groundwork for the family's interest in travel, first throughout the United States and Canada, and then abroad. We took one, sometimes two, major trips annually, and many of our most warm, positive, and fun memories are from these travels.

When we were planning a tourist trip to Asia in 1973, Florrie was invited to present a full-day workshop at the family court in Tokyo (Kaslow, 2000a). This marked not only the first time she was to lecture in a very different culture, but also her first contribution to the field of international family therapy (Kaslow, 1982b). We had an experience on that trip that set the stage for the whole family's enthusiasm for accompanying Florrie around the world. Specifically, the host for her professional presentation at the modern courthouse in Tokyo invited us to his home for dinner, an honor we could not refuse. At his home, we sat on tatami mats on the floor and ate with our host. In traditional Japanese style, his wife and daughter-in-law served us dinner, while the grandchildren peeked in and giggled at us. They kept their heads bowed, were very deferential, and it appeared that they did not speak English. However, the women were very different when they took us on a guided tour of the home, and we saw our hostess' office at one end of the home, where she practiced as a pediatrician. At the other end of the home, we saw the daughter-in-law's office, and learned that she was an otolaryngologist. During the tour, the women spoke in English and assumed a very different and more empowered stature. They indicated that they were able to compartmentalize their professional and personal lives with seemingly minimal marital conflict. After this tour, we were all able to sing together in the den area, as Nadine played the piano. Interestingly, even when the couple visited us in the States, the wife walked respectfully behind her husband, despite the fact that in Japan at that time, as a physician, she had a higher status position than did her husband. This entire experience left an indelible mark on all of our lives, as it demonstrated how people from diverse cultures negotiate family relationships very differently and yet how many commonalities we have in terms of balancing personal and professional responsibilities, having fun as families singing and dancing, and experiencing a profound sense of family loyalty.

Since that time, the four of us initially, and in more recent years, Florrie and Sol alone, have traveled around the world as Florrie has been invited to speak, teach, and consult in more than 40 countries. From these experiences, Florrie has highlighted some of the key differences in customs and cultures she has observed, while recognizing that within any country there are variations and uniquenesses (Kaslow, 1991, 2000a, 2000b, 1982b). Specifically, in writing and in the media, as a guest expert on a Voice of America radio segment entitled "Psychological Consultation," she has underscored differences in customs related to physical distance and closeness, levels of formality, role of age and wisdom, value placed on individualism and the pursuit of self-actualization versus adhering to family and group beliefs systems and loyalties, and gender roles (Kaslow, 1997b, 2000a). Florrie has highlighted for us the importance of learning as much as we can about the culture, values, and customs of the places and people that we visit; familiarizing ourselves with and behaving in a manner consistent with the expectations and social and professional protocol of each country; becoming bi- or trilingual; and developing some comfort with being in a marginal position (Kaslow, 2000a).

Sol accompanied Florrie in 1987 to the first East-West Bridging Conference in Family Therapy held in Prague, Czechoslovakia, where Florrie presented on the self of the therapist in different cultures. The outgrowth of this conference was the formation of the International Family Therapy Association (IFTA), of which Florrie was elected as the founding President. Since then, IFTA has grown to include over 700 people from more than 50 countries. Members of IFTA are interested in families and think globally. Sol has attended every IFTA conference with Florrie and has participated with her at all of the meetings of the International Academy of Family Psychology, another international group of which Florrie has held multiple leadership roles. In addition, he accompanied her when she led two People to People trips through the Citizen Ambassador Program, one to Mainland China and the other to Australia and New Zealand (Kaslow, 2000a).

Nadine has shared her mother's interest in culturally competent family interventions (Celano & Kaslow, 2000; Kaslow, Celano, & Dreelin, 1995; Kaslow, Wood, & Loundy, 1998). She has published extensively on this topic, and much of her current research focuses on African American families, particularly low-income families. Nadine and Florrie enjoy engaging in dialogues regarding Nadine's clinical-research endeavors on culturally competent interventions for the abused and depressed adolescents (Griffith, Zucker, Bliss, Foster, & Kaslow, 2001), abused women and their children (Kaslow et al., in press), and suicidal and abused women (Heron, Twomey, Jacobs, & Kaslow, 1997) that Nadine works with at Emory/Grady.

CONCLUDING COMMENTS

As Florrie so aptly said in her chapter in her edited book *Voices in Family Psychology* (Kaslow, 1990), in authoring this type of treatise, one faces the question of what to disclose and why. We sought to be appropriately selective and honest and reasonably objective, while simultaneously protecting the confidentiality of our family. It is our hope that we have been able to convey a number of important ways in which Florrie's contributions to family psychology and international psychology have impacted upon us as individuals and as a family system. Florrie is gifted in ferreting out where the action will be and in contributing to the advancement of the field, has a propensity for clinical and theoretical integrationism, and is talented in terms of communicating both orally and in writing. We take joy in her accomplishments, as she does in ours.

She has been supportive to us in good times and in bad, and we trust that as our family continues to negotiate future family life cycle stages that family support and loyalty will persist and deepen. Our family values, initially developed and elaborated upon during fascinating dinnertime conversations and long family trips, have served all of us well. A citizen of a professional world that has no geographic borders (Kaslow, 2000a), Florrie has instilled in all of us, as well as her grandchildren, the value of being citizens of the world. We will be curious to discover Florrie's reaction to this article, as it is our surprise and gift to her.

REFERENCES

Celano, M. P., & Kaslow, N. J. (2000). Culturally competent family interventions: Review and case illustrations. *American Journal of Family Therapy, 28,* 217-228.

Griffith, J., Zucker, M., Bliss, M., Foster, J., & Kaslow, N. (2001). Family interventions for depressed African American adolescent females. *Innovations in Clinical Practice, 19,* 159-173.

Heron, R. L., Twomey, H. B., Jacobs, D. P., & Kaslow, N. J. (1997). Culturally competent interventions for abused and suicidal African American women. *Psychotherapy: Theory, Research, Practice, Training, 34,* 410-424.

Kaslow, F. (1995). *Projective genogramming.* Sarasota: Professional Resource Press.

Kaslow, F. W. (1981). Profile of the healthy family. *Interaction, 4,* 1-15.

Kaslow, F. W. (1982a). Portrait of the healthy couple. *Psychiatric Clinics of North America, 5,* 519-527.

Kaslow, F. W. (1986a). Consultation with the military. In L. C.Wynne, T. T. Weber & S. H. McDaniel (Eds.), *Systems consultation* (pp. 383-397). New York: Guilford Press.

Kaslow, F. W. (1988). Sexuality in May-December marriages. In D. Kantor & B. Okun (Eds.), *Intimate environments: Sex, intimacy, and gender in families* (pp. 321-345). New York: Guilford Press.

Kaslow, F. W. (1990). A multifaceted family psychology potpourri. In F. W. Kaslow (Ed.), *Voices in family psychology* (Vol. 1, pp. 281-322). Newbury Park, CA: Sage.

Kaslow, F. W. (1991). Family psychology and family therapy abroad: A personal odyssey. *American Journal of Family Therapy, 19,* 291-301.

Kaslow, F. W. (1993a). Relational diagnosis: An idea whose time has come? *Family Process, 31,* 255-259.

Kaslow, F. W. (1993b). Relational diagnosis: Past, present, and future. *American Journal of Family Therapy, 21,* 195-204.

Kaslow, F. W. (1995). Descendants of Holocaust victims and perpetrators: Legacies and dialogue. *Contemporary Family Therapy, 17,* 275-290.

Kaslow, F. W. (1997a). A dialogue between descendants of Holocaust perpetrators and victims: Session two. *Israel Journal of Psychiatry, 34,* 44-54.

Kaslow, F. W. (1997b). The voice of America: Culturally sensitive radio. In D. A. Kirschner & S. Kirschner (Eds.), *Perspectives on psychology in the media* (pp. 141-156). Washington, DC: American Psychological Association.

Kaslow, F. W. (1998). A Holocaust dialogue continues: Voices of descendants of victims and of perpetrators. *Journal of Family Psychotherapy, 9*, 1-10.

Kaslow, F. W. (2000a). Establishing linkages through international psychology: Dealing with universalities and uniquenessess. *American Psychologist, 55*, 1375-1388.

Kaslow, F. W. (2000b). History of family therapy: Developments outside of the USA. *Journal of Family Psychotherapy, 11*, 1-35.

Kaslow, F. W. (Ed.). (1982b). *The international book of family therapy.* New York: Brunner/Mazel.

Kaslow, F. W. (Ed.). (1984). *Psychotherapy for psychotherapists.* New York: The Haworth Press, Inc.

Kaslow, F. W. (Ed.). (1986b). *Supervision and training: Models, dilemmas, and challenges.* New York: The Haworth Press, Inc.

Kaslow, F. W. (Ed.). (1987). *The family life of psychotherapists: Clinical implications.* New York: The Haworth Press, Inc.

Kaslow, F. W. (Ed.). (1993c). *The military family in peace and war.* New York: Springer.

Kaslow, F. W. (Ed.). (1996). *Handbook of relational diagnosis and dysfunctional family patterns.* New York: John Wiley and Sons, Inc.

Kaslow, F. W. (Ed.). (2000c). *Handbook of couple and family forensics: A sourcebook for mental health and legal professionals.* New York: John Wiley and Sons.

Kaslow, F. W., & Cooper, B. (1984). A family therapy approach to understanding and accepting a learning disabled child. In C. E. Schafer, J. M. Briesmeister & M. E. Fitton (Eds.), *Family therapy techniques for problem behaviors of children and teenagers* (pp. 22-25). San Francisco: Jossey-Bass.

Kaslow, F. W., & Hammerschmidt, H. (1992). Long term "good" marriages: The seemingly essential ingredients. *Journal of Couples Therapy, 3*, 15-38.

Kaslow, F. W., Hansson, J., & Lundblad, A. M. (1994). Long-term marriages in Sweden: And some comparisons with similar couples in the US. *Contemporary Family Therapy, 16*, 521-537.

Kaslow, F. W., & Kaslow, S. (1992). The family that works together: Special problems of family businesses. In S. Zedeck (Ed.), *Work, families, and organizations* (pp. 312-361). San Francisco, CA: Jossey Bass.

Kaslow, F. W., & Ridenour, R. I. (1984). *The military family.* New York: Guilford Press.

Kaslow, F. W., & Robison, J. A. (1996). Long-term satisfying marriages: Perceptions of contributing factors. *American Journal of Family Therapy, 24*, 153-170.

Kaslow, F. W., & Schwartz, L. L. (1987). *The dynamics of divorce: A lifecycle perspective.* New York: Brunner/Mazel.

Kaslow, F. W., & Sussman, M. B. (Eds.). (1982). *Cults and the family.* New York: The Haworth Press, Inc.

Kaslow, N. J., Celano, M., & Dreelin, B. (1995). A cultural perspective on family theory and therapy. *Psychiatric Clinics of North America, 18*, 621-633.

Kaslow, N. J., & Friedman, D. (1984). Interface of personal treatment and clinical training for psychotherapist trainees. In F. W. Kaslow (Ed.), *Psychotherapy for psychotherapists* (pp. 33-37). New York: The Haworth Press, Inc.

Kaslow, N. J., Heron, S., Roberts, D. K., Thompson, M., Guessous, O., & Jones, C. K. (in press). Family and community factors that predict internalizing and externalizing symptoms in low-income, African American children: A preliminary report. *New York Academy of Sciences.*

Kaslow, N. J., Kaslow, F., & Farber, E. (1999). Theories and techniques of marital and family therapy. In M. B. Sussman, S. K. Steinmetz & G. W. Peterson (Eds.), *Handbook of marriage and the family* (pp. 767-792). New York: Plenum.

Kaslow, N. J., & Kaslow, F. W. (1981). Dynamics of relationship between career mothers and young adult daughters. In A. S. Gurman (Ed.), *Questions and answers in the practice of family therapy* (pp. 368-372). New York: Brunner/Mazel.

Kaslow, N. J., Wood, K., & Loundy, M. (1998). A cultural perspective on families across the life cycle: Patterns, assessment, and intervention. In A. S. Bellack & M. Hersen (Eds.), *Comprehensive clinical psychology: Diversity in clinical psychology* (Vol. 10, pp. 173-205). Oxford: Pergamon Press.

Roizblatt, A., Kaslow, F. W., Rivera, S., Fuchs, T., Conyers, C., & Zacharias, A. (1999). Long lasting marriages in Chile. *Contemporary Family Therapy, 21,* 113-129.

Schwartz, L. L., & Kaslow, F. W. (1997). *Painful partings: Divorce and its aftermath.* New York: John Wiley and Sons, Inc.

Sharlin, S. A., Kaslow, F. W., & Hammerschmidt, H. (2000). *Together through thick and thin: A multinational picture of long-term marriages.* Binghamton, NY: The Haworth Press, Inc.

Index

BOOK ORDER FORM!

Order a copy of this book with this form or online at:
http://www.haworthpress.com/store/product.asp?sku=5217

Family Therapy Around the World
A Festschrift for Florence W. Kaslow

____ in softbound at $27.95 (ISBN: 0-7890-2515-9)
____ in hardbound at $39.95 (ISBN: 0-7890-2514-0)

COST OF BOOKS _____

POSTAGE & HANDLING _____
US: $4.00 for first book & $1.50
for each additional book
Outside US: $5.00 for first book
& $2.00 for each additional book.

SUBTOTAL _____

In Canada: add 7% GST. _____

STATE TAX _____
CA, IL, IN, MN, NY, OH & SD residents
please add appropriate local sales tax.

FINAL TOTAL _____
If paying in Canadian funds, convert
using the current exchange rate,
UNESCO coupons welcome.

❑ BILL ME LATER:
Bill-me option is good on US/Canada/
Mexico orders only; not good to jobbers,
wholesalers, or subscription agencies.

❑ Signature _____

❑ Payment Enclosed: $ _____

❑ PLEASE CHARGE TO MY CREDIT CARD:

❑ Visa ❑ MasterCard ❑ AmEx ❑ Discover
❑ Diner's Club ❑ Eurocard ❑ JCB

Account # _____

Exp Date _____

Signature _____
(Prices in US dollars and subject to change without notice.)

PLEASE PRINT ALL INFORMATION OR ATTACH YOUR BUSINESS CARD

Name _____

Address _____

City _____ State/Province _____ Zip/Postal Code _____

Country _____

Tel _____ Fax _____

E-Mail _____

May we use your e-mail address for confirmations and other types of information? ❑ Yes ❑ No We appreciate receiving
your e-mail address. Haworth would like to e-mail special discount offers to you, as a preferred customer.
We will never share, rent, or exchange your e-mail address. We regard such actions as an invasion of your privacy.

Order From Your **Local Bookstore** or Directly From
The Haworth Press, Inc. 10 Alice Street, Binghamton, New York 13904-1580 • USA
Call Our toll-free number (1-800-429-6784) / Outside US/Canada: (607) 722-5857
Fax: 1-800-895-0582 / Outside US/Canada: (607) 771-0012
E-mail your order to us: orders@haworthpress.com

For orders outside US and Canada, you may wish to order through your local
sales representative, distributor, or bookseller.
For information, see http://haworthpress.com/distributors

(Discounts are available for individual orders in US and Canada only, not booksellers/distributors.)

Please photocopy this form for your personal use.
www.HaworthPress.com

BOF04